Exploring Creation

with

Zoology 3

Land Animals of the Sixth Day

by Jeannie K. Fulbright

Exploring Creation With Zoology 3: Land Animals of the Sixth Day

Published by
Apologia Educational Ministries, Inc.
1106 Meridian Plaza, Suite 220
Anderson, IN 46016
www.apologia.com

Manufactured in the United States of America
Second Printing 2009

ISBN: 978-1-932012-85-9

Printed by Courier, Inc., Kendallville, IN

Cover photos © Getty Images, © Ecoprint, © Radovan Spurney, © Patrick Johnson, © Cathy Keifer, © Wojciech Plonka, © Hans-Peter Naundorf, © Ivonne Wierink
[Agency for all but the Getty Images Photo is www.shutterstock.com*]*

Unless otherwise stated, all Scripture quotes come from the New American Standard Bible (NASB)

Need Help?

Apologia Educational Ministries, Inc. Curriculum Support

If you have any questions while using Apologia curriculum,
feel free to contact us in any of the following ways:

<u>By Mail</u>:   Curriculum Help
Apologia Educational Ministries, Inc.
1106 Meridian Plaza, Suite 220
Anderson, IN 46016

<u>By E-MAIL</u>:   help@apologia.com

<u>On The Web</u>: http://www.apologia.com

<u>By FAX</u>:   (765) 608 - 3290

<u>By Phone</u>:   (765) 608 - 3280

*Illustrations from the MasterClips
collection and the Microsoft Clip Art
Gallery*

Scientific Speculation Sheet

Name _____   **Date** _____

Experiment Title _____

Materials Used:

Procedure: (What you will do or what you did)

Hypothesis: (What you think will happen and why)

Results: (What actually happened)

Conclusion: (What you learned)

Introduction

Congratulations on choosing *Exploring Creation with Zoology 3: Land Animals of the Sixth Day*. You will find this to be an easy-to-use science curriculum for your whole family. The text is written directly to the student, making it very appealing to kids from six to thirteen. The material is presented in a conversational, engaging style that will make science enchanting and memorable for your students, creating an environment in which learning is a joy.

Lesson Increments

The lessons in this book contain quite a bit of scientific information. Each lesson should be broken up into manageable time slots depending on your children's age and attention span. This will vary from family to family. There are 14 lessons in this text, covering the different kinds of land animals. Most lessons can be divided into two-week segments. You can do the reading and the notebook assignments during the first week, and you can do the experiments and the data recording during the second week. If

you do science two or three days per week, you can read four to six pages a day to finish a lesson and begin the experiment. This will give you 32 weeks for the entire book. Older students can work through the book more quickly if they wish.

For record keeping and evaluation, narrations and notebooking replace the traditional and less effective method of filling in blanks in a workbook. We believe notebooking and narrations are a superior method of facilitating retention and providing documentation of your child's education.

Narrations

Older elementary students can do the entire book and most experiments on their own, while younger students will enjoy an older sibling or parent reading it to them. Each lesson begins with a reading of the text. Throughout the reading, the students will be asked to retell or narrate the information they just studied. This helps them assimilate the information in their minds. The act of verbalizing it in their own words propels them forward in their ability to effectively and clearly communicate with others that which they know. It also serves to lock the information into their minds.

Communication skills are necessary no matter what interests your children pursue, so please don't skip the narrations. Though they may seem to take up valuable time, they are vital to your child's intellectual development. Persevere through the first attempts; the more narrating the child does, the better at it he will become. The better at narrating the child becomes, the better at writing, researching, and clearly communicating his beliefs he will be. Some parents encourage their child to take notes as they listen to them read. You may or may not want to try this.

Notebooks

At the end of each lesson, notebook activities are used to give the child further experience with the material. The notebook is an important tool that will provide you and your child with a record of what was learned. The notebook activities generally occur at the end of a lesson, but they are sometimes used to break up lessons. Older students are given additional assignments in some of the notebooking segments for more challenge.

Projects and Experiments

In this text there are a wide variety of projects and experiments. Every single lesson ends with an opportunity to further ground your child in real science by doing projects or performing experiments. These activities will help your children to develop the skills needed to conduct valid and scientifically accurate science experiments.

The projects and experiments in this book use mostly common, household items. As a result, they are fairly inexpensive, but you will have to hunt down everything that you need. To aid you in this, pages viii-ix contain a list of the materials that you need for the experiments and projects in each lesson.

The Immersion Approach
Is it Okay to Spend a Year on Just a Part of Zoology?

Many educators promote the spiral or survey approach to education, wherein a child is exposed over and over again to minute amounts of a variety of science topics. The theory goes that we just want to "expose" the child to science at this age, each year giving a bit more information than was given the year before. This method has been largely unsuccessful in public and private schools, as National Center for Education Statistics (NCES) data indicate that eighth graders are consistently less than 50% proficient in science.

This method assumes the young child is unable to understand profound scientific truths. Presenting a child with scant and insufficient science fails to develop a love for the subject. If the learning is skimpy, the subject seems monotonous. The child is simply scratching the surface of the amazing and fascinating information available in science. Sadly, students taught in this way are led to believe they "know all about" that subject, when in reality the subject is much richer than they were allowed to explore. That is why we recommend

that kids, even young children, are given an in-depth, above their perceived grade level exploration into each science topic. You, the educator, have the opportunity to abandon methods that don't work so that your students can learn in the ways that have been proven effective. The immersion approach is the way everyone, even young kids, learn best. That is why we major in one field in college and take many classes in that field alone. If you immerse your child in one field of science for an entire year, he will develop a love for that subject and a love for learning in general.

Additionally, a child that has focused on one subject throughout an entire year is being challenged mentally in ways that will develop his or her ability to think critically and retain complex information. This will actually benefit the child and give him an advantage on achievement tests. He will be able to make more intelligent inferences about the right answer on science questions, as God has created an orderly world that works very similarly throughout all matters of science. A child who has not been given the deeper, more profound information will not understand how the scientific world operates.

Course Website

If your child would like to learn more about the animals discussed in this course, there is a course website that allows the student to dig even deeper into these aspects of zoology. To go to the course website, simply type the following address into your web browser:

http://www.apologia.com/bookextras

You will see a box on the page. Type the following password into the box:

Godmadethemcrawl

Make sure you capitalize the first letter, and make sure there are no spaces in the password. When you hit "enter," you will be taken to the course website.

Items Needed To Complete Each Lesson

Every child will need his own notebook, blank paper, lined paper, and colored pencils.

Lesson 1

- A laundry basket or large plastic container
- A bag of M&M's (you can also use Skittles® or any other candy that comes in a variety of colors)
- A plain sheet of white paper
- Clean paper towels
- 21 sheets of construction paper in three different colors matching three of the candies
- 6 (or more) extra sheets of construction paper to line the laundry basket or container.
- A stopwatch or some other kind of timer

Lesson 2

- A box of lemon gelatin (Jell-O® brand works best)
- Sugar
- Hot water
- Red food coloring
- Two bowls
- Serving cups or dishes

Lesson 3

- Masking tape
- Tape measure
- Two thermometers that read room temperature and above
- A white trash bag and a black trashbag (They need to be the same size and thickness.)
- Some small stones

Lesson 4

- Two blindfolds
- Colored tape
- Cellophane tape or glue
- A surface on which you can mark off a 2-foot by 2-foot square with tape
- Several pieces of cardboard
- Paper
- Scissors
- A ruler
- Six drawings (or small pictures) of a cougar. They can all be copies of one drawing or picture.

Lesson 5

- Copy of a world map you can cut up
- Protective eyewear
- Breathing mask or surgical mask
- A shallow, wide, disposable foil baking pan
- Cement mix and water (amount depends on the size of your pan)
- A strong piece of cardboard or small piece of wood (A cement trowel would be ideal.)
- A small disposable container, such as a margarine container or a short plastic cup
- Bait (such as peanut butter, peanuts, sunflower seeds, mealworms, or scraps of meat)

Lesson 6

- Tape measure

Lesson 7

- Stopwatch or some other kind of timer
- Ruler or tape measure
- Owl pellets (You can buy these at science supply houses. The course website, discussed in the introduction to the book, has links to several places that will send them to you in the mail.)
- Paper plate
- Bamboo skewer or toothpick
- A blank sheet of paper
- Tweezers
- Latex or rubber gloves

Lesson 8

- A folder or poster board
- Cutouts of every continent (except Antarctica)
- Index cards
- Beads in different colors (You need several beads of each color.)

Lesson 9

♦ A small plastic bottle (like the kind drinking water comes in)
♦ A pin
♦ A balloon
♦ Water

Lesson 10

♦ A lizard to raise and the things needed to care for it.

Lesson 11

♦ A turtle to raise and the things needed to care for it.

Lesson 12

♦ Two plastic bags (large, zippered bags are best)
♦ Several small stones
♦ Several leaves
♦ Two cardboard cylinders, like those used in toilet paper rolls
♦ A few metal coat hangers your parents will allow you to destroy
♦ Pliers
♦ Wire cutters or very strong scissors
♦ A timer, like a stopwatch

Lesson 13

♦ A ball of yarn
♦ Tape
♦ A long, sturdy wooden dowel or broom handle
♦ A foam board about 1½ feet long and 1½ feet wide
♦ Marker
♦ An adult with sharp knife (like an X-ACTO® knife) or sharp blade
♦ Duct tape or glue
♦ A flashlight
♦ A shoebox
♦ Oil-based paint (yellow is best, but any bright color will do)
♦ A paint brush (one with a small tip, like what an artist would use)
♦ A yardstick or measuring tape
♦ Chalk

Lesson 14

♦ Glass baking pan or bowl
♦ Ruler
♦ Bucket
♦ Large spoon, a spade, or a shovel
♦ Five-gallon bucket with a lid
♦ Newspaper (just the black and white sections)
♦ Water
♦ Earthworms
♦ An oblong baking tray
♦ Moist paper towels
♦ Heating pad
♦ Ice pack

Exploring Creation With Zoology 3: Land Animals of the Sixth Day
Table of Contents

Lesson 1
Introduction to the Animals of Day Six

Have you ever gone on a **safari** (suh far' ee)? A safari is a journey across a stretch of land, usually made to observe or hunt wild animals. Your safari begins today. This will be an unusual safari, because you will travel all over the world – from the jungles of Asia to the rainforests of South America. Your journey will even take you to your own backyard as you study the animals God created to crawl, walk, leap, gallop, run, jump, creep, and slither across the land.

The people in this jeep are on a safari.

You're going to have a great time learning all about animals across the world, identifying their tracks, and investigating what makes them a part of God's animal kingdom. You'll discover many animals that have such incredible features that they cry out in praise of their Maker. You'll keep records of all you learn, and do experiments and projects along the way. This will be a safari you'll never forget!

God Made the Animals

Are you familiar with the days of creation? Do you know what God made on each day? Do you remember what He made on day five of creation? If you studied Zoology 1 and 2 in this series, you explored all the animals God created on the fifth day. In this book, you are going to discover the animals God made on the sixth day. Let's find out exactly what the Bible says God created on the sixth day. Genesis 1:24–25 says:

And God said, "Let the land produce living creatures according to their kinds: livestock, creatures that move along the ground, and wild animals, each according to its kind." And it was so. ***God made the wild animals according to their kinds, the livestock according to their kinds, and all the creatures that move along the ground according to their kinds.*** *And God saw that it was good.* [NIV, emphasis added]

Let's read the sentence in bold again. It separates the creatures God created into three groups: **wild animals**, **livestock**, and the **creatures that move along the ground**. Since that's how the Bible describes the animals God made on the sixth day, that's the order in which we will study them.

Did you notice that God separates the wild animals from the livestock? Do you know what livestock are? Livestock are animals that we own, care for, and use for food or to help us with our chores. Can you think of examples of livestock? I can think of many: horses, donkeys, oxen, sheep, cattle, and pigs. Isn't it interesting to think that God actually created animals to help us? Horses and donkeys help us by carrying us or our things from place to place. They can also help us by pulling plows as we plant crops. Oxen are used for that as well, and sheep give us wool for clothing. Cattle are eaten and milked. Pigs are also eaten. In some countries, camels help people with their work and carry them from place to place, so we'll study camels when we study livestock. Can you think of one thing these animals have in common? They all have hooves. Animals with hooves are called

The adult oxen in this picture are helping this man plow his field. Oxen are livestock.

ungulates (un' gyoo litz). In the livestock section, we'll study every ungulate, even though some of them (like zebras and gazelles) are not really livestock.

Of course, we'll also study animals that aren't livestock. The Bible calls them "wild animals" and "creatures that move along the ground." When someone says "wild animals," what do you think of? I immediately imagine lions and tigers and bears (oh my!). These animals, of course, are not usually kept for us to eat or to help us work. Most of them don't make good pets, either.

When my brother was in college, he was given an **ocelot** (os' uh lot) as a pet. How cute that ocelot kitten was! It played and scampered about, climbing up the furniture and attacking toy mice, just like any young housecat. As it grew, however, its playful bite became more powerful, and its claws grew longer and sharper. One night, as my brother was sleeping, the ocelot saw his feet hanging off the edge of the bed, twitching. After a few minutes of crouching on the floor, the ocelot leapt up and grabbed my brother's feet with both claws, hanging on for dear life. My brother was hurt so badly he had to go to the hospital! Although it made him sad, he had to find a new home for his ocelot. Most wild animals are not meant to be pets. However, some have been bred

Some animals were meant for the wild, like this beautiful ocelot.

to become pets over the years. Can you think of any? Dogs and cats come to mind. Since dogs and cats are pets that came from wild animals, we'll include them in our wild animal section.

Do you know what I mean when I say that an animal "comes from" another animal? Well, if you look back at the Bible verse we read a little while ago, you will see that God said that all the animals reproduce *after their own kind*. That word "**kind**" is very important. You see, there are many different *species* of animals, but not nearly as many *kinds* of animals. For example, there are calico cats and Siamese cats that live in people's homes, and there are also lions and tigers that roam the wilds of Africa. Even though they are very different from one another, creation scientists can show that most likely they all came from a pair of cats that walked off the ark after the worldwide flood.

In other words, God created each kind of animal, and He created them with the ability to adapt and change over time. So after the two cats walked off the ark and began to reproduce, their young were similar to, but not exactly the same, as they were. As time went on, the differences between the young and their parents continued to "pile up," until there were many different species of cats – from the cute little Siamese to the dangerous lion.

Some people argue that the story of the worldwide flood can't be true because all the different animals of the world could not fit on the ark. However, Noah took only two of each *kind* of animal onto the ark. He didn't have to take two of each of the different species of cat, for example. He just had to take two from the cat *kind*, and they would eventually be the great, great, great, great, great grandparents of all the different species of cats we see today. So Noah just had to take two of each *kind* of creature, and there was plenty of room on the ark for them. You'll learn more about this as you work through this course.

This green anole (uh noh' lee – a type of lizard) is probably an example of what the Bible calls a creature that moves along the ground.

When the Bible mentions creatures that creep, it is most likely talking about reptiles (such as snakes and lizards), amphibians (such as frogs and salamanders), arthropods (such as spiders and scorpions), and all the worm-like creatures that move along and under the ground.

As I mentioned, you'll study the wild animals first, livestock second and then all the creeping creatures third. Since dinosaurs were probably reptiles, we'll place them into the creeping section, though most of them did not creep. Many tromped slowly along or scurried about on two legs.

Since you have most likely studied Zoology 1 and Zoology 2, you already know a lot about animals. You know about animal classification, nocturnal and diurnal animals, herbivores, carnivores, habitats, endangered species, arthropods, annelids, parasites, and many other things. So I won't repeat the information you already know, except to occasionally remind you of things you may have forgotten. At the end of this lesson, you'll do a fun activity that will teach you a little bit more about camouflage, which is something else you learned about in the first two zoology books. This experiment will encourage you to think about how camouflage helps some animals survive, sometimes at the expense of others that do not. This is called **natural selection**, which is something we have not talked about in the other books. However, it will come up quite a bit in this book, so it will be important for you to do an experiment that helps you understand the concept.

Predators and Prey

In this book, we'll study a lot of **predators** (pred' uh turz) and their **prey** (pray). This means we'll have to learn about animals (the predators) chasing, capturing, and eating other creatures (the prey). This might bother you. It might make you sad to learn about an animal and then learn that it gets eaten by other animals. Do you know why this bothers you? It's because you were created in the image of God and have emotions that are similar to God's emotions. The Bible says God notices when a single sparrow falls to the ground. He cares about the animals, just like you do. It is a sad thing to God that animals are now predators and prey. But did you know that this was not the way it was originally meant to be?

This tiger has a rabbit in its mouth. It hunted the rabbit, caught it, and will soon eat it. The tiger is the predator, and the rabbit is its prey.

Creation Confirmation

After God finished His work of creation, He said something very important about what all the animals should eat. Let's read what God said in Genesis 1:29-31:

Then God said, "I give you every seed-bearing plant on the face of the whole earth and every tree that has fruit with seed in it. They will be yours for food. And to all the beasts of the earth and all the birds of the air and all the creatures that move on the ground—everything that has the breath of life in it—I give every green plant for food." And it was so. God saw all that he had made, and it was very good. And there was evening, and there was morning—the sixth day. [NIV]

All the animals were given plants to eat. That means all animals were all originally herbivores (creatures that eat only plants). To God, this wasn't just good; it was *very* good.

Many Christians believe that there was no animal death on the earth right after creation. That's because in the beginning, animals weren't supposed to die. Death and decay came as a result of Adam and Eve's sin in the Garden of Eden. Because of their sin, all of creation, including animals, was subject to death and decay. Apparently, some animals (especially the ones that had the right kind of teeth) began to develop a taste for other animals. As a result, some animals stopped eating the plants God had made for their food, and they began eating other animals.

Romans 8:20-22 tells us that all of creation waits for the day when the world will be restored to its original state:

> *For the creation was subjected to futility, not willingly, but because of Him who subjected it, in hope that the creation itself also will be set free from its slavery to corruption into the freedom of the glory of the children of God. For we know that the whole creation groans and suffers the pains of childbirth together until now.*

The Bible promises that one day Jesus will return and remove death from the earth, rescuing creation from its groans and suffering. In 1 Corinthians 15:24-26 we read:

then comes the end, when He hands over the kingdom to the God and Father, when He has abolished all rule and all authority and power. For He must reign until He has put all His enemies under His feet. The last enemy that will be abolished is death.

Perhaps when Jesus destroys death, the world will look something like what is described in Isaiah 11:6-9:

And the wolf will dwell with the lamb, and the leopard will lie down with the young goat, and the calf and the young lion and the fatling together; and a little boy will lead them. Also the cow and the bear will graze, their young will lie down together, and the lion will eat straw like the ox. The nursing child will play by the hole of the cobra, and the weaned child will put his hand on the viper's den. They will not hurt or destroy in all My holy mountain.

Perhaps it's easier to picture the perfect world that God created when we see situations like this. The snake in this picture typically eats rodents (like hamsters). However, he refused to eat the hamster in the picture, even though it was put in the snake's cage as food. Instead, these two animals have become close friends, to the amazement of zoo visitors in Tokyo, Japan.

Can you imagine lions that will only eat plants, and poisonous snakes that will be harmless? Wolves playing with lambs, and leopards with goats is hard to picture, but that's what it was like when God originally created the animals. The Bible also promises that someday it will be like that again!

You might be wondering, "But what about the fact that carnivores only eat meat and can't survive on plants? Aren't their sharp teeth meant for tearing flesh?" This is something you might have been taught, but isn't necessarily true. You see, many animals with extremely sharp teeth, like fruit bats, certain monkeys, and some bears, eat only fruit and other plant parts. Their teeth are perfect for tearing into the flesh of the thick skin of fruits, or ripping tough leaves off a branch. The panda bear's sharp teeth, for example, are perfect for peeling the flesh off the bamboo shoots it eats. Furthermore, there have been reports of carnivorous animals, such as dogs and lions, that will eat only plants. In fact, Georges and Margaret Westbeau had a lion they named "Little Tyke." This interesting animal refused to eat any kind of meat. The Westbeaus were worried by the false notion that lions have to eat meat to survive, so they tried everything they could to coax the lion to eat meat. Nevertheless, it survived its entire life on grain, rice, milk, and eggs.

A panda bear eats only plants. It has very sharp teeth, however, because they are ideal for eating its favorite food: bamboo.

Though it's hard to imagine a world without death and decay, we are promised that this is the way it will be one day. So as you are reading this book and learning about predators and their prey, just remember: It won't always be like that.

Studying Animals

Have you ever studied an animal? I don't mean just watching or playing with an animal. I mean, have you observed an animal, taken note of its behavior, and thought about the reasons it does what it does? Have you ever read a book about an animal's anatomy or behavior and tried to remember what you learned? If so, you are probably someone who would enjoy a career in zoology.

Zoologists (zoh awl' uh jists) study animal behavior, habitats, anatomy, and everything else they can about animals. Most of what we know about animals is the result of scientists studying them. Zoologists learn more about animal behavior when they are able to study them in the wild. An animal studied in a zoo doesn't really behave the way it would act in the wild. A zoo is a false habitat, and the animal adjusts its behavior to the zoo environment. Although scientists can learn a lot about animals in a zoo, they won't understand much about their normal behavior unless they study creatures in their natural habitat and environment.

Studying animals in their natural habitat is tricky. When an animal encounters a human, it will usually behave differently than normal. It might be nervous and on guard. If a scientist wants to learn how animals act on a daily basis, how animals form relationships with one another, and about animals' normal habits, he must either be hidden from the animals or get the animals used to his presence. Because many animals have keen senses, it is often hard to hide from them. As a result, zoologists often try to get animals used to people, a process called **habituation** (huh bich' oo aye' shun).

Habituation

Meerkats, like the one shown here, are typically easily frightened by humans. However, scientists from Cornell University habituated them to the presence of humans so they could be studied.

To habituate animals, scientists will slowly get closer and closer to the animals, then remain there – causing no harm or disruption, day after day – until the animals get used to their presence. In the beginning, the animals hide and are cautious. After a time, however, the animals no longer see the scientists as a threat, and they begin to go about their usual business. The scientists can then begin studying them. One famous scientist, Dr. Jane Goodall, habituated chimpanzees to her presence and studied them for many years in a wildlife park in Africa. This was also done by scientists at Cornell University with a group of meerkats in an African desert. The study lasted for ten years, and much was learned about meerkats during this time. Habituating animals is a common way students and scientists study them in the wild.

In most such circumstances, animals become habituated to the sight, smells, and sounds of the particular scientists that have been there day after day, week after week, month after month, and even year after year. The animals are habituated to these individual scientists only. It's important to note that the animals are not *tamed* by these scientists, though the creatures might trot right up to the scientists and investigate them, even crawling on their laps, considering them friends. However, they are still wild animals that will fiercely bite and hurt anyone they don't trust. These animals have learned to trust only a few particular scientists. If a new scientist approaches, the animals go back to their fearful, cautious behavior.

Habituating animals to humans can be risky for both the animals and the people. If an animal becomes habituated to many people, it can come to think that all humans are somewhat safe. This is dangerous for an animal, because it could walk right up to a hunter that would shoot it.   On the other hand, if the animal seems tame to a person, the person might start trying to treat it like a pet. Since a wild animal is not used to such treatment, it might think the person is trying to hurt it, and it could harm the person, thinking it must defend itself. So once again, a habituated animal is *not tame*. The animal is only unafraid of some humans. General habituation often happens with bears in national parks. Some bears become used to humans feeding them, even though people are told not to. As a result, bears sometimes approach people looking for food. Even though they may look friendly, the bears are still *very, very dangerous* wild animals. People sometimes make the mistake of thinking such bears are tame and start feeding them. When a person runs out of food, however, the bear may become violent. One swipe from a bear claw can result in death. We'll learn more about that later.

Many of the animals you will learn about in this book, such as monkeys, have been studied for hundreds of years, whether through habituation or through observing them from afar. Others, such as certain species of salamanders, have only been studied by a very few scientists because they are difficult to find. There are some animals we know almost nothing about, typically because they are difficult to track and because they live in a habitat not frequented by people. If you completed the Zoology 2 course, you might remember that blue whales and male sea turtles fall into this category.

Even though there are many things we do not know about animals, you will learn a great deal about what we do know as this book takes you on a tour through the world, looking at the different orders and families of animals. However, there isn't room to tell you about every animal species in creation. If you want to learn more about a particular species of animal, check out books from the library or do some research on the Internet. The course website I told you about in the introduction to the book is a great place to start. If there is a lot known about this animal, you will find a lot of information. If little is known or understood about a particular animal, there probably has not been a scientist dedicated to studying it. Perhaps you will be the one who does that when you grow up!

Animal Careers

If you have a special love for animals, you may want to consider a career that will give you the opportunity to work with them. There are many ways for people to work with animals as a career. All of them can be rewarding, if you love animals. Some require degrees or certification; others don't require any special education, but they do require training. Let's take a look at a few of the jobs you could get working with animals.

The most obvious career for a person who loves animals is to become a **veterinarian** (vet' ur uh nair' ee uhn), a doctor who works with injured and ill animals. Most veterinarians either specialize in small animals, like dogs and cats, or large animals, like horses and cows. A very few will specialize in exotic animals like marine animals, zoo animals, or chickens. I know chickens don't seem all that

This veterinarian is examining someone's pet dog.

exotic, but once a veterinarian knows about chickens, she can treat parrots and injured birds in the wild. A veterinarian who specializes in exotic animals can also work in zoos or animal parks, with wildlife organizations, or with animal research organizations. An exotic veterinarian can even work in chicken plants, treating the chickens that will one day be served on someone's dinner table! One interesting veterinary career involves working with politicians and health organizations, educating people and creating programs dealing with **zoonotic** (zoh uh not' ik) **diseases**. Zoonotic diseases are illnesses transmitted between animals and people, like avian flu, mad cow disease, west Nile fever, and Lyme disease.

While there are more than 150 medical schools in the United States, there are less than 30 veterinary schools. This means a person has a better chance of becoming a doctor than a veterinarian. However, you have a greater likelihood of getting into veterinary school if you have experience working with different types of animals. There are many places to get this experience. You could volunteer as a vet's assistant or in a laboratory that studies animals. You could also volunteer for a few years on a farm, zoo, or nature preserve. The more experience you have with different kinds of animals, the better your chance of being accepted to veterinary school.

Zoologist

This zoologist is studying a pine snake he found hiding under a board.

Zoologists are people who usually have a degree in zoology or biology and intend to work with animals. A zoologist will often work in the field, specializing in one type of animal. This often involves capturing, tagging, or recording the number of animals found in a specific location. Studying animal populations is a very important part of zoology. Zoologists often work for government agencies or private companies, helping people decide how to preserve the animal population in that area. You will do an experiment in a later lesson that will help you understand population growth and decline.

Also, zoologists can become zookeepers or aquarium keepers. Zookeepers usually begin by caring for specific types of animals and their habitats. Eventually they can add more and more animal exhibits to their responsibilities, working their way up to being in charge of the entire zoo. At that point, they are often called zoo curators. In addition to making sure the animals are properly cared for, zookeepers watch for unusual behaviors or illness. They also make sure the animals are groomed, exercised, and trained (if necessary). Zoologists can also get animals for a zoo, usually from other zoos or breeding programs. Other zoologists work in the zoo as animal behaviorists. These people train other zookeepers on how to interact with and care for the animals. They have experience working with animals, and usually hold a degree in animal behavior.

Zoologists can also spend time as animal educators, helping people understand animals and their habitats. Wildlife parks, sanctuaries, aquariums, and museums hire educators to create brochures, videos, tours, and exhibits. These zoologists often live on the park grounds and study, research, and explore wildlife behavior. They usually write books or magazine articles, which is another way for them to make a living as a zoologist. Animal educators and program directors need a strong background in writing and speaking.

As a zoologist, you can also be a wildlife rehabilitator. In this case, you would work for the government (or some other agency) to care for ill, injured, or orphaned animals with the hope of one day being able to release them back into the wild. Sometimes, wildlife rehabilitators (or other zoologists) become animal trainers at theme parks like SeaWorld or Disney's Animal Kingdom.

These wildlife rehabilitators are capturing an ill sea lion. Once it is nursed back to health, they will hopefully be able to release it back into the wild.

Zoologists can also make wildlife documentaries. These are the informative shows about animals you might watch on Animal Planet or the Discovery Channel. It is a good idea to have experience with filmmaking if you want to make documentaries.

If you plan to become a zoologist, it is important that you learn good communication and writing skills. You will need these skills to help others understand how to protect the animals you study.

Pet Careers

Even if you don't want to get a degree in biology or zoology, there are a lot of careers that involve working with animals. For example, you could become a certified dog trainer, training dogs for all kinds of work, such as guide dogs, police dogs, or inspection dogs. You could also expand your career to include many other kinds of animals. Animal trainers are often hired to train animals to be in movies or television shows. Also, you could become an animal control officer, work at an animal shelter, work at a pet store, or work as a veterinarian technician. Although most of these careers do not require college degrees, they do require lots of knowledge and experience with animals.

Because horses are a favorite animal for many, there are several careers in the equine (horse) field. In addition to becoming a large-animal veterinarian, you could become a horse breeder or a horse trainer. You could also work at a race track or rodeo. Some jobs involving horses are very specific. For example, you could become a farrier (far' ee ur), which is a person who cares specifically for horses' hooves.

These are only a few of the many kinds of jobs you could get working with animals. Many places that work with animals use student volunteers to help them. Volunteers may clean cages, exercise the animals, or even assist with operations or training. Though volunteers don't get paid, they get a lot of the experience necessary to get a paying job someday.

As you study zoology this year, you might begin to develop your own ideas about what you want to do when you grow up. Whether you choose to work with animals or not, it's a lot of fun to study them.

What Do You Remember?

Each lesson will have a section like this. It is designed to help you remember some of the important things you learned in the lesson. For this lesson, explain what animal habituation is. What is a safari? What does it mean to be a predator? What does it mean to be prey? Have there always been predators and prey? What is a zoonotic disease? Name a few careers that involve working with animals.

Map It!

You will be learning about a lot of different types of animals as you go through this book. Each lesson will give you an opportunity to place on a world map small images of the animals you studied. To start this project, get a large world map you can hang on your wall. Throughout the rest of the book, there will be "Map It!" sections that will tell you to map the important animals you have studied. When you reach one of those sections, you need to get a small image of the animal (such as a tiny photograph you printed from the Internet or a tiny drawing you make) and put it on your map over a location where you can typically find the animal. The course website I told you about in the introduction to the book will have links to many websites that contain such pictures.

Track It!

Many lessons will have a "Track It!" section that will include pictures or drawings of animal tracks related to the lesson. These sections will focus on the tracks you might find in North America. You may want to trace or draw these tracks, creating a separate book you can carry with you on hikes or walks in wooded areas. That way, when you come across some tracks, you can try to identify what animal made them. Please note that if you live outside North America, you should check the course website I told you about in the introduction to the book. There you will find links to pictures and drawings of animal tracks that might be found in your area of the world.

Notebook Activities

As you work through this course, you will create your own zoology "Book of Knowledge," also known as your Zoology Notebook. At the end of every lesson, you will have an opportunity to write down what you learned and make an illustration to go along with it. Sometimes you will also be given a creative assignment.

At this time, I want you to create the cover page for your Zoology Notebook. You can cut pictures of animals out of magazines, or print them from the computer if you don't want to draw them yourself. Once you have made your cover, start your zoology notebook with a page about a few of the careers that involve working with animals. Also, draw a picture of two animals that are usually predator and prey, but draw it so that they are enjoying each other's company, much like the picture of the snake and hamster on page 5. If you are having a hard time thinking of animals to draw in the picture, read the Scripture verse next to the picture.

Experiment

Remember how we discussed animals that are either predator or prey? Well, predators and prey need to blend in with their environment so they aren't seen. Prey don't want to be seen so they don't get eaten; predators prefer not to be seen so they can sneak up on their prey. Let's do a little experiment with M&M® candies to see what happens to animals that are well camouflaged and those that are not.

Since you probably like to eat M&M's, you can think of yourself as an M&M's "predator." In this experiment, then, you (the predator) will be hunting for the M&M's (the prey) in a special habitat you create. Then you can discover which M&M's are best suited to survive in this habitat.

You will need:

- Scientific Speculation Sheet (found on page iv of this book)
- A laundry basket or large plastic container
- A bag of M&M's (you can also use Skittles® or any other candy that comes in a variety of colors)
- A plain sheet of white paper
- Clean paper towels
- 21 sheets of construction paper in three different colors matching three of the candies (we used 7 brown, 7 green, and 7 orange.)
- 6 (or more) extra sheets of construction paper to line the laundry basket or container.
- A stopwatch or some other kind of timer

1. On the plain sheet of white paper, make a table like the one below:

	Red M&M's	Brown M&M's	Green M&M's	Yellow M&M's	Orange M&M's	Blue M&M's
Starting Number						
Number Found						
Number Not Found						

2. Lay some paper towels on the floor or on a table and pour your M&M's onto the paper towels.

3. Separate the M&M's into groups according to their color.

4. Count the number of M&M's in each color group. Whichever color has the least number in it will tell you the number of M&M's you will use in each color group. For example, if there are 18 brown, 16 red, 17 yellow, and 14 green M&M's, you will use 14 M&M's in each group.

5. Take the extra M&M's from the other groups so that all the groups have the same number in them.

6. With a parent's permission, eat the rest of the M&M's you will not need.

7. Write the number of M&M's you have in each group (it should be the same number for each color) in the first row of the table you made in step #1.

8. Now you are going to make the habitat. Cover the bottom of the laundry basket with some of the extra sheets of construction paper. They can be all one color or different colors. It doesn't matter.

9. Using the seven sheets for each color, tear each sheet of construction paper into six pieces. It does not matter which way you tear it. Just make six pieces out of one sheet.

10. Crumple up each piece of construction paper and toss it into the basket.

11. After all seven sheets of construction paper of each color have been torn up and the pieces crumpled and put inside the basket, place the other sheets of construction paper on the sides of the basket to cover the holes.

12. Pour the M&M's into the basket, spreading them around evenly.

13. You will have two minutes to search for M&M's in the habitat. Make a hypothesis about what you will find in two minutes. Will you find more of one color than another? If so, which colors will you find the most of? Which will you find the least of? Write down your hypothesis on the Scientific Speculation Sheet.

14. Set the timer for two minutes and begin searching for M&M's.

15. After your time is up, separate the M&M's into color groups and count the ones you found. Record the number of each color you found in the second row of the table you made in step 1.

16. For each color, subtract the number you found from the number you started with. That will be the number you didn't find. Write that number in the third row of the table.

17. Was your hypothesis correct? Complete the rest of the Scientific Speculation Sheet.

Think about what the results of your experiment mean. If M&M's could reproduce and create other M&M's, which M&M's in your habitat would be most likely to reproduce? Which M&M's would have a hard time reproducing? After many years, which M&M's would be most abundant in that habitat? Which M&M's would probably become extinct?

This rabbit blends in well with its snowy surroundings, making it hard for predators to find it. Most likely, natural selection will ensure that such rabbits will thrive in that habitat.

You have just learned a lesson about camouflage and a special process that happens in nature called natural selection. Animals that are best suited for a particular environment, especially those that are able to hide themselves well, are naturally able to survive and reproduce in that environment. Those that cannot hide themselves well tend not to survive. That's called natural selection, because it is almost like the habitat "selects" those animals that are best suited to survive there.

Now if you have heard of evolution before, do not get natural selection and evolution confused. They are two completely different things. Evolution is a idea that some scientists believe in despite the fact that there is very little evidence for it and a lot of evidence against it. Natural selection is a well-documented scientific theory that helps us understand how creation determines what kinds of animals will survive in specific habitats. You will learn more about these things as you go through the rest of this course.

Lesson 2
Carnivorous Mammals

Quick! Name three animals. Which animals did you name? If you are like most people, all the animals you named had hair. Few people ever say "spider," "salamander," or "tick," although those are animals as well. Why is that? Well, one reason may be that there are so many interesting and different kinds of animals with hair. Do you remember what an animal with hair is called? It is called a mammal. When you go to the zoo, you spend most of your time looking at mammals. And, just like the zoo, most of the animals covered in this book will be mammals. In fact, the first nine lessons will be about mammals!

When people think of animals, they usually think of animals with hair, like this lioness. Animals with hair are called mammals.

Creature Features

Think of all the things you already know about mammals. You know that mammals are chordates (in phylum Chordata) with vertebrae (backbones). They are endothermic (warm-blooded), and they must breathe oxygen from the air, even if they spend a lot of time underwater. Because mammals nurse their young with mother's milk, you might think they all give birth to living young, but you will soon see that this isn't always true. Although you already know a lot about mammals, you need to learn more about them now.

Jaw

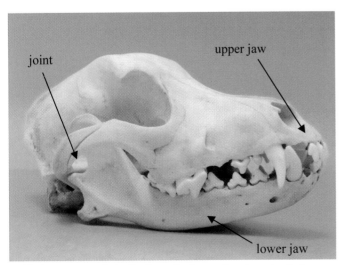

This is a mammal skull, since the lower jaw is a single bone.

Suppose you found a skull that might have belonged to a reptile or mammal. How could you tell which it was? Interestingly, you can always tell a mammal from a reptile by looking at its jaw. Mammals have a lower jaw made of only one bone. The lower jaw of a reptile, however, is made up of several bones. Not only that, the way the lower jawbone moves is very different in reptiles as compared to mammals. In reptiles, the joint that connects the lower jawbone to the rest of the skull is like a simple hinge. Do you know what a hinge is? Look at the door to your house. It is attached to the wall with hinges. Those hinges keep the door stuck to the wall, but they also allow the door to open and close. It can *only* open and close, however. It cannot move from side to side. In mammals, the joint that connects the lower jawbone to the skull allows it to not only open and close, but also move from side to side.

What's the big deal? Well, because of their jaw structure, reptiles cannot chew. Instead, they must swallow their food whole. Not so with mammals; they can chew their food. This actually makes a big difference. You see, after you eat food, you must **digest** it. This means your body breaks down the food so that it can be turned into energy you use to walk, run, play, breathe, etc. Well, it is easier to digest food that has been chewed, so mammals digest their food easily compared to reptiles.

Those Pearly Whites

What would you do without your teeth? Well, you would probably have to mash your food into soup or paste and then slurp it down. If you don't brush and floss your teeth every day, you may have to do this one day, because teeth that aren't cared for can rot and fall out! If animals lose their teeth out in the wild, they'll probably die. They are very dependent on their teeth for both catching and consuming prey. Do you know that you have different kinds of teeth in your mouth? There are four major kinds of teeth God created for mammals: **incisors** (in sye' zerz) for biting, **canines** (kay' nines) for tearing and gripping, and both **premolars** (pree moh' lurz) and **molars** for grinding.

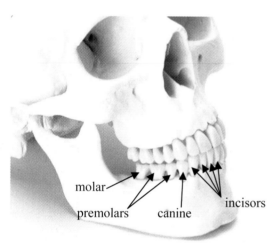

This closeup of a person's skull shows the different kinds of teeth you have.

You can often guess an animal's diet by the shape, size, and kind of teeth it has, but not always. An animal that eats meat will usually have long, sharp canine teeth, pointed incisors, and molars and premolars that have jagged edges. A plant-eating animal, on the other hand, will often have no canines, broad, flattened incisors, and square, flattened molars and premolars. However, as you learned in the previous lesson, this isn't always the case. An animal like a panda bear can have long, sharp incisors and canines (see picture on page 6) but still eat only plants.

Your Epidermis Is Showing!

When I was a child, I would walk up to people and say, "Your **epidermis** (ep' ih dur' mis) is showing." If the person did not know that "epidermis" means "skin," he would look embarrassed, checking himself over to make sure everything was fastened properly. Although I was just trying to fool people, it was true that their epidermis *was* showing. Every mammal has two layers of skin: the epidermis and the dermis. The epidermis is the outer layer of skin that has hair on it. The **dermis** (dur' mis) is the layer of skin that gets bruised and bleeds, and it is under the epidermis. Most

mammals have so much fur that the epidermis is hidden. There are some mammals, however, that do show their epidermis. Elephants and rhinos have a few little bristles of hair sticking up here and there, but their epidermis is definitely showing!

The dermis is hidden beneath the epidermis. It is a very important part of the skin, because it is the part that is alive! Believe it or not, most of a mammal's epidermis is made of dead tissue. The dermis, however, is made of living tissue. This living

These rhinoceroses have some hair, because they are mammals. However, they don't have much, so you can see their epidermis.

tissue can replace the epidermis if it gets cut or injured in some other way. The dermis also houses several very important **glands**.

Do you know what glands are? They are organs in the body that make and release chemicals. Animals have many glands in their dermis, including glands that release odors. They are called **scent glands**. Though we sometimes aren't very fond of the smells that a mammal's skin produces, other mammals love them. In fact, they depend on those smells, because they use them to communicate. When many mammals are born, for example, their eyes are shut for a while. However, they can always find their mother by the smell that she produces, because each mammal produces its own, individual smell! Have you ever noticed a cat rubbing the side of its face against things in the house? The cat is doing that to communicate. It has glands on the side of its face designed to produce its own, unique smell. It is putting that smell around the house, letting other cats know that it lives there. A cat also has glands like that on its sides and tail. In fact, when a cat comes up to you and rubs its face, side, and tail against you, it is actually mixing its smell with your smell to let you know that it considers you a part of its family. Communication by smell is very important for many animals, including mammals.

Cooling Off

Animals also have **sweat glands** that produce and release a watery mixture we call "sweat." Do you know why you sweat? It's kind of a strange thing, isn't it? Well, sweating is what our bodies do to cool off. Mammals also sweat to cool off. When a mammal is hot, its sweat glands will produce sweat and release it onto the epidermis, where it eventually evaporates. The evaporation cools the epidermis. It's like a built-in air conditioning system! To understand this better, try the experiment on the next page.

Try This!

Blow on your hands for a moment. Does that feel cool? Now run some water from the sink on one of your hands. Blow on the wet hand. Does that feel even cooler than it did before? Blow on the dry hand and the wet hand. Which one is cooler? The wet hand feels cooler when you blow on it because water evaporated from your hand as you blew. That cooled your hand even more than just blowing on it would. That's how sweat helps to cool a mammal's body.

Unlike us, many mammals don't have sweat glands all over their body. They usually have only a few on certain parts of the body. For example, dogs and cats have sweat glands only on their feet, and rabbits have them only on their lips. With so few sweat glands, then, some mammals resort to other ways to cool off. Panting, for example, is how a dog helps to cool itself off. Of course, a hot mammal will often try to find a nice shady spot and stay there in hopes of cooling off and staying cool.

But what does a mammal do if it is cold? Well, what do you do? Imagine being outside with your bathing suit on in Antarctica. How would your body respond? You would shiver. Shivering makes our muscles move, and that generates a lot of heat, which helps to warm us. Mammals shiver when they are cold. Another thing they do is huddle together with other mammals, trying to share whatever warmth they have.

Now that we know a little more about mammals in general, let's travel into the wilderness and explore a few of our favorite kinds of mammals, like dogs and cats and other ferocious creatures. I know you don't normally think of dogs and cats as wild and ferocious. However, they belong to order **Carnivora** (kar nih' vor uh), which contains many of the ferocious predators of the animal kingdom.

Order Carnivora

I'm sure you can guess what a carnivore eats, especially if you speak Spanish. The word "carne" in Spanish means "meat," which comes from the Latin word that means "flesh." Not all animals that eat meat are in order Carnivora, and there are some animals in order Carnivora that don't eat meat. They are classified in this order, however, mostly because of their teeth. Even if they don't eat meat, all animals in order Carnivore have molars and premolars specially designed to cut meat. They are called **carnassial** (kar nas' ee uhl) **teeth**.

molar designed for cutting meat

The molar pointed out in this tiger's mouth is one of its carnassial teeth. The fact that a tiger has teeth like this puts it in order Carnivora.

Generally speaking, members of order Carnivora are the ferocious predators of the animal kingdom. They are the hunters, while other animals are the hunted. They are often quick, powerful, and fierce in their hunting methods, and the sight of them strikes an understandable fear in all the meek and mild creatures of the world. They usually have keen senses of sight, hearing, and smell. Their senses help them find prey, which they chase down and eat with the help of their carnassial teeth. Different carnivores have different means of killing their prey. Cats kill prey by biting the neck or throat, while dogs shake their prey viciously back and forth to dislocate the neck. A weasel bites the base of its prey's skull. These carnivores can be frightening creatures! They often teach these methods to their young by playing roughly with them as they mature. If you've ever watched a mother cat play with her kitten, you've seen this training in action.

Order Carnivora can be split into at least two groups: **caniforms** (kayn' ih formz) and **feliforms** (fel' ih formz). "Caniform" sounds a little like "canine," while "feliform" sounds a bit like "feline." Are you familiar with the words "canine" and "feline"? Well, if so, then it'll be easy for you to remember that caniforms are dog-like carnivores and feliforms are cat-like carnivores. So, we really are going to be studying dogs and cats – and all the animals that are like them. In the next few lessons, we'll explore the family **Canidae** (kan' ih day), which is made up of true dogs, as well as other caniforms, like bears, raccoons, and otters. Then we'll study the family **Felidae** (fel' ih day), which are cats, and then we'll study other feliforms like hyenas and mongooses. Be careful not to get out of your vehicle during this part of our safari, because these creatures carry a powerful bite!

Tell someone everything you remember about mammals and carnivores.

Family Canidae

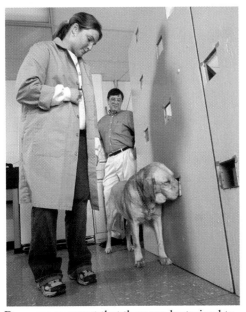

Dogs are so smart that they can be trained to do many useful things. This dog is being trained to use his keen sense of smell to find bad-tasting catfish. His work will end up saving fish processors time and money.

Have you ever heard someone say "sly as a fox" or "wily as a coyote"? "Sly" and "wily" are adjectives describing cleverness and intelligence. Foxes, wolves, and coyotes belong to the class of intelligent animals we call canines, which are in family Canidae. Jackals and (of course) man's best friend (domesticated dogs) are also in this family. We can all agree that an animal would have to be pretty smart to be man's best friend. In fact, dogs are some of the smartest creatures in God's creation. Dogs save children from burning buildings, rescue drowning people, lead the blind, find people lost in the woods, catch criminals, and so much more. Few other animals can boast of such heroics.

Every year, dogs perform amazing feats for people. In 2007, a man came out of his house on a dark night and was attacked by a bear. His dog, named "Dude," jumped between them and fought the bear off. A true hero, the dog gave up his life for his owner. Also, in the same year, a German shepherd that got out of its yard was wandering around the neighborhood when it found a woman injured in her car. The car had run off the side of a road and into a ditch. No one could see the car from the road. The escaped dog pulled the lady out of her car and dragged her up to the road where he let her lean against him so she could signal a passing car. Around the same time, a golden retriever named Toby saved his owner, who was choking on a piece of apple. When she started choking, she tried to beat on her own chest, but she couldn't get the piece of apple out of her throat. Toby pushed her to the ground and began jumping up and down on her chest until the piece of apple was dislodged. These are only a few of the heroic dog stories that happened in just one year.

Amusingly, though the domesticated dog is one of humankind's most beloved animals, most other canines are considered pests. Why? Wild animals need food, and dogs like an easy meal. They will steal lambs in a flock, chickens from a pen, or calves from a farm. Yes, jackals, foxes, coyotes, and wolves are notorious for sneaking in to "fleece the flock." Even the Bible refers to evil people who trick others into believing lies as "wolves in sheep's clothing" (see Matthew 7:15, for example). Wolves are disliked so much all over the world that some have been hunted to near extinction. However, some canines, like the red fox and the coyote, are more plentiful now than they have ever been. Yet, of all the canines, the domestic dog is still favored – even if it sometimes chews up the furniture and chases the mailman.

It's Still a Dog

Family Canidae seems very diverse, and yet all the dogs in the family are the same kind. The tiny teacup Chihuahua, the enormous English Mastiff, and the timber wolf wandering the countryside are all the same basic kind of creature. What does that mean? It means that when God created animals, He created a single doglike creature, and all the members of family Canidae come from that doglike creature. So, why do all the members of family Canidae look so different from one another? It's similar to the reason many people look different from one another. The 4-foot-tall Pygmy Indians of South America and the 7-foot-tall Watusi Africans all came from two people: Adam and Eve. God created His people (and His animals) with the ability to change and adapt. This led to many different types of people, even though they all come from just two: Adam and Eve.

Even though this timber wolf is not the same *species* as the dogs you and I keep as pets, it is a member of the same family, and it probably descended from the same created kind.

In the same way, God most likely created only one type of dog, but He built into that dog "kind" the ability to change and adapt over the years. As a result, even though there are different *species* of dog, they all are a part of the same *kind*. For example, the dogs that you and I love to pet and keep in our homes are often called "domesticated dogs" and are members of the species *Canis familiaris* (familiar dogs). The timber wolf, on the other hand, is a member of the species *Canis lupus*. Nevertheless, domesticated dogs and wolves are probably all the descendants of the dog kind that God originally created.

In fact, many of the differences among domesticated dogs have actually been chosen by humans. Humans have bred dogs to look a particular way and have particular characteristics. There are specific dogs for herding, hauling, guarding, hunting, or companionship. As these traits appeared, man continued to breed dogs with these characteristics until the breed was very specialized. Sometimes these specialized characteristics are somewhat harmful for the dog. For example, pugs are dogs that have been bred with a flattened face and a severe underbite. The lower jaw protrudes uncomfortably forward, and the flattened nose causes the dog difficulty in breathing. Despite the many unusual breeds of domesticated dog and even the different species in family Canidae, the members of this family are most likely all descendants of the same original dog kind created by God.

Creation Confirmation

Sadly, some people mistake changes that have taken place in dogs for evolution. This is absolutely not the case. The fact that so many different breeds and species of dogs exist today has nothing to do with evolution. It just shows how God has designed His creation to adapt to changes. Let me explain this in a way that will help you understand.

First, we need to have a basic understanding of **genes** (jeens) and **DNA**. Don't worry; I won't make this too complicated. DNA is a wonderful molecule that exists in every living creature. It stores

This is a model of DNA, the molecule that contains information (stored in the form of genes) about a creature.

a lot of information that helps the creature be what it is supposed to be. It stores that information in the form of genes. A dog of species *Canis familiaris*, for example, has thousands and thousands of genes. Every creature is given *two* copies of each gene – one from each parent. So a mother dog will give one of each of her genes to her pup, and the father dog will give one of each of his genes to the pup. Most of the time, each gene is either **dominant** or **recessive**. If it is dominant, it will win, and its information will be used. Even if the recessive gene is in the dog, is not used when the dominant gene is present. It is like the recessive gene is "masked." It is there; it just doesn't do anything for the animal.

Let me give you an example of what I mean. Chihuahuas can have very short hair or long hair, and the length of the hair is determined by the dog's genes. The short-hair gene is dominant, and the long-hair gene is recessive. If a pup gets one short-hair gene from one parent and one long-hair gene from the other, its hair won't be of medium length. It will be short. Even though it has the long-hair gene, it is recessive (masked) and doesn't do anything. So…let's suppose two short-hair dogs have puppies. It is possible for one (or more) of the puppies to have long hair, even though both parents have short hair. Why? Because even though both parents have short hair, they could each have a recessive long-hair gene. If a pup gets its mother's long-hair gene

A Chihuahua with one long-hair gene and one short-hair gene will have short hair (left). However, if a Chihuahua has two long-hair genes, it will have long hair (right).

and its father's long-hair gene, it will have long hair, because there is no dominant gene to mask the recessive long-hair gene.

So, now you understand how genes work. Let's take a look at how dogs can change features over time either by natural selection or by breeding. Imagine that Noah had two wild dogs on the ark. Both of these dogs together had dominant and recessive genes for many different features (short nose, long nose, short hair, long hair, curly hair, straight hair, short legs, long legs, short ears, long ears, and on and on). These two dogs may have even looked very different from each other; but they were the same kind, so they could mate and have puppies. After the ark landed, these dogs produced offspring with many different features, populating the earth, forming new packs and spreading all over. As dogs spread to different locations, the different features of those dogs were taken to those locations.

In the wild, dogs that had better features for survival – long, thick hair in cold regions and gray coloring for better camouflage in the woods – lived to produce puppies with those features. Any dog born that didn't have those needed features would not be able to survive in that region. Over time, only dogs with the best features for survival would be left. They did not evolve long hair to survive in the cold regions. They did not evolve gray fur for camouflage in the woods. These features were already in their genes. Their genes just kept mixing each time they reproduced, and the dogs that had the best "mix" of genes for their environment were the ones that ended up surviving.

Even though dogs have changed considerably since the Flood, they have never changed into another kind of animal like a horse! Dogs can produce other dogs, because their genes only allowed for them to be dogs. Remember, the Bible says that animals reproduce after their own *kind*. Over time, however, nature ended up selecting the best mix of genes for the dogs in a given habitat. The dogs that lived in cold regions, for example, developed long hair because the short-hair dogs kept dying from being too cold. As a result, the short-hair genes were eventually lost in the dogs that lived in those regions.

So do you see how natural selection works? Nature selects the genes that work best for a given animal in a given region, because those animals without the best mix of genes end up dying. People can actually do the same thing. If you want to make a new breed of dog that is very tiny, for example, you can get two small dogs and let them have puppies. Then you can keep the smallest male and smallest female from the litter and let them have puppies. If you keep doing this over a long period of time, you will probably end up having dogs that are much smaller than the ones you started with. This is called "artificial selection," and it is the way most breeds of dogs were produced. Once again, however, don't confuse natural selection or artificial selection with evolution. Evolution is the idea that one kind of creature (a dog, for example) can eventually produce another kind of creature (a horse, for example). Such an idea contradicts what we know about DNA and genes. DNA and genes indicate that (as the Bible says) animals reproduce after their own kind. Nature (or people) may select among the many features that the DNA allows that kind to have, but the kind cannot change.

Explain what you learned about genes, natural selection, and artificial selection.

What Are Dogs Like?

This is an alpha female timber wolf with two of her pups.

No matter how well bred, a dog is still a dog. If you have one, you already know that dogs like to be with people. With few exceptions, canines crave companionship. That's because dogs are pack animals; they need a leader and prefer to live in groups. The social behavior of most dogs resembles that of a wolf, and even a domesticated dog would behave a lot like a wolf if it were left in the wild.

Wolves and domesticated dogs have an inborn knowledge of the rules of the pack. These rules are reinforced in the first weeks of life, when the pup is with its litter. What are those rules? Well, the basics are pretty simple. One dog, usually a male, is the leader (called the **alpha male**). The alpha male has a mate that is the second in command. These two leaders, the alpha male and the **alpha female**, are called the **dominant pair**, and they are the only dogs allowed to have puppies. The female digs a large hole in the ground, called a den, where she gives birth to her pups, and the entire pack helps to take care of them. Every dog has a position in the pack, from greatest to least. A dog quickly learns who is above it and who is below it in this "pecking order." This is done by playing tug of war and wrestling. Whichever dog wins these tussles is above the dog that lost. Any day of the week, one of the dogs might challenge another dog for position.

Canine Communication

In addition to leaving their scent around their territory, dogs also communicate through body postures and facial expressions. It's easy to tell when a dog is feeling aggressive, fearful, playful, or submissive. For example, it's a sign of aggression when a dog stands tall with its ears pricked up and its head held high. It will also bare its teeth and erect the fur along its spine to appear bigger. It might even give a threatening growl or an angry bark.

Submissive, frightened canines lower their bodies, flatten their ears, tuck their tails, and close their mouths. Whimpering or silent, they may roll onto their backs and lie there, exposing their belly. This is a very submissive position because they are exposing the most sensitive area of the body. If you see a dog roll over on his back, exposing his belly when he meets you, that means he believes you are dominant (above him in the pack). When dogs want to play, they raise their rear and lower their forelegs in a kind of bow. This posture says, "I'm ready to play! Let's see who wins!"

This steppe wolf is saying, "Let's play!" to another wolf.

Canine Construction

Most canines are muscular. Their legs are strong and powerful for hunting and running. They actually walk on their toes (four on each paw), so each toe has its own pad to absorb shock from the ground and make it easier to get traction. Animals that walk on their toes are called **digitigrades** (dij' ih tih graydz), and this gives them the ability to run swiftly. Many dogs have a fifth toe, usually on the two front legs, but it doesn't touch the ground. Compared to other carnivores, canine claws are not very sharp. All canines in the wild have a long, pointed jaw with fang-like canine teeth used to kill prey.

Canine Senses

You may already know that a dog's hearing is keen, even better than its ability to see. However, a canine's sense of sight is pretty good as well. Most people have been taught that canines see only in black and white. That isn't true. They are able to see color, but they don't have as many color sensors in their eyes as people have. As a result, they cannot see the range of colors we see. For example, while dogs can tell the difference between yellow and blue, they cannot tell the difference between red and green.

What do you suppose is the most important sense for a dog? Have you ever heard the phrase, "Follow your nose"? Well, that's how a canine finds its food. Canines have amazing **olfactory** (ol fak' tuh ree) organs (organs of smell). In fact, they have about 25 times more olfactory sensors than humans do! Their sense of smell is the most important sense they have. If they catch a whiff of an animal they would like to eat, they can track it for miles and miles until they find their prey. Their keen sense of smell also makes dogs great at finding people who are lost or hiding, as well as things people try to hide, like drugs and explosives.

Hunting

Canines hunt for prey in packs. As a result, they can bring down animals that are many times their size and weight. After trailing a herd for a while, they work together to separate one straggler (an old or sick individual, for example) from the rest. This animal is chased while the dogs nip at it with their sharp teeth until it falls. Once their prey is down, the pack stands back and waits for the dominant pair to eat first. This is where we get the phrase, "The big dog eats first." When every dog in the pack has had its fill, they return to the den and regurgitate (vomit) meat for the pups to eat.

What new things have you learned about dogs? Describe those things to someone else.

Wolves

Timber wolves like these have been hunted for so long that they are in danger of becoming extinct.

Now it's time to talk about some of the different canines we see in God's creation. Let's start with **wolves** (*Canis lupus*). Throughout history, wolves have been pests for livestock farmers and a source of fear for travelers at night. They frequently attack chickens, goats, sheep, and cows that are raised by farmers, and old stories tell of horrifying run-ins with wolves in the woods. Because of this, many breeds of wolf have been hunted almost to extinction.

In addition, as people have built cities, wolves have been "squeezed out," because they require large areas of solitary land. The timber wolf was once the most easily found canine in the world. Today, however, its numbers are so low that it is now on the endangered species list, which means scientists who work for the U.S. government think that without special protection, it could become extinct.

These amazingly smart animals form packs of about ten dogs, claiming large pieces of territory that span hundreds of miles. They mark the boundaries with their scents and are like police on patrol, continually covering the area over and over to make certain no intruder wolves come near.

The dominant female usually has about seven pups. Like all dogs, they are born helpless, with their eyes shut, but they grow like wildfire. After about a month of nursing from the mother, they emerge from the den ready to eat food other dogs regurgitate from their most recent meal. After a few months, they'll begin hunting with the pack. By the following season, most of these pups will be sent off to form their own pack. Though the dominant female keeps having pups, they only keep about ten dogs in any one pack.

Wolf howls can be heard up to six miles away, and even farther away by other packs of wolves. They howl to warn other packs of their presence and to define their territory. Although they howl, wolves rarely bark. It is believed that domesticated dogs have been bred to be barkers, because quiet dogs aren't very helpful as watchdogs.

Coyotes

Though many species of wolves are in danger of becoming extinct, **coyotes** (*Canis latrans*) are thriving. Unlike wolves, coyotes do not have need of large areas of solitary land. When people built towns and cities on their terrain, the coyotes didn't move out – they simply changed their diet. They started hunting the kinds of animals you find near cities, like rats, moles, and even stray pets. We call this mode of living "**opportunistic**." In addition, coyotes sometimes eat fruits and other plant parts to supplement their diet. Thus, even though they are in order Carnivora, they are actually omnivores.

As night hunters, coyotes can form small packs, but they are often alone. When a coyote finds small prey, like a rat, it stands still with its legs stiff, watching and listening. Then, when the moment is

This coyote is howling to tell others that this is his hunting territory.

right, it leaps straight up in the air and brings its front feet down on the tiny animal, pinning it to the ground before biting it. This is the typical "coyote pounce." Some domesticated dogs play this way. When coyotes find larger prey (like a deer), the whole pack is needed to bring it down. They typically take turns chasing the poor animal until it wears out and becomes an easy kill. Coyotes are the night howlers, commonly depicted in Southwestern art in the howling stance, like the coyote in the picture above. Like wolves, they howl to let other coyotes know that this is their hunting ground.

Foxes

The **red fox** (*Vulpes vulpes*) is another opportunistic canine. Red foxes can eat anything (including fruit), but they really prefer small animals like mice and rabbits. Unlike many canines, the

This arctic fox has its "winter coat" so it blends in with the snow.

red fox does not generally travel or hunt in packs. Instead, it is usually a solitary animal, pouncing on small prey much like a coyote does. Since red foxes do eat plant parts (like fruit) from time to time, they are technically omnivores, even though they are a part of order Carnivora.

Although the red fox is by far the most common species of fox, there are several others. The **arctic fox** (*Vulpes lagopus*) lives in the arctic regions of Europe, Asia, North America, Greenland, and Iceland. It changes from a bluish-gray color in the summer to pure white in the winter so it is camouflaged against the snowy world in which it lives.

Jackals

For some reason, the **jackal** seems eerie to many people. It is referenced 19 times in the Bible, usually to refer to wastelands or wilderness. Jackals are often the villain in comics or movies, and I guess it's no wonder. Their howls sound more like shrieks that frighten both adults and children. They are associated with evil and death, probably because they tend to "pick over" the remains of other animals' prey. Like foxes and coyotes, they are opportunistic omnivores that can live near or even in cities. They look a lot like small wolves with really big ears. They can only be found in Africa, parts of Asia, and parts of Europe. There are no jackals in North or South America.

This is a black-backed jackal (*Canis mesomelas*).

Dingoes

This dingo looks a lot like a German shepherd.

It's thought by many Australians that **dingoes** (ding' gohz) were once pet dogs owned by Indonesian traders who fished in the waters of Australia and landed on shore thousands of years ago. Even though they are considered a subspecies of domesticated dogs (*Canis familiaris dingo*), they are wild dogs. In fact, they are the only wild dogs in Australia. These German shepherd lookalikes are anything but shepherds; they've been known to eat young children or babies left unsupervised. They are also implicated in causing many species of marsupials to become extinct or threatened. Their reputation is so dreadful that frightening movies have been made about them and their antics. They are a feared predator in the Australian wild. A dingo's color is determined by where it lives. Golden yellow dingoes are found in sandy areas, while darker black and tan dingoes are found in forests. Can you think of why this may have happened? Think about the M&M's experiment you did in Lesson 1.

Raccoon Dogs

Is it a raccoon or a dog? This crazy creature that lives only in Japan is oddly both! It looks just like a raccoon, eats the same foods as a raccoon, is nocturnal like a raccoon, and doesn't even bark. Unlike other canines, it doesn't claim territory. To top it all off, it even climbs trees! So, how do we know it's not a strange species of raccoon? Well, the **raccoon dog** (*Nyctereutes procyonoides*) has the feet of a dog, not the hand-like appendages of a raccoon. It can't hang by its feet like a raccoon can. It also has the same teeth that dogs have. In the end, it is simply a dog that looks outlandishly like a large raccoon!

Although it looks like a raccoon, the animal in this cage is actually a dog.

African Wild Dogs

Can you see why the African wild dog is called a "painted wolf?"

The painted wolf, as the **African wild dog** (*Lycaon pictus*) is often called, is the most social of all the canines. These beautifully colored dogs live in packs of up to one hundred animals. That's a lot of dogs! But it's helpful to have so many when they are hunting the wildebeest, zebras, and impalas that cross the plains in Africa. As is often the case with canines, only the dominant pair in the pack breeds and has pups, and the pack cares for the pups once they are born. These large-eared dogs have a small head; long colorful legs; and only four toes on each foot.

What Do You Remember?

What characteristics do mammals have? How can you tell the skull of a mammal from the skull of a reptile? Which sense does a dog use the most? What are some of the ways dogs communicate? What four major kinds of teeth do mammals have? How many of each gene do you have? Where did you get them? If a gene is recessive, what does that mean? How does a pack of dogs usually hunt prey? What do we call the male leader of a pack? What do we call the female leader? Why are wolves so rare today? What is a digitigrade?

Map It!

If you are doing a map of the animals we saw on our safari, put the timber wolf on the map in Alaska, Canada, and Russia. Dingoes live in Australia. African wild dogs should be placed in South Africa. Raccoon dogs live in Japan. Jackals live in Africa and Asia, and coyotes live all over the place, as do foxes.

Track It!

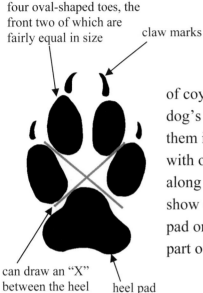

four oval-shaped toes, the front two of which are fairly equal in size

claw marks

can draw an "X" between the heel pad and toe pads

heel pad

When hiking through the woods, it's not uncommon to find the tracks of coyotes and domestic dogs near streams and on trails. It's easy to tell a dog's tracks from the tracks of other animals. The first thing to notice about them is that dog toes are oval-shaped. The two front toes are usually even with one another and equal in size. You can also draw an imaginary "X" along the ridges between the toes and heel pad. Also, dog tracks will usually show claw marks, since dogs cannot retract their claws. The top of the heel pad only has one lobe, which is much higher than the bottom. The bottom part of the heel pad has two lobes.

Notebook Activities

Today, you are going to create a canine newsletter, detailing all the information you learned in a newsy fashion. This can be done on paper or on the computer, if you know how to use a computer in that way. If you choose to use the computer, there are free newsletter templates you can download for Microsoft Word or Microsoft Publisher. Check the course website for help with this. If you prefer to do your newsletter by hand, you can use one of the templates provided with the Notebook Pages found on the course website.

Give your newsletter a catchy name. Write several articles detailing the information you've learned about dogs. Be sure to put it all in your own words! If you would like, do some research on a dog breed and put that information in your newsletter as well.

Older Students: Do some research on recent dog rescue stories and include that in your newsletter.

Experiment

We discussed a dog's highly sensitive sense of smell in this lesson. Humans can smell pretty well too. However, it may be that humans are more influenced by sight than by smell. Let's do an experiment to find out if this is true. If you change the color of lemon Jell-O® from yellow to red, do you think a person will think the Jell-O was a flavor usually associated with red, or do you think that

person's nose can smell the lemon smell in spite of the color change? Make your guess and use a Scientific Speculation Sheet to write down your hypothesis.

You will need:

♦ Scientific Speculation Sheet
♦ A box of lemon gelatin (Jell-O brand works best)
♦ Sugar
♦ Hot water
♦ Red food coloring
♦ Two bowls
♦ Serving cups or dishes

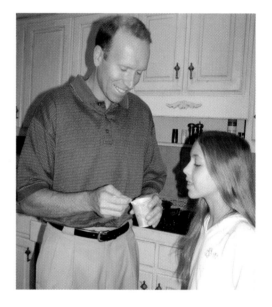

1. Using the directions on the box, make some lemon Jell-O.
2. While it is still liquid, pour the gelatin into two different bowls.
3. Mix red food coloring into the Jell-O in one of the bowls.
4. Place both bowls in the refrigerator.
5. After the Jell-O sets, put a serving of each in two different serving cups or dishes.
6. Experiment on a family member or friend. Without letting the person see the yellow Jell-O, ask him to smell the red Jell-O and have him guess the flavor. Record the answer. You might want to use a table like the one given below.
7. Have your subject taste the red Jell-O and guess the flavor. Record the answer.
8. Repeat steps 6 and 7 with the yellow Jell-O. Repeat the experiment with some other people to see how they do.
9. Was your hypothesis correct?

Name		Yellow Jell-O	Red Jell-O
Dad	Smell	Lemon	Cherry
	Taste	Lemon	Raspberry
Mom	Smell	Lemon	Strawberry
	Taste	Lemon	Strawberry

Lesson 3
Caniforms Continued

Unparalleled Ursidae

In the Bible, God asks Job, "Can you bring forth the constellations in their seasons or lead out the Bear with its cubs?" (Job 38:32, NIV). If you have studied astronomy, you know that the bear and cubs mentioned here are the constellations Ursa Major and Ursa Minor. "Ursa" is the Latin word for "bear," and all bears are classified in the family Ursidae (ur' sih day).

Bears are considered caniforms, even though they do not behave like dogs.

Looking at the bear on the right, can you see why bears are considered caniforms? This particular bear has a very dog-like look, doesn't it? Well, bears may look a bit like dogs, but they don't act like dogs. Bears prefer to live alone, unless it's a mother bear with her cubs. Bears share many features with other kinds of animals. This is because the same Designer, God, created all the animals and used similarities in design when creating them, just like the way all the pictures of a particular artist look similar.

Unlike dogs, bears are able to stand on two legs comfortably. They also sit with their legs straight out in front of them. Also, unlike dogs, they are **plantigrades** (plan' tih graydz). Can you guess what that means? Think about a similar word you learned in the previous lesson: digitigrades. That referred to animals that walk on their toes. Plantigrades are animals that don't walk on their toes. They use the entire bottom of the foot. Monkeys, raccoons, and rabbits are also plantigrades.

As creationists, we think that the bears we see today probably all descended from one pair that God saved on the ark. From there, bears have spread throughout the whole earth. Though bears today have many specialized features or variations, such as the partially webbed paw and the white fur of the polar bear, all bears share similar genes. There have even been bears found that are part grizzly bear and part polar bear – named pizzly bears! So, different species of bears are able to mate and produce young. In God's creation, then, there is probably only one bear *kind*, though scientists have separated them into different species.

Even though most bears are predominantly vegetarians, their teeth classify them in order Carnivora.

You may be surprised to learn that bears are mostly vegetarians. In fact, they can survive, and even thrive, eating only vegetation. So why on earth are they classified in order Carnivora? Do you remember what feature scientists look for to put an animal in order Carnivora? If you said their teeth, you have a great memory. Bears have carnassial teeth, but most bears prefer fruits, roots, shoots, and nuts, as well as the occasional insect and fish. Because such a huge animal lives on a diet of mainly vegetables, it spends almost every waking moment looking for and eating food.

Most bears will eat meat if it's an easy catch or they have a hankering for something more substantial. The polar bear is the only bear that must eat meat, as that's the main kind of food available in the frozen area in which it lives. The panda, on the opposite end of the food spectrum, will rarely eat anything but bamboo. It's an herbivorous carnivore. Imagine that! We'll learn more about each of these bears in a moment.

Have you ever heard the nursery rhyme "Fuzzy Wuzzy was a bear, Fuzzy Wuzzy had no hair, Fuzzy Wuzzy wasn't fuzzy, was he?" Well, in addition to not being fuzzy, Fuzzy Wuzzy was likely not even a bear, because all bears have hair! Actually, Fuzzy Wuzzy could have been a newborn bear, because cubs are born with almost no hair. They begin to grow hair not long after birth. The hair comes in four basic varieties, depending on the species: brown, black, gold, or white. Bears are predominantly one color, with other colors providing distinctive markings.

Bears can smell as well as or better than dogs, but they can't see or hear as well. They tend to be nearsighted, which means they see things better the closer they are, and their ears are rather small for such a large creature. The most prominent feature on a bear's face is…you guessed it…the mouth, which opens wide in a lengthy growl when the bear is threatened. Inside that big bear mouth are the teeth that place it in order Carnivora. Except for polar bears, however, the back molars are not nearly as sharp as those found in most meat-eaters. They are blunter, like a plant-eater's teeth, for grinding up vegetation.

How big do you think the biggest bear grows? If you have a tape measure, measure out 11 feet from the ground up. That may be higher than the ceiling in your house. Imagine in that space, standing before you, a fully grown brown bear. That's how big they grow! Yes, that might be a bit frightening. Even if it were just teasing you, one swipe with its powerful paw, and you would be a mess. In fact, that is all it takes for a bear to kill a small animal – a single blow from its paw.

Most bears are smaller than the brown bear, but all bears are fairly big when fully grown.   Even the sun bear, the smallest species of bear, can weigh almost 150 pounds when fully grown. To make themselves seem even bigger, they can stand up on two legs and even walk a few steps. Thankfully, bears tend to stay down on all fours most of the time. They only get up on their hind legs when they feel threatened, need a better look, or are trying to reach something high in a tree. They tend to lumber around slowly unless they really need to run. They only run if they are chasing another creature or being chased themselves. Some bears can run faster than 30 miles per hour, so they usually catch what they chase. Most bears also have the ability to climb trees.

Most bears are good tree-climbers. This is very useful for bear cubs, because they can escape danger by climbing up a tree.

Even though they can seem cute and even cuddly, bears are rather gruff and rough, particularly when they encounter another bear. Male bears are especially willing to clash with other males during mating season. Since they do not help the female raise the cubs, they may kill (and even eat) their own cub if they encounter it alone in the forest. However, there are some times when bears come together in peace to hunt for salmon in the rivers.

Do you know what many bears do during the winter? They sleep! Because of this, some people say they **hibernate** (hi' bur nayt), but that's not really true. If you took Zoology 1, you know that when an animal really hibernates, its breathing slows down a lot, and its body temperature lowers to a point where it is almost the same temperature as the surrounding air. Bats hibernate like that; bears do not. After filling up with all they can eat from spring to fall, bears retreat to a special den and lie down for a long winter's nap, living off their body fat the entire time. Because their breathing and body temperature decrease only a little during this period, we say that bears experience **dormancy** during the winter. Dormancy is a state of temporary inactivity – a long, quiet nap. An animal that is truly in a state of hibernation, like a bat, is not easily awakened. A bear, however, is quite easily awakened from its winter's rest. A mother bear can even give birth to cubs during dormancy. The nearly hairless cubs snuggle up next to mother bear, keeping warm in her thick fur.

Because bears can't live in harmony with people, their survival becomes threatened when people develop cities on their territories and chase them out of the area. They are also hunted for their fur. In China, bears are more endangered than in other areas. This is because bears are hunted for their gall bladder and pituitary gland, which are used in Chinese folk medicine. Though many bears are threatened, conservation laws have completely changed the endangered status of two bears. Because of strict laws that have been made to protect them, the American black bear and the polar bear are no longer endangered. Now these two bear species are found in large numbers in their specific habitats.

If you see a polar bear in the wild, it's a good idea to get to a safe place. Polar bears will consider any large creature to be food. If you see an American black bear in the wild, it will probably be looking for food as well. However, it isn't interested in eating people; it is interested in eating the things people eat, like chips, hot dogs, and hamburgers. Don't feed them! Read on to learn why.

Do Not Feed the Bears

This black bear knows there is yummy food in the trash bin, and he is looking for a way to get in.

People love the outdoors. They enjoy camping in natural habitats where bears live. The American black bear has learned something about these people: they bring lots of yummy food with them. They have learned that this food is found in containers, like coolers and trash cans. Sometimes, the containers are left outside. Sometimes they are inside but are easy to get to, because they are in tents or because a door has been left open.

For years, campers have enjoyed feeding bears from their car windows, or leaving food out and watching the bears come close to eat. Guess what has happened to those bears? They have become habituated. Remember that habituated means unafraid of people, *not* tame. Bears that have become habituated to humans are a big problem. They lose their natural fear of people. They seem so calm and tame to campers and hikers. This deceives the campers. Many of them begin to hand-feed the bear. However, once the food is gone, the bear will often swipe or bite the person that fed it. This is often the way a bear behaves once it has been fed. It isn't usually trying to kill the person. It just swats or bites to show its displeasure. You see, this is how a bear acts towards another bear if it is mad. Because of this behavior, bears that are habituated and attempt to get too close to people must be trapped and relocated to a place people don't frequent. Almost always, the bear finds its way back – even across hundreds of miles. When it returns to the same location, the unfortunate result is that the bear must be killed so that it won't harm people. This is why many states with big bear populations use the slogan, "A fed bear is a dead bear." Can you understand why a bear that is fed by people must eventually be killed?

If You See a Bear

Have you ever wondered what you should do if you see a bear out in the wild? Should you run? Grab a weapon and fight? Play dead? Scream and holler at it? Wildlife experts say never turn and run away from a bear. It will feel compelled to chase you, and most bears can run a lot faster than people. Running away is never the answer. Don't climb a tree either, because most bears are better climbers than you are. A bear can also push down smaller trees. What you should do is face the bear without looking it in the eye and slowly back away. Don't run – simply keep backing away and look confident and commanding. If you are in a group, huddle together to make yourselves look bigger. This should be sufficient to make the bear leave you alone – unless you are between a cub and its mother.

Mother bears are very protective. NEVER get between a mother bear and her cubs!

If the bear rises up on its hind legs, it may just be trying to get a better look or smell the air. This is not a sign of aggression. If it begins making a popping sound with its jaw, it is warning you. If it runs after you, don't panic. This is usually a bluff, where the bear is just pretending to charge at you, hoping to frighten you off. If this happens, wave your arms and shout at the bear. If the bear doesn't stop before it reaches you, you need to fight back. Use whatever you have at hand to punch the bear in the nose – the tenderest part of a bear. However, the top and side of the head are very tough. Aim for the face. This will probably make the bear feel the fight isn't worth it. When it stops fighting, begin backing away again.

Some people have been told to play dead. This isn't a great idea if you are facing an American black bear, as it would probably bite you more or drag you away. A grizzly bear might leave you alone if you played dead. With grizzly bears, the best way to ward off an attack is to drop down, roll into a ball like a baby in the womb, and put your hand behind your neck. This has been the most effective posture to calm a grizzly bear.

Try This!

You never know when you may find yourself face to face with a bear. You may be hiking or camping and be surprised by a large shape lumbering nearby. I hope you would remember everything you just learned. Well, the best way to remember it is to do it. Why don't you practice what you would do if you saw a bear in the wild? Choose someone to be the bear; that person will do all the things a bear may do. Someone else will do all the things a person should do if he sees a bear. First, pretend that the bear is not a grizzly. Then pretend it's a grizzly. Of course, please don't punch your pretend bear!

Brown Bears

hump

This brown bear is almost cream-colored. You know it is a brown bear, however, because of its muscle hump.

There are several types of **brown bear** (*Ursus arctos*), including grizzly bears, Kodiak bears, and Mexican brown bears. Although they are called "brown bears," they do not always appear to be brown. A brown bear's fur can come in many shades of brown, from cream to a brown that is so dark it appears to be black. The best way to identify a brown bear is to look for a large hump above the shoulders. This hump contains muscles that allow them to dig effectively. Though they will usually avoid humans, brown bears have long been the most dangerous bears to people. They are extremely aggressive, especially a mother bear that thinks her cubs are being threatened. Can you imagine one of these fearsome creatures, reared up on its hind legs, roaring and chasing people through the woods? These bears have become the object of many tall tales.

Though a large part of their diet comes from roots, shoots, leaves, and fruits, brown bears do eat meat, especially at certain times during the year. They will eat insects and fish, as well as mammals like squirrels, young deer, and young bison. In some regions, they even steal cattle from ranchers. Brown bears in Alaska and Russia also enjoy a nice salmon dinner…or lunch…or breakfast. These lumbering giants are comfortable in water and are quite adept at fishing for salmon. As you learned in Zoology 2, salmon make an annual migration upstream to spawn. During this time, the normally solitary brown bears form huge groups that congregate along the rivers

This brown bear in Alaska is about to have a fresh salmon dinner!

through which the salmon travel, eating to their hearts' content. Salmon season is a very important time for these bears, providing the nutrients needed for the bear's survival through the winter. In fact, during that season, salmon is almost the only thing a brown bear in Alaska or Russia eats!

American Black Bears

This cartoon, drawn by Clifford Berryman in 1902, is credited with starting the teddy bear craze.

Did you ever have a teddy bear? Well, you may not know that the **American black bear** (*Ursus americanus*) was the inspiration for the original teddy bear. In 1902, President Theodore Roosevelt was in Mississippi to settle a border dispute. While there, his hosts took him hunting, an activity he was known to love. However, the hunting was so poor that his hosts captured a female black bear and tied her to a tree. They tried to get President Roosevelt to shoot her, but he refused to shoot a helpless target. An editorial cartoonist, Clifford Berryman, read the story and drew a cartoon about it. After this, little stuffed bears were made and called teddy bears, after Theodore Roosevelt.

American black bears are the most abundant bears in North America. They live in most states of the United States, in Canada, and even down to central Mexico. Some states have a huge number of black bears, like Alaska (with about 100,000) and Oregon (with 25,000). Other states, such as Texas and Alabama, may have only 50 bears or so in the entire state. You aren't as likely to run into a bear in the Southern or Midwestern regions of the United States. However, the further north or west you go, the more common American black bears become.

If you do happen to see a bear in the wild, it's probably a black bear. It might be hard to tell it from a brown bear, however, because American black bears are sometimes very light brown colored, and brown bears can be so dark that they look black. To tell the difference, you can look at three things. First, remember that brown bears have a large hump on the back. Black bears can have a hump as well, but it is usually small. Second, black bears have larger and less furry ears than brown bears. Third, a black bear's face has a rather straight profile, while a brown bear's profile has a dip between the eyes and the snout. Finally, if you look at their tracks, you can see that a brown bear's claws are longer than the claws of a black bear. The black bear's short claws make it an

Despite its brown color, this is an American black bear. Notice the long ears and lack of a hump.

excellent climber, while the brown bear's long claws make it great at catching slippery prey, like salmon. Black bears are smaller than brown bears, which is sometimes the best way to tell them apart.

American black bears don't usually rear up on their hind legs like brown bears do. They're most often found walking along the ground on all fours like a dog. However, they are as strong as any bear; one swipe from a paw can cause instant death to a small creature. American Black bears will also eat almost anything; they especially love the easy-to-get people food brought by campers.

Polar Bears

The snout of the adult polar bear in this picture shows that its skin is black.

Polar bears (*Ursus maritimus*) are black. I know that doesn't seem right, but it is. Their *skin* is black, which allows them to soak up as much warmth as possible from the sun. Over that black skin, these bears have clear, air-filled hairs that appear whitish-yellow. This helps them blend in with the snowy surroundings of their Arctic habitat. They are one of the largest carnivores in the world. Males can weigh more than 1,500 pounds and can stand up to 11 feet tall. Females are smaller, but they are still impressive. Because grizzly bears and polar bears sometimes have overlapping territories, they have been known to mate, producing "pizzly bears." Scientists classify polar bears and brown bears as different species because of their different features. However, as creationists, we think these bears are all part of the same "kind" that God created on the sixth day.

Polar bears have adapted to swimming quite well and can hold their breath for almost two minutes. They use their huge front paws that are slightly webbed between the toes to paddle through the water. In addition, their long hairs stick together when they are wet, forming a watertight barrier that protects the skin.

In the summer, polar bears often eat plants, but they never give up eating meat. Their favorite food is the ringed seal. They'll swim up to 60 miles from shore looking for this delicacy. They often wait around breaks in the ice. When a seal comes up to the surface of the water to breathe, it is grabbed. Also, during the spring, mother seals build little snow piles on top of the ice. That's where they put their pups. Polar bears sniff out the pups, breaking into the chamber and eating them.

Because seals, walruses, and whales must come to the water's surface to breathe air, polar bears often prey on them as well. Once again, a polar bear will wait near breaks in the ice for these mammals to surface and breathe. When they come up, the bear claws or bites the animal, dragging it onto the ice. Sometimes, if the bear spots a seal on the ice, it will slowly and silently move toward it. Once it is about 50 feet away, it charges at top speed before the creature can escape. Though these creatures are enormous and heavy, they can run at almost 25 miles per hour.

Some people say that the earth is experiencing a global warming because of pollution, and this threatens the polar bears. That's not really true. Careful measurements of earth's average temperature over the past 30 years show no significant warming trend, so the idea that the globe is warming has little scientific support. If you want to learn more about global warming, visit the course website I told you about in the introduction. But for now, let's just talk about polar bears. Because polar bears live on the ice, some people are afraid they will become extinct if the ice begins to melt in the Arctic. Although I don't think there is scientific evidence to support the idea that the earth is warming up enough for this to happen, let's discuss what would happen to polar bears if it did.

Polar bears survive just as well on land as they do on ice. In fact, many of them spend the summer on land. Often, seals "haul out" on land rather than ice, so polar bears could still hunt seals, even if ice were not around. Further, polar bears in captivity thrive on fish, fruits, and vegetables. This is not their normal diet, but if a lack of ice made it impossible for them to hunt seals, they could easily adapt to the kinds of food polar bears in captivity eat. The polar bear population is not in danger because of melting ice. In fact, the polar bear population has

This polar bear is waiting for a mammal to surface at a break in the ice. However, this is not the only way polar bears hunt, so a loss of ice would not necessarily mean a loss of polar bears.

exploded in the last forty years – growing from 5,000 bears to 25,000. After doing a huge study of the worldwide polar bear population, widely respected polar bear authority Dr. Mike Taylor said, "We're seeing an increase in bears that's really unprecedented…" [*The Scotsman*, February 7, 2005] So we need not worry about these white giants.

Sun Bears

The short, sleek fur and golden markings tell you this is a sun bear.

Perhaps Winnie the Pooh was modeled after a **sun bear** (*Helarctos malayanus*). These slow, sleepy bears are about the size of a large dog (standing only 3 or 4 feet high), making them the smallest bears on earth. This is why they are also called "dog bears" and sometimes kept as pets. They are omnivores, mostly craving bees (and their honey), termites, and worms. Sun bears extract their food from holes and crevices with a long (up to 10 inches) tongue. With their sleek, short hair, they are perfectly suited for the tropical forests of Southeast Asia in which they live. They are usually black in color with a golden face and a golden sun shape on their chest. Being nocturnal, they spend most of the day in trees, sleeping in the lower branches and eating the fruits that grow there.

Giant Pandas

Giant pandas (*Ailuropoda melanoleuca*) are adored by most animal lovers. These creatures are probably the most docile bears in the woods (the woods of China, that is). Pandas seem so endearing with their little black ears perched high on their furry white heads. Perhaps it's the panda's droopy eyes, set deep inside sloping black patches, that make it so adorable.

Although they eat mostly bamboo, giant pandas are omnivores.

Although these bears prefer bamboo, most people are surprised to learn that they will eat other animals now and again, just like any other bear. Giant pandas are slow creatures, so when they eat meat, they usually choose grubs, which they find under the ground. They will also eat carrion (the remains of dead animals). When eating bamboo, the panda uses what look like **opposable** (uh poh' zuh bul) **thumbs**. This is rare, because most mammals don't have opposable thumbs. However, you have them! This just means that your thumbs can move around and be placed across your fingers to help you grab things. The Panda's "thumb" is actually just an extended wrist bone, so it is not really a thumb. However, the panda uses it like an opposable thumb, grasping bamboo between the "thumb" and its claws so it can strip the bamboo shoot of its leaves.

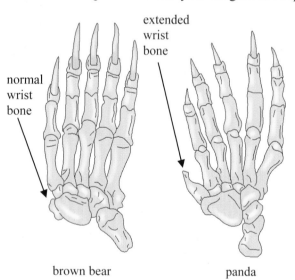
normal wrist bone

extended wrist bone

brown bear   panda

These drawings of paw bones show you the difference between a brown bear's paw and a panda's paw. The panda uses its extended wrist bone as a thumb.

Oddly, giant pandas do not have a single predator in the forests of China. However, they are still seriously endangered because of habitat loss. Wildlife conservationists have worked to increase the population by both protecting their habitat and breeding them in captivity. There are almost 200 giant pandas kept in zoos around the world. Sadly, zoos have not been very successful in breeding them. Only three out of ten captive-bred giant panda cubs live for more than six months.

In the wild, giant panda reproduction isn't much better than in zoos. As cute and docile as these giant creatures are, they sometimes lack parenting skills. Occasionally, for example, the mother simply won't care for her young. Also, if twins are born, the mother chooses one twin to raise and abandons the other. Some researchers believe that some pandas may live their whole life without ever bearing young. These problems may be the result of a mutation that occurred in the panda population. We'll learn more about mutations in the next lesson.

The panda cub is only 6 inches long when born, and like all bear cubs, it is born blind and helpless. The mother must keep it warm, clean, and fed. It requires so much care that the mother often doesn't leave her cub for any reason for almost a month; she often doesn't even eat during that time. In a little over two months, the cub can stand and walk a few steps. By the time it is four months old, the cub is very active, running around and climbing on its mother's back. When the cub is five months old, it follows its mother around, copying what she does. This is how it learns to eat bamboo, climb trees, and all the other things a good panda must do. By the time the panda is about 18 months old, it is ready to live on its own and will leave its mother.

If bears are predominantly one color, is a panda white with black spots or black with white spots? What do you think? Well, panda cubs are born with sparse, white hair, so it is most reasonable to think of pandas as white bears with black spots.

Try This!

How easy do you think it would be to live without an opposable thumb? You might be surprised how dependent you are on this one little feature God has given you. Why don't you try and see what it would be like to live without the use of your thumb for a few hours. Wrap some masking tape around your index finger and thumb so your thumb is stuck to your index finger and cannot move on its own. Spend a few hours doing what you would normally do throughout the day. Definitely try to eat a snack or a meal before you take the tape off. Aren't you glad God gave you opposable thumbs?

Explain to someone what you have learned about bears.

Musky Mustelidae

Now that you've had a good introduction to family Ursidae, I want to move on to another family of caniforms. Many years ago, it was considered a mark of wealth for a woman to own and wear **mink**. What is mink? Well, a mink (*Mustela vison*) is a little, ferret-like creature with unusually soft fur. It belongs in family **Mustelidae** (mus' tih luh day'), which is also called the weasel family. These carnivores are considered more dog-like than cat-like, though they are very different from either dogs or cats.

Minks have soft fur that is highly prized by hunters.

Most of the members of family Mustelidae, often called **mustelids** (mus' tuh lidz) are blessed with luxuriously soft fur, making them a favorite among hunters. For hundreds of years, people in cold climates have longed for mink, sable, ermine, and even otter coats. Even though they have been fanatically hunted for hundreds of years, the sable and certain otters are the only mustelids that are considered endangered today.

A badger's burrow is a mass of tunnels and underground caves called a **sett**. As portrayed in the *Wind in the Willows*, the sett is kept meticulously clean and passed down from one generation to the next

God created many different kinds of mustelids, including badgers, wolverines, otters, martens, ferrets, and weasels. In fact, the family name comes from the Latin word "mustela," which means "weasel." They are all part of the same family, because they are similar in many aspects. However, there are many differences, as well. For example, many of these mustelids live and hunt in different ways. Badgers dig holes and burrow under the ground, while martens live in trees. Otters spend almost all their time in the water, while minks only spend part of their day swimming.

So why are these creatures all part of the same family? Well, despite their differences, they also have many things in common, like a big stink! Mustelids have scent glands that reek of a strong, distasteful odor. Many mustelids use their scent glands when threatened. They turn their behind to the enemy, raise their tail, and spray noxious liquid at the offending creature. Some mustelids even scream or stand on their front paws while doing this. Sounds like the behavior of skunks, doesn't it? Well, at one time, skunks were considered mustelids because of this very fact. In addition, the striped polecat and the African striped weasel (which are mustelids) actually look like skunks, with a white stripe going from their head to their tail. Nevertheless, skunks are no longer considered mustelids. They are now in their own family, which we'll study next.

What else, besides stink glands, makes an animal a mustelid? Well, mustelids sport short legs and long bodies – though some, like the badger and wolverine,

The wolverine is a thick-furred mustelid that looks like a small bear. It lives in colder regions of the world like Siberia and Alaska and is able to crush frozen meat and bone with its powerful jaws. It lives in caves, burrows made by other animals, or under the snow.

have a wider body than others. Also, most mustelids, except otters and badgers, are loners. Much like bears, they usually don't run in packs or spend time with other mustelids, unless they are mating or raising young. Unlike bears, however, almost all the mustelids are primarily carnivorous, always on the hunt for small or big animals to eat. Since we don't have time to discuss all the different mustelids in great detail, let's just examine one of the cuter members of this family: the **otter**.

Otters

Like children, otters love to play. They scamper about on their webbed feet, frolicking in and out of water, playing chase or tug of war with fellow otters. Not surprisingly, then, a group of otters is called a **romp**. Each romp of otters typically has its own territory where the members hunt, live, and play together.

There are many difference species of otters, and they can be found in rivers, streams, and oceans all over the world. Being carnivorous, they typically feast on aquatic animals like fish, clams, and crabs. They return to land only to rest in their small home, which is called a **holt**.

Northern river otters like these (*Lontra canadensis*) can be found in the waterways of North America.

At more than half a million hairs per square inch, their dense fur keeps their skin dry as they swim in the water. It also traps a layer of air against the skin, which helps insulate them from the cold. While this wonderful fur keeps them healthy in cold water, it has caused them trouble in another way. You see, this fur has been highly valued by people, and as a result, many species of otter have been hunted to the point where they were considered in danger of becoming extinct. Thankfully, however, many species (like the **sea otter**, *Enhydra lutris*) are now protected by conservation laws. As a result, their numbers are growing.

The variety among otters is astounding! Some, like the **northern river otters** pictured above, live in freshwater, while others, like the sea otter, swim in saltwater. Some otters have long, thick tails, while others have flatter, paddle-like tales. Most otters are fairly small, growing up to 3 or 4 feet in length. The **giant otter** (*Pteronura brasiliensis*) found in South America, however, can grow to be 6 feet long. That's a huge creature! Imagine an otter that is as long as your dad is tall!

Sea otters often swim on their backs. This allows them to eat, use tools, and even cradle young while they stay in the water.

Otters are rare among animals in that many of them regularly use tools to get things done. Primates (monkeys and apes) often use tools as well, and some other specific animals have been shown to use tools from time to time. However, tool use is rare among animals. Like primates, however, otters have developed the ability to find the right tools for the job, and that job is getting food. Sea otters, for example, use stones to bash open the clams they want to eat. With their excellent eyesight, sea otters find just the right rock from the bottom of the ocean and bring it up to the surface. They then set a clam or similar shellfish on their stomach and use the rock to pound on the shell until it cracks open.

The sea otter's webbed feet have **retractable claws**, which means it can pull its claws in and out of its paws. It uses its claws for combing and water-proofing its thick fur as well as for catching prey. In fact, the most important thing a sea otter pup learns is how to clean and groom its fur. This process helps coat the fur with oils that the otter's skin glands produce, and it helps keep a layer of air trapped against the skin. This makes the fur waterproof, so the otter stays warm and its skin stays dry as it scampers about in the waves.

The sea otter spends almost all its time in the water. Otters love kelp (seaweed) beds. The kelp hides many sea creatures that the otter likes to eat and offers it a leaf bed upon which to rest. Sea otters also wrap themselves in long strands of kelp anchored to the seafloor. That way, they can sleep without floating out to sea.

As shown in the picture above, a sea otter spends a lot of time floating on its back. This allows the otter to use its stomach as a table for its food, a workplace for its tools, and even as a crib for its pups. A sea otter's pups are born in the water and can float, but they cannot swim at first. Thus, their mother often carries them on her stomach. Interestingly enough, most otters that live in freshwater give birth to their pups in their holts on land, and the pups stay in their holts for several months.

The Great Hunt

A few hundred years ago, sea otters were hunted mercilessly all over the world. It all started in 1741, when a sea captain (Vitus Jonassen Bering) working under Russian czar Peter the Great started exploring the Siberian Pacific to see whether or not Asia and North America were connected by land.

His ship was wrecked, and in order to survive, his crew hunted and ate sea otters. They also noticed that the sea otter fur kept them very warm. As a result, they brought almost a *thousand* sea otter pelts (skins with fur) back to Russia. Many of those pelts reached Chinese markets, and the Chinese *loved* them. The pelts came to be in such high demand that a single coat or belt made with sea otter fur could be worth *a full year's pay*. Needless to say, hunters constantly navigated the icy waters from Russia to Alaska in pursuit of otter pelts.

Soon, there were almost no more sea otters in Alaska. The Russians – having no more use for a frozen land with few sea otters – sold the region to the United States. Americans also joined the hunt for otters, causing the population of otters to decrease even more. By 1911, scientists became worried about the sea otter becoming extinct in that region, so a treaty was signed protecting them. Today, otters are on the comeback thanks to laws that continue to protect them from hunters. Although you can still find them in Alaska, sea otters are mostly found along the California coast, especially near Monterey.

If you want to learn more about other mustelids, like the wolverine, mink, sable, or ermine, go to the course website I told you about in the introduction. There you will find links to information about these specific mustelids.

Mephitidae Stink

Because skunks have their own nasty smell, scientists used to classify them in family Mustelidae. However, once scientists compared skunk genes to other mustelid genes, they noticed that skunks had too many genetic differences to put them in the same family as otters, minks, etc. So, they have now moved the skunks into their own family, **Mephitidae** (mef' ih tih day'). This family name makes sense, since the Latin word *mephit* means "foul odor." This new family includes several species, such as the hog-nosed, striped, and spotted skunks of North America and the "stink badger" of Asia. Although skunks are usually black and white, some skunks are brown or gray, and a few are

Striped skunks (*Mephitis mephitis*) can be found throughout most of North America.

cream-colored. All skunks are striped. They may have a single thick stripe across their back and tail, or two thinner stripes instead of one. Even the spotted skunk has a series of broken white stripes that make it look more spotted than striped.

When skunks feel threatened, they can spray their noxious, sticky spray up to 20 feet away. They warn their victims first by hissing and/or stamping their feet. One kind of skunk, the spotted skunk, will raise itself into a handstand and walk toward you with its hind legs in the air. The goo in their spray contains several chemicals, some of which can actually cause temporary blindness if they get in your eyes. Their smell is so powerful that it can be detected by humans over a mile away. So, if you ever spot a skunk with its back to you and see it stamping its feet, run away as fast as you can.

Most skunks live in North and South America, but the stink badger, which is a type of skunk, lives in Indonesia and the Philippines. These animals have great digging feet, which they use to hollow out their dens and to search for food. Like mustelids, these creatures are mostly carnivorous, but they do eat plant material from time to time. They prefer eating eggs, insects, and other small mammals, but they are also scavengers. Skunks will break into your garbage, just like the raccoons you are about to study. Skunks are also notorious for carrying rabies. In the year 2000, there were more than 2,200 cases of rabies from skunk bites in the U.S. and Puerto Rico. You'll learn about rabies in a moment.

Prying Procyonidae

Notice the front paws that give the raccoon its name.

Mischievous and crafty, the rascally raccoon has long been a neighbor to folks living in the New World. Have you ever seen a picture of Daniel Boone wearing his signature coonskin cap with its ringtail hanging down? Even though raccoons have been hunted since the days of old, they still dwell in abundance in many parts of North and South America, from southern Canada to northern Argentina.

Raccoons make up the genus **Procyon** (prah' see ahn) of the family **Procyonidae** (prah' see ahn' uh day). Animals in this family have medium or long tails, most of which are ringed. They have five toes on each foot and are plantigrades – which is important to know if you are looking for their tracks! There are three main species of raccoon: the common **northern raccoon** (*Procyon lotor*), the **crab-eating raccoon** (*Procyon cancrivorus*), and the **Cozumel raccoon** (*Procyon pygmaeus*). The name "raccoon" comes from the Native American word "arakum," which means "he scratches with his hands." If you've ever seen a raccoon's front paws up close, you can understand why Native Americans focused on their "hands" when they named this creature.

Raccoons have five digits on each paw, and they use their front paws ("hands") with amazing dexterity. So you see, people aren't the only creatures that God created with hands that can do fine work! Raccoons also have them, as do primates (like monkeys), which we'll learn about in another lesson.

Raccoons walk like bears, but only grow to be the size of a small dog. They prefer to live in trees and are easily recognized by the black fur that lines their eyes, making them look like some kind of bandit. It seems that God had a sense of humor when He placed that "bandit patch" across the raccoon's eyes, because these animals are notorious for stealing things. In fact, some friends of mine had the biggest trouble with raccoons coming into their kitchen at night through the cat door. The raccoons opened their drawers and cabinets and ate all their dry food. They even opened boxes of cereal and ate the contents! In many areas of the United States, raccoons go so far as to move into the house, making their home in people's attics. They're also bad about sifting through trash cans left outside and spilling the contents all over the ground in their search for food.

If you've ever read *Where the Red Fern Grows*, you already know something about raccoons. They are curious and fearless, and rarely pass up the opportunity to explore an interesting smell or crevice. They will probe a crack with their front feet and pull anything of interest from the hole for closer inspection. For years, they have been hunted by people and their coon dogs. Their pelts were so valuable that in the early history of the United States, they were used as a substitute for money. However, for coon dogs, hunting raccoons is risky business. It's been said that raccoons are so crafty, they'll lure dogs into the water and then drown them!

Raccoon males hunt and live alone. A raccoon female, however, forms a family group with her young. The family group does everything together so that the mother can teach her young how to hunt, climb, and swim. Usually, the family group stays together until the mother raccoon has her next set of babies. During mating season, these creatures become quite noisy, with screams and loud chirping noises that fill the night. Baby raccoons (called **kits**) are especially noisy.

Of course, raccoons aren't the only members of family Procyonidae. The South American coati is found from the southern United States to northern Argentina. It looks like an orange raccoon with a doglike head. The kinkajou (kink' uh joo) and the olingo (oh' lin go) live in Central and South America. These two members of family Procyonidae have unusually long tails, and the kinkajou can actually use its tail to grasp things, like the branch of a tree. Scientists call this kind of tail **prehensile**. Can you think of another animal with a prehensile tail? Like the kinkajou, a monkey can wrap its tail around a tree branch and hang from it.

This picture shows a kinkajou using its prehensile tail to hang from a limb.

You can see why red pandas are put in the same family as raccoons.

Family Procyonidae also has an Asian member: the **red panda** (*Ailurus fulgens*). It can be found in many parts of Southeast Asia, but it is generally associated with China. It is not a bear, but like the panda bear, it eats bamboo. It also eats berries, flowers, leaves, and bird eggs. There is another thing these two cute animals have in common: a "thumb." Like the panda bear, the red panda has an extended wrist bone it can use like a thumb to strip branches from bamboo shoots. Unlike the panda bear, however, it has the ringed tail and face markings of a raccoon.

Raccoon Rabies

I told you earlier that many skunks have rabies. Well, even more raccoons do. In the year 2000, there were more than 2,700 cases of rabies in the U.S. that could be traced back to raccoons. What is rabies? It is a potentially deadly disease caused by a **virus**, which is a tiny agent of infection. The virus is carried in an animal's saliva and is spread to other animals (or people) when an infected animal's saliva gets into an open wound or moist tissue (such as the nose, mouth, or eyes) of another animal. The most common way it gets transferred is by an infected animal biting another animal (or a person). Since it can cause death if not treated soon enough, it is important to avoid animals that have the disease.

You can sometimes tell if an animal has rabies by the way it behaves. If an animal acts differently than it normally does, it might have rabies. Wild animals with rabies, for example, may become friendly and approach you, or they may be unusually aggressive. Pets can get rabies when they get in a fight with an animal that has it. A pet with rabies will sometimes lose its appetite and later become aggressive. Sometimes a rabid dog's bark will also sound different. A rabid animal sometimes moves strangely, with an awkward, stiff walk. Some animals become paralyzed in the face or legs, have a drooping jaw, or have a strange facial expression. Animals with rabies sometimes gnaw on their own legs or attack everything, even unmoving objects. Sometimes, a pet with rabies will just slobber more than usual. Unfortunately, *it is impossible to tell if an animal has rabies just by the way it behaves*. That's why the best thing to do to avoid rabies is to keep your pets free of rabies and avoid situations where a wild animal can bite you. Never, ever try to pet a wild animal, no matter how friendly it appears.

The best way to keep your pet from getting rabies is to keep its rabies vaccinations up to date. If you think you have come into contact with a rabid animal, wash off any saliva with hot, soapy water and call your doctor immediately. If you were bit by *any animal*, clean the wound immediately and thoroughly, squeezing it to make any saliva bleed out. The animal that bit you should be tested, which unfortunately means killing it. The only way to tell whether an animal has rabies is to examine its brain, and that cannot be done on a living animal.

What Do You Remember?

What is a plantigrade? Do bears eat mostly meat? What do bears do instead of hibernating? Should you ever feed a bear? Name one way to tell the difference between a black bear and a brown bear. What color is polar bear skin? What is different about a panda's wrist compared to a brown bear's wrist? What kind of otter spends almost all its time in the water? Which is more likely to have rabies: a skunk or a raccoon?

Notebook Activities

Make a notebook page for each of the families you studied in this lesson. Draw, cut out, or print pictures from the Internet for a few members from each family. Write down interesting facts about each. Also, create a comic strip showing people what to do if they see a bear in the wild.

Track It!

Bears and raccoons both walk flat-footed, like people. As you already learned, they are called plantigrades. Finding bear tracks would be an exciting discovery in nature. Bears are one of the few animals that actually prefer to use man-made trails, because it's easier to travel on a trail than through underbrush. So you might see bear footprints on trails in the woods. Also, look for other signs of bears: claw marks on trees, rotten logs that are ripped apart, or hair on tree bark where a bear rubbed against it. Their droppings are large and usually contain leaves and berries.

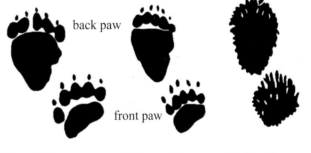

back paw

front paw

Black Bear   Brown Bear   Polar Bear

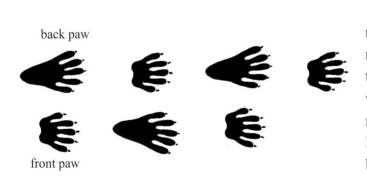

back paw

front paw

Raccoon tracks are common, even in neighborhoods. The back foot looks like a miniature human footprint with really long toes. The front foot looks like a human hand with ballooned fingers. There are usually claw marks above all the prints. The tracks they leave show us that they walk so that the left back foot is almost beside the right front foot, and vice versa.

Map It!

Mark the animals you studied in this lesson on your animal map. **Polar bears**: Alaska, Greenland, and Siberia. **Brown bears**: Alaska, east through the Yukon and Northwest Territories, south through British Columbia and through the western half of Alberta. Also, there are some in the state of Washington, northern Idaho, western Montana, and northwestern Wyoming. **American black bears**: throughout the United States. **Pandas**: central China. **Sun bears**: Southeast Asia. **River otters**: throughout North America. **Sea otters**: the Pacific coasts of Alaska, Canada, and California. **Skunks**: throughout North and South America. **Raccoons**: throughout North America and northern South America.

Experiment

Polar bears have black skin. I told you this is to help keep them warm. In this experiment, you will measure how hot a black trash bag gets when it lays out in the sun and compare that to how hot a white trashbag gets in the sun. Do you think there will be a difference? If so, which do you think will get hotter? Record your hypothesis on a Scientific Speculation Sheet.

You will need:
- Scientific Speculation Sheet
- Two thermometers that read room temperature and above
- A white trash bag and a black trashbag (They need to be the same size and thickness.)
- A sunny patch of sidewalk or driveway (It needs to be sunny for this experiment to work.)
- Some small stones

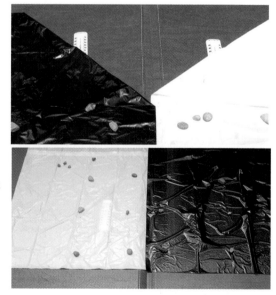

1. Lay the two trash bags on the sidewalk.
2. Put a thermometer under each trash bag, near the center.
3. Arrange some stones on each bag so that the bags do not blow away.
4. Wait about 20 minutes.
5. Pull the thermometers out and read them. Was there a difference in temperature? If so, which bag got hotter? Was your hypothesis correct?
6. Fill out the rest of your Scientific Speculation Sheet.

Different colors absorb different amounts of light. In general, the darker the color, the more light it absorbs. If exposed to the same sun, then, darker-colored objects will get warmer than lighter-colored objects. A polar bear's dark skin helps it to stay warm because it absorbs a lot of light from the sun!

Lesson 4
Feliform Carnivores

We've had an exciting start to our safari through the world of carnivores, but we've only just begun! Let's move on to the interesting carnivores known as feliforms. As we study these fascinating creatures, you'll uncover truths about some mysterious animals, such as cats and hyenas. For example, you'll find out that meerkats are a type of cat and why the mongoose is the most dangerous animal on the earth. Buckle up and let's go!

Family Felidae

As a kitten, even a snow leopard looks cute and playful.

Even people who don't like cats usually can't deny the charm of playful kittens. Every kitten plays, whether it is a tabby, an ocelot, a lynx, or a lion. A kitten is still a kitten, and playing teaches it how to stalk and catch prey as well as defend itself. Kittens (and all true cats) are members of the family **Felidae** (fee' luh dee), which comes from the Latin word "felix," which means "happy." Perhaps it's their tendency to purr or the fact that kittens spend their hours in unending play that earned them the name "happy." Whatever the case, a happy housecat is a purr-fect friend to have around, but a hungry lion…well, that's another story. As you learn about all the wild cats in God's creation, think about a housecat (yours, if you have one). Does it behave like these fierce creatures? You may find domestic cats (*Felis catus*) to be virtually the same as some wild cats in everything but size and color. The wild cats even purr, just like a housecat!

Cats depend on their claws to help them survive. They use their claws when pouncing on prey, fighting with an enemy, and climbing up trees. Most cats have retractable claws, which means they can pull their claws into their paws when they don't need them, and they can extend them out of their paws when they need to. Most caniforms cannot perform this amazing feat (pun intended).

Flexible skeletons allow cats to squeeze through difficult passageways or jump down from tall trees. If you toss a dog out of the house, it will often smack its chin against the ground. If you toss a cat, it will generally land on its feet. Contrary to popular belief, cats don't *always* land on their feet if they fall from a high place, nor do they have nine lives. However, because of their supple body and flexible skeleton, they can survive falls from high places better than many animals.

Cats have acute senses. They can see well both during the daytime and at night because their eyes are very sensitive to light. During the day, their pupils contract into little slits, while at night their pupils dilate so wide that the moonlight makes them appear to glow. They also can hear exceptionally well. Their ears turn toward the source of the noises they hear, even while they appear to be sound asleep.

Cats have an extra sense organ that few animals share. Can you guess what it is? It's their whiskers! A cat's whiskers are not just hairs. They are amazing "sensors" that allow the cat to learn about its surroundings even when it is pitch black. A cat's whiskers actually detect tiny changes in the way air moves. Even in the darkest night, if a cat approaches an obstacle (like a big log, for example), it will sense the slight changes in air movements caused by the presence of the obstacle. It will even know how to move to avoid the obstacle just by sensing the air! A cat's whiskers also tell it whether or not it can fit through an opening. If it can get through the opening without touching the edges with its whiskers, it knows the rest of its body will fit through as well. Since a cat uses its whiskers so much, you should *never* cut a cat's whiskers!

A cat's sense of smell is also very important. Do you remember that I said mammals have scent glands? A cat's scent glands are located on its cheeks, forehead, sides, tail, and paws. Cats rub these glands on trees, rocks, and even on other cats to communicate with them, whether friend or foe. Your housecat will even mark you with its scent as it rubs against your legs. This tells you the cat thinks of you as a part of its family. Like dogs, the males claim territories as off-limits to other males.

Proficient Predators

This cougar is ready to pounce on its prey.

Possessing a powerful body, sharp teeth, piercing claws, and swift reflexes, cats are quite good at what they do best – hunting. Although the Bible indicates that one day, predators and prey will lie down peacefully together, in the fallen world that we are studying, feliforms are more likely to eat than lie down with most other animals. With knife-like molars that can slice through bones, these silent stalkers deliver a powerful bite with their heavy lower jaw. Sometimes they skulk around scoping out possible prey, and other times they conceal themselves awaiting the next passerby. With the tip of its tail slowly wagging back and forth, a cat lowers its front paws, raises its back legs up, and springs when the unsuspecting mouse (or moose) happens by. For a wild cat, that's dinner. A domestic cat usually brings its prey to its leader to eat first – that's you! It's actually an insult to your cat when you don't take its dead mouse inside and eat what you can, giving the leftovers back to the skilled hunter.

All cats have coats that give them a hunting advantage. Just as hunters wear camouflage clothing when they enter the forest, wild cats sport camouflage specially suited for the environment in which they live. Lions and cougars are buff-colored like the dry, grassy fields and savannas in which they roam. A tiger's stripes blend with the tall jungle grasses, while the lynx, ocelot, cheetah, jaguar, and leopard are spotted and speckled to match the way sunlight hits the forest floor as it shines through the trees. The snow leopard is white with black spots so that it blends in with the snow.

Can you explain why these different kinds of cats, all descending from one kind of cat, would look so different from one another today? Remember what you have learned about natural selection.

Specific Spots and Stripes

The larger, spotted cats are often confused with one another. Though **leopards**, **jaguars**, and **cheetahs** have similar markings, there are ways you can tell them apart. Cheetahs are recognized by the black "tear stains" that go from their eyes to their mouth. A leopard is stockier than a cheetah, with lightly colored fur in the center of its rosette-shaped spots. The jaguar is shorter and even stockier than a leopard, and its rosettes are larger, with small black spots sprinkled within a few of them. Another way you can tell the jaguar and leopard apart is by where you find them. Unless you are in a zoo, the leopard is found only in Africa and Asia, while the jaguar lives only in the Americas.

Based on what you just read, identify each cat as a leopard, jaguar, or cheetah. The answers are found with the "Answers to the Narrative Questions" at the back of the book.

Leopards can have kittens that are completely black. They are called **black panthers**, but they are really just black leopards. The black color comes from a chemical called **melanin** (mel' uh nin). Black panthers have more melanin in their fur than most leopards. Black panthers even have leopard spots, but you can only see them if you look closely in the right light. Other cats can have black kittens as well, and they are also sometimes called "black panthers," too. People also have melanin, and if you have dark skin, you have more melanin in your skin than someone with light skin.

Family Names

Family Felidae is usually split into two smaller "subfamilies" called **Felinae** (fel' ih nay) and **Pantherinae** (pan' thuh reen' ay). Subfamily Felinae contains the "small" cats like housecats and lynxes, while Pantherinae contains the "roaring" cats, like lions, tigers, jaguars, and leopards. Some zoologists put the cheetah in subfamily Felinae, but many put the cheetah in its own subfamily, called **Acinonychinae** (uh sih' noh nich' ih nay). This name comes from two Greek words that mean "thorn" and "claw." Can you guess what this refers to? Well, cheetahs can't retract their claws. As a result, their claws are a bit like thorns – they always stick out.

Are you wondering how this special characteristic may have developed in cheetahs over time? Well, cheetahs live on the open plains among the some of the fastest animals in the world – gazelles. In order for cheetahs to have dinner, they need to run faster than their prey. Cheetahs born with claws that did not retract were probably able to catch prey better than the cheetahs with retractable claws, because extended claws give them more traction as they run. This would, most likely, make cheetahs without retractable claws better able to survive. As time went on, the number of cheetahs without retractable claws increased until all living cheetahs had non-retractable claws.

The cheetah is the fastest land animal living on earth. Guess how fast the fastest man can run? The fastest man on earth runs for short distances at a speed of about 23 miles per hour. That is slower than cars are allowed to drive in town. Guess how fast a cheetah can run? It can run at speeds of about 70 miles per hour! That's faster than cars are allowed to drive on most highways! However, cheetahs don't like to work too hard. If they don't catch their prey within a few seconds, they stop and look for something else to eat. Cheetahs can run that fast only over short distances.

The Top of the Food Chain

Enormous, armed, and dangerous, the big cats (subfamily Pantherinae) are not afraid of people. In fact, they aren't afraid of anything. These creatures are **apex predators**. An animal is an apex predator if the other animals around it do not consider it to be their typical prey. Obviously, no animal considers a lion possible prey!

Even though they are fierce hunters, some big cats are endangered, and a few are even extremely endangered. How can they be both dangerous and endangered at the same

This lioness is showing you one reason big cats are apex predators!

time? Well, some big cats are endangered because they are hunted. Many times they are hunted for their pelts, but more often, it's because of the danger they pose to people living in the area. Lions and leopards, for example, have been known to attack people. Leopards are bold enough to confidently saunter right into a busy village and attack! In fact, the **Bengal tiger** of India is the cat with the worst reputation for man eating. This tiger has been preying on unfortunate Indians for thousands of years. In the 1930s, Bengal tigers killed more than a thousand people every year. One renowned tiger, named Champawat, killed over 200 men, women, and children in a few short years before being driven out of Nepal. She then relocated and added 200 more people to her record until she was tracked down and killed in 1937. Even today, more than 50 people are eaten by tigers in India each year. Conservationists want to help save the tigers, while the people of India want to save their children. It's quite a quandary for conservationists in the area. What do you think should be done?

Inform someone of all you know about cats in general before moving on to learn about specific cats.

Lions

With its luxurious mane, the male of this pride is easy to recognize.

With a ferocious roar that can be heard for miles, a **lion** (*Panthera leo*) lets all the animals know that he is the predator, and they are his prey. Of course, male lions are easy to recognize with their mane and the tuft of fur at the end of their tail. In addition, lions are unlike other cats in many ways. You see, lions form strong, supportive, and caring social groups that stick together and nurture one another. This is rare among cats.

A social group of lions, called a **pride**, can have up to 40 or 50 members. It usually consists of several females (lionesses) that are related to each other, their cubs, and a small number (sometimes only one) of males that have actually fought and won the right to be in the pride. The pride does everything together and for each other. Generally, the female lions hunt for the pride, bringing their prey back for everyone. Usually, the males eat first, the females second, and the younger lions last. Each cub is not only cared for by its mother, but also every other female in the pride. Females may even nurse cubs that are not their own. Unlike dogs (that, remember, only allow one female to reproduce), every lioness in the pride is allowed to have cubs. Each lioness lives for about twelve years. Male lions have a shorter lifespan because they spend a lot of time fighting other males for leadership in the pride or the right to become a part of the pride.

Although lions take wonderful care of their cubs, male cubs are not given the security of long-term membership in the pride. Once a male cub reaches three to four years old, he's out of the pride. He will either become a loner or fight to become part of a new pride. Another option would be for him to join with other male lions to form a coalition. If several males are turned out of their pride together, they'll often form their own coalition. A coalition of male lions can fight the male lions of another pride. The winners become the new males of the pride.

The top male in the pride only keeps his position as long as no other males challenge him. If one does challenge him and wins the role of the top male in the pride, it will then destroy all the cubs sired by the former top male. This practice is called **infanticide** (in fan' tih side). Why does the new top male do this? It's because he wants to have cubs, and females will not mate if they are nursing offspring. If the new leader removes the cubs, the females will mate with the new leader and have cubs by the new leader.

Prides claim a large piece of land or territory and don't allow other prides or coalitions to hunt on their land. The females do most of the work, including the hunting. Every female in the pride is given a different job during a hunt. Some will chase the prey, some direct the prey away from its herd, and another will be the one to ambush and grab the victim. When the cubs wrestle and play with one another, it's not just for fun. The way a female plays during her formative cub years will impact which job she gets when she is old enough to hunt. In addition to practicing for real-life hunts, their abilities are evaluated and their social order is decided during these playful tussles.

These lions are about to enjoy a zebra dinner.

While the females are gathering up the grub, the male (or males) patrols the borders, defending the territory against intruders. One particular intruder that lions hate is the **spotted hyena** (*Crocuta crocuta*). Spotted hyenas prey on cubs and injured lions and often try to steal the kill from a pride or coalition. In the same way, lions will often try to chase hyenas away to gain the hyenas' latest kill. Though lions are powerful and quick, spotted hyenas are ferocious animals with the most powerful bite in the animal kingdom. Lions hate spotted hyenas, and vice versa. In fact, lions sometimes chase and kill hyenas without even eating them. Their purpose in doing so is only to rid the world of hyenas.

Lions inhabit almost any climate in Africa except deserts and rain forests. Lions don't like to live in heavily forested areas. Perhaps they have found it difficult to camouflage themselves there, or they are too large to make their way through underbrush. Interestingly, lions also lived in southern

Europe around the time of Christ. There is also a small number of lions, called **Asiatic lions**, that live in India. They are smaller than African lions with shorter manes, and there are far fewer Asiatic lions than there are African lions.

Let's leave Africa now and head east, crossing the Indian Ocean. We'll travel up through the Bay of Bengal and then climb into another jeep to enter the jungles of Southeast Asia. This is where we'll find our next feline to study.

Tigers

Bengal tigers, like the one pictured here, are the most common type of tiger.

The fearsome **tiger** (*Panthera tigris*) is several hundred pounds heavier than the lion. Unlike lions, tigers prefer the jungle, where their striped coat enables them to blend in with the strips of light that streak through the forest. Stalking silently, this solitary hunter is able to hide from its prey until just the right moment, when it leaps from a tree or from behind a thicket. The tiger disables its prey with a potent bite.

Like all big cats, tigers prefer large prey, which sometimes take an entire week to eat. They will eat any prey available, and the larger it is, the better. How does baby elephant sound for breakfast? Tigers are the only animals that can single-handedly attack and bring down a grown Asian elephant. Tigers are immense creatures, weighing as much as 600 pounds and measuring up to 11 feet long.

There are several different types (subspecies) of tigers. There are Bengal tigers, Siberian tigers, Indochinese tigers, South China tigers, and Sumatran tigers. With so many subspecies of tigers, you would think there would be many of them all over the world. The truth is, there are only about seven thousand actual tigers alive today in their natural habitats. Whether the natives like it or not, India is home to more than 80% of those tigers, and all of them are Bengal tigers.

Perhaps, with the Bengal tiger prowling about, you would rather take this safari through the jungle in the safety of a riverboat. After all, cats hate water, right? Unfortunately, no place in the jungle is safe from tigers. In fact, tigers *enjoy* a romp in the water. They can often be found bathing in lakes, rivers, and ponds. They'll swim out into the water to catch their prey if need be. They've even been known to overturn fishing boats to consume the prey driving the boat. However, the water is just where the tiger could meet his demise. You see, there is one animal that can kill a tiger. Can you guess what animal that is? It's the crocodile.

In addition to being great swimmers, tigers are also amazing jumpers. They can easily jump over a fence that is 7 feet high. This isn't very good for those living in areas where tigers roam. It's difficult to keep them out of a city or homestead. However, it is nice that tigers aren't like lions – they don't rove in groups. They are solitary cats, living and hunting alone. The only time you will find two tigers in the same area is when they are fighting, mating, or caring for young. Most cubs stay with their mother for two or three years, never

Tigers seem to enjoy a good swim from time to time.

encountering their father. That's a good thing, since male tigers are also known for practicing infanticide. Most tigers live ten to fifteen years.

If we journey north, out of the rainforests of Southeast Asia, we will eventually enter the cold pine forest of Siberia, where the Siberian tiger resides. These tigers are lighter in color and larger than the species in the rainforest. In fact, Siberian tigers are the largest type of tiger. They are critically endangered. In 2005, it was estimated that only 431 to 529 existed in the entire world!

Try This!

The tigers stalk the jungles of Southeast Asia, where the forest is very dense. They cannot depend completely on sight to find their food. Try this activity to experience how difficult it is to catch prey when you can't see. Blindfold two people. One will be the predator, the other will be the prey. Then, both people will walk around a room (the jungle). The predator should pursue the prey. When the prey is touched by the predator, the prey has been captured. There is no need to grab; simply touch and the prey is captured. Is it difficult to do this without the sense of sight? What other sense does the predator use? What tactics are used by the prey to avoid capture?

What do you remember about lions and tigers?

North America's Three

There are about forty different species of wild cats all over the world. However, only three inhabit North America: the **Canada lynx** (*Lynx canadensis*), the **bobcat** (*Lynx rufus*), and the **cougar** (*Puma concolor*). There are other cats that live in South America, but let's learn about these three North American cats.

Note the short tail, black tufts at the tips of the ears, and the double-pointed "beard" that mark this as a Canada lynx.

With an eccentric, double-pointed beard hanging off its chin; a short, stubby tail; and noticeable tufts of black hair on the top of each ear, the Canada lynx lives in the colder regions of North America. Because of this, it has very dense fur that turns a bit red in the summer. A Canada lynx always seems to be hunched over, because its front legs are shorter than its back legs! It comes equipped with its own "snowshoes" – large, furry paws that make it much easier for the lynx to walk through the snow. Like most cats, these lynxes are loners. The only "family" groups you will see consist of a mother raising her cubs, which usually stay with her for about a year.

The population of these cats is dependent on how abundant the snowshoe hare is. If there are a lot of snowshoe hares, there will be a lot of lynxes. If the snowshoe hare population decreases, so does the population of lynxes. Why? Because snowshoe hares are the main prey for Canada lynxes. Even though they will eat other small animals such as rodents, birds, and fish, they prefer snowshoe hares. If the population of the snowshoe hare decreases, there will not be enough food to go around, and some Canada lynxes will die as a result.

Bobcats are smaller than lynxes. Often called "wildcats," they are abundant in the United States, with over a million scattered throughout the nation. Their abundance is partially due to the fact that they can eat almost anything, from birds to reptiles to rabbits. Each male bobcat claims about 60 square miles of territory for itself, sometimes less. If one bobcat crosses into another bobcat's territory, there will be trouble. They mark the borders of their territory with scent and droppings.

This bobcat looks a lot like a housecat, doesn't it?

These tan cats have tabby-like streaks of black throughout their spotted coat. Bobcats are only about 3 feet long from the tip of their nose to the tip of their stubby bobbed tail, from which they get their name. That's about twice as big as most housecats. Also like a housecat, bobcats prefer to avoid water, but they will swim when they have to.

This cougar might also be called a puma, a mountain lion, or even a catamount.

When a loud shriek pierces the night air, campers huddle together in fear. Is it a puma or a cougar? Perhaps it's a mountain lion. Actually, all three of these animals are one and the same. Since they were once found all over North America, Central America, and even northern South America, they've been given different names by different people. These cats are the largest, fiercest cats in the New World. They're bigger than leopards, growing more than 7 feet long and weighing more than 160 pounds. They are so powerful they have been seen jumping up onto a ledge that's 12 feet high with a fully grown deer in their mouth. They eat a wide variety of animals (even bobcats and coyotes), but they prefer deer and elk. Cougars are amazing runners as well, clocked at almost 45 miles per hour. No wonder campers tremble when they hear its telltale shriek!

Over time, cougars have become less and less common throughout the New World. This is because a male cougar requires a large territory, sometimes more than 200 square miles! If another male cougar enters that territory, there will be a fight to the death. The more territory people take to build houses and so forth, the less there is available for cougars. As a result, cougars are becoming concentrated in remote, mountainous regions, like those you find in the western United States and Canada. A small population can still be found in Florida.

Try This!

If cougars lived in your area, there would only be one male for every 200 square miles. With this information, can you figure out how many male cougars could live in your state? How about in your city? Male bobcats claim about 60 square miles of territory. How many male bobcats could live in your state? Sample calculations are given for the state of Indiana in the "Answers to the Narrative Questions" at the back of the book.

Explain all that you remember about lions, tigers, Canada lynxes, bobcats, and cougars.

Hyaenidae

What looks like a cross between a mule and a German shepherd but acts like a cat, a vulture, and a shark? A hyena! Its face is dog-like, but its neck is thick and long like a mule. Yet, like a cat, it purrs when it is nursing. Like a vulture, it is a scavenger, cleaning up dead animals in the wild. Given this animal's strange mix of characteristics, you should realize we have stopped talking about true cats (family Felidae) and have moved on to the feliform family called **Hyaenidae** (hi' in uh day).

Since God designed hyenas to be a part of His "cleanup crew," He provided them with special tools for the trade. You might remember that the hyena has the most powerful jaws in the animal kingdom. These animals can easily crush the enormous bones of the large prey they consume. They are even designed with a special ability to digest bones, which is a rare thing in the animal kingdom. Like birds of prey, they form pellets and cough up materials (like hoofs and hair) they can't digest.

The brown hyena (*Hyaena brunnea*) was the inspiration for the hyena characters in the Disney movie *The Lion King*.

Hyenas have a strange configuration of long front legs and short hind legs, which tilts their body upward. This makes them look like they are always running uphill. There are four species of hyenas, named for their coat. The **spotted hyena** (*Crocuta crocuta*) has spots (of course). The **brown hyena** looks more like a sloped-backed wolf, with its shaggy fur and pointed ears (see the picture above). The **striped hyena** (*Hyaena hyaena*) looks much like the brown hyena, but it has more stripes. The **aardwolf** (*Proteles cristata*) looks more like a wolf. The brown hyena lives in southern Africa. While the spotted hyena once ranged throughout Europe and Asia, it is now confined to sub-Saharan Africa. The striped hyena is native to northern Africa, the Middle East, and Asia. There are two populations of aardwolf, one in the southern parts of Africa and the other in the northern parts of Africa.

I said that hyenas also behave like sharks. How's that? Well, spotted hyenas are like shark pups because, from the moment they are born, they try to destroy their siblings, just like sharks do in the womb. These brown, bearlike cubs have an unusual drive to fight for power. The spotted hyena mother might try to intervene, but it does no good. You see, the newborn cubs soon begin digging small tunnels that branch off from the main birthing den, and those tunnels are too small for the mother to fit inside. The cubs crawl into the tunnels and destroy one another if they can. Weaker cubs hide in their tunnel, too afraid to come out and nurse, so they starve to death. If the cubs don't annihilate each other, they'll develop a pecking order, with one being more dominant than the next.

Spotted hyenas behave differently from most other hyenas. Most hyenas are peaceful scavengers, eating carrion and any fruits and vegetables they can find. The spotted hyena doesn't eat any vegetation and, though it will eat carrion, it is an apex predator (in the absence of lions), chasing down prey. Although they form packs (called **clans**), hyenas don't behave like pack animals, which work together to benefit the pack by organizing group hunts and caring for one another's young. The spotted hyenas typically hunt alone, but the food is shared with the more dominant members of the clan. Interestingly enough, females are dominant over males in a spotted hyena clan. If a male makes a kill, for example, females actually get to eat from it first. The most vicious females in the clan are the more dominant ones. Is it any surprise that her offspring are particularly fierce?

Spotted hyena behavior and anatomy are so strange that it seems there may be **mutations** in their gene pool that work against the poor creatures. What exactly are mutations? Mutations are changes to an animal's (or plant's) genes. These changes often cause deformities or diseases, and they can be passed on from parent to offspring.

This spotted hyena female is carrying the one cub that survived from her litter. Notice how bearlike it appears.

So why do I say that spotted hyenas may have mutations in their genes? The most obvious problem is the female's **birth canal**. The birth canal is the passage that a mammal must pass through when it is being born. In most female mammals, the birth canal is short and wide, allowing the babies to come through fairly easily. The spotted hyena, however, has a birth canal that is long and thin. This seeming deformity makes it very difficult and painful for these poor creatures to give birth. About 10% of first-time mothers die giving birth, and about 60% of first-born pups die in the birthing process. Furthermore, before the cub is born, the mother produces a surge of a chemical called **testosterone** (tes tos' tuh rohn). This chemical is common in male mammals, but the large amount of it produced by the mother during pregnancy causes aggression in the cubs. This is one of the reasons the cubs come out ready to fight.

Creation Confirmation

When God created the world, every creature was formed in a way that was good and healthy. However, because of the Fall, disease, deformities, and mutations have entered the world. Mutations are different from natural selection. Remember, natural selection "selects" genes that make an animal (or plant) more likely to survive. However, those genes were already in the animal (or plant). Mutations *change* the genes, either putting something in the genes that wasn't there to begin with or eliminating something that was there.

So what happens when an animal gets a mutation? Is it good for the animal or bad? Well, scientists have studied this question for a long time. For example, scientists have done many, many experiments where they have caused mutations in fruit flies – those tiny flies that are attracted to fruit. When such experiments are done, all sorts of things happen. For example, some mutated fruit flies end up having crinkled wings, unusually small wings, or even no wings at all. Many times, the mutated fruit flies were unable to reproduce. Imagine a fruit fly that can't fly or reproduce! Sometimes, a mutation causes no observable effect to the fruit fly. That's the typical result you see with mutations.

Although scientists have found a few very special cases where mutations can be helpful to a creature, the vast majority of mutations either do not affect the creature or are harmful to it.

Now if you think about how God works, this should make perfect sense. After all, once God created, He pronounced it to be very good. Since God is all-powerful, you would expect that He would design His creation well. Mutations are changes that occur to the creatures God created, but they are not changes made by God. What do you expect to happen when a great design is tampered with by someone or something unfamiliar with the design? Well, suppose you decided to "help" your parents out by "fixing" their broken-down car. You probably don't know much about cars, but you start fooling around with the engine, trying to get it to work. Do you think you would really be helping? Of course not! Most likely, your "help" would result in more damage to the engine. A well-designed engine must be repaired by an expert who understands the design. In the same way, the very fact that most mutations do not help a creature in any way shows that the genes a creature has are *very* well designed. As you would expect with any well-designed system, a change to a creature's genes will rarely have a positive effect on the creature.

This is why I say that the spotted hyena might have mutations in its genes. I seriously doubt that it is good for hyena cubs to be so aggressive when they are born, so I doubt that this was originally a part of God's design. However, a mutation in a hyena's genes long ago could have caused the mother to release large amounts of testosterone to her unborn cubs. The unusual amounts of testosterone would then result in overly aggressive young. These young would quickly kill most of the others in the clan, and as a result, they would be the ones to reproduce, passing this mutation on to their children as well. Over time, more and more aggressive hyenas would be born, and they would wipe out the less aggressive ones, until eventually the only hyenas left were the aggressive ones. It's also possible that the strange birth canal in spotted hyenas is related to the same mutation.

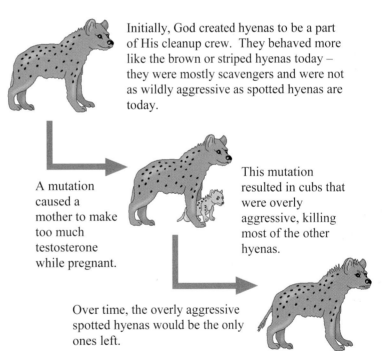

This diagram shows one possible explanation for the unusually aggressive behavior observed in spotted hyenas today.

Initially, God created hyenas to be a part of His cleanup crew. They behaved more like the brown or striped hyenas today – they were mostly scavengers and were not as wildly aggressive as spotted hyenas are today.

A mutation caused a mother to make too much testosterone while pregnant.

This mutation resulted in cubs that were overly aggressive, killing most of the other hyenas.

Over time, the overly aggressive spotted hyenas would be the only ones left.

The important point to all of this is that scientific experiments have shown that mutations rarely help a creature. As a result, if mutations get passed down from generation to generation and get "selected" by natural selection, the result is probably not going to be positive for the creature involved.

Aardwolves

Aardwolves are the smallest of the hyena family.

The only hyena that won't be found eating large mammals is the **aardwolf**. Why? Because its favorite food is quite a bit smaller. Can you guess what it might be? You probably didn't guess correctly if you named a smaller mammal. You can't get much smaller than termites, and that's what the aardwolf prefers to any other food. Termites! In fact, they have special, sticky tongues that are perfect for consuming the 200,000 termites they eat every night. They live in the sandy plains and brush country of Africa, where their termite treats are found.

Though they look almost identical to a miniature hyena, aardwolves seem more like a cross between a skunk and an anteater. Like a skunk, they can spray noxious chemicals from their rear end to ward off predators. Like an anteater, they have a tongue designed specifically to eat small, crawling insects. Interestingly enough, however, while most insect eaters actually burrow into the earth in search of their prey, the aardwolf is happy to simply wait outside a termite mound and lick the termites up as they come out.

The name "aardwolf" comes from the Afrikaans (a language in Africa) word meaning "earth wolf." They received this name when they were noticed coming out of burrows dug into the earth at night. Interestingly enough, while the aardwolf is nocturnal during most of the year, it changes to be diurnal (active during the day) in the winter. Why does it do this? Because termites also change from nocturnal to diurnal during the winter. Since aardwolves wait for their food to come to them, they must change their habits when their food changes its habits!

Viverridae

Imagine walking through the rainforest and seeing kitty cats up in the trees. Well, that could happen in Africa, Asia, or southern Europe, because a group of feliforms that look and act a lot like long-nosed cats lives there. They belong to the family **Viverridae** (vih ver' ih day). Though they are often referred to as African or Asian cats, they aren't kept as pets. They are mischievous and wild and have glands that produce a foul smell.

This large spotted genet (*Genetta tigrina*) is an example of the members of family Viverridae.

Most of the members of this family are nocturnal hunters, spending most of their lives in trees. They eat small animals, like insects and worms. Those that live near water often eat shellfish, and some species supplement their diets with fruits and roots. Their senses of sight, smell, and hearing are sharp, making them fierce and effective predators. Like most cats, they tend to hunt and live alone. Although this is an extremely large group of animals with many different species, less is known about them compared to many other families because they are nocturnal and sneaky. As a result, they are hard to study.

Herpestidae

The yellow mongoose (*Cynictis penicillata*) is a fierce hunter.

Meerkats and mongooses belong to the last family of feliforms you'll study in this book, called **Herpestidae** (her pes' tih day). These carnivores eat a wide variety of animals, including insects, small mammals, birds (and their eggs), and reptiles (especially snakes). Some even eat crabs! Most members of this family live in underground tunnels, which they dig themselves. Because of their habit of digging, most of their meals are made up of beetles and other creatures that live in the dirt.

Some people say that this family is home to one of the most dangerous animals in the world: the **mongoose**. For example, in his famous book *Rikki-Tikki-Tavi*, Rudyard Kipling says, "It is the hardest thing in the world to frighten a mongoose." It may seem that the large lion is the king of the jungle, but the mongoose could easily fight for this title. You see, when a lion faces off against a cobra, the lion will likely end up running away. Not so for the mongoose. No snake is safe in the presence of a mongoose. Because of its speed, a mongoose is able to avoid most of the quick strikes of a snake. It can then kill the snake by sinking its teeth into the base of the snake's skull.

Because of their fierce snake-fighting abilities, mongooses are a favored pet and "watchdog" in the snake-infested places where they live. However, when people have tried to import them into areas where they don't naturally live, they often end up causing more problems than the snakes they were brought in to hunt. They were imported into the West Indies, for example, in an effort to control snakes. However, they ended up destroying many native animals.

This is a colony of banded mongooses (*Mungos mungo*).

Similarly, mongooses were introduced into Hawaii to control the rat population. Unfortunately, they did nothing to help decrease the rat population. Why? Well, rats are nocturnal, but mongooses are generally diurnal. So…rats are hidden away sleeping during the day, which is when mongooses hunt! Instead of eating rats, then, the mongooses ate other animals as well as the eggs of certain birds that nest on the ground. As a result, they have been rightly blamed for the destruction of several native Hawaiian species.

There are many different species of mongooses. They are social creatures, hunting with the entire colony and forming close relationships with each member. Some species live in colonies of up to 40 animals. They are caring and kind toward all the colony members. These relationships are so close that some will even risk their own lives to save another mongoose from the clutches of a raptor's talons or the grip of a jackal's jaws.

One interesting species is the dwarf mongoose that lives in Africa. It tends to live in small colonies that often use a termite mound as a home, and it has an interesting relationship with the Hornbill (a bird) that also lives there. These two animals are often seen foraging together for food. In fact, Hornbills are so eager to forage with dwarf mongooses that they will squawk down the holes of the dwarf mongooses' home in the morning, telling them to get up because it's time for breakfast. The Hornbills keep watch for predators, calling out warnings if they see an animal that is a predator for *either* Hornbills or dwarf mongooses. Why do they do this? Because the mongooses scratch up animals that live in the dirt, and the Hornbills will dive in and eat the animals that escape the mongooses. As you learned in Zoology 2, this kind of relationship is called **symbiosis** (sim by oh' sis). It is a common occurrence throughout God's creation, reminding us that God originally created creatures to work and live together so all could benefit!

Meerkats

These meerkats are busy cleaning each other.

Meerkats are also in family Herpestidae, and are also called **suricates** (soo' rih kayts). Disney's movie *The Lion King* brought fame to the meerkat with the character named Timon. However, unlike the meerkat in the movie, real meerkats are never found without other meerkats. Like mongooses, these social creatures form colonies of many meerkats that are usually all related to one another.

In fact, meerkats are so dependent on their colony that they are likely to die without it. Why? Well, there are many reasons. First, meerkats live underground in tunnels dug by the entire colony. These long, complex tunnels keep the individuals safe from predators all night long. The members of the colony also help protect one another from disease, cleaning each other daily and removing ticks, mites, and fleas. Probably the most important reason meerkats are dependent on their colony, however, is the protection it provides. When meerkats are out hunting for food, one or more of the meerkats will stand watch, warning the hunters of any predators they see. That way some of the meerkats can concentrate on hunting, while the rest concentrate on making sure they don't become the hunted.

One meerkat is the head female and is often the mother to all in the colony. None of the other meerkats are allowed to bear young, but they all must care for the young born to the dominant female, treating them like their own offspring. Once the pups are old enough to leave the burrows, older brothers and sisters train them. They teach the youngsters how to clean the burrow entrance, dig holes and hunt for insects, stand watch for the colony, etc.

Every morning, meerkats emerge from their burrow to hunt for food. One or more in the hunting party will stand guard, climbing up on rocks or hills to reach the highest vantage point. They stand up on their hind legs to get the best view of the terrain. Their ability to stand on their hind legs is one of the most distinctive marks of meerkats. They can stand for hours, and when they sit, they tend to sit up on their haunches. If a meerkat on watch sees a threat, it barks, alerting the hunters, who will then dive for cover into a hole or under something. These holes are so important that the meerkats dig many of them throughout their hunting territory, keeping them meticulous for just such emergencies.

These meerkats look like they are posing for a picture, but they are just doing what they do naturally – standing on their hind legs to get a better view of something that has caught their interest.

What Do You Remember?

What special sensory organ do cats have? If a leopard or jaguar is black, what is it often called? Which cat cannot retract its claws? What is an apex predator? Which cat forms strong family bonds? Which cat is the most dangerous to humans? Which cat is the fastest runner? Name the three wild cats that live in North America. Which requires the largest hunting territory? How is a hyena similar to a dog? How is it similar to a cat? How is the spotted hyena different from other hyenas? What does an aardwolf eat? What is a mutation? What kind of homes do creatures from the family Herpestidae create for themselves? Which animal is the mongoose famous for being able to kill? How do meerkats care for their family members?

Map It!

Include these animals on your map:

Lions – Africa and Asia

Tigers – Southeast Asia and Siberia

Bobcats – Throughout the United States

Cougars – Western United States, Florida, and Canada

Canada lynxes – Canada, Alaska, Montana, Idaho, Washington, Utah, Minnesota, and New England

Spotted hyenas – Sub-Saharan Africa

Striped hyenas – Northern Africa, Middle East, India, and Asia

Brown hyenas – Southern Africa

Aardwolves – Southern and northern (but not central) Africa

Viverridae – Africa, Asia, or southern Europe

Mongooses – Asia, Africa, southern Europe, and Hawaii

Meerkats – Africa

Track It!

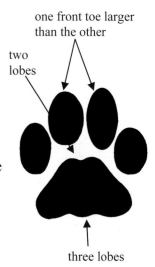

one front toe larger than the other

two lobes

three lobes

Knowing the tracks of an American wildcat is quite important for anyone hiking in North America. The first thing to notice about cat tracks is that they are more circular in shape than dog tracks. The two front toes do not line up evenly, as one is usually bigger than the other. The top edge of the heel pad has two lobes, while the bottom edge has three lobes. Also, you can't make an "X" mark through the mid section as you can with a dog's track. Because their claws are retractable, they aren't visible above the toe pads, unless the cat was running or pouncing.

Notebook Activities

Create a storyboard for a documentary or movie about the relationship between spotted hyenas and lions. Show what happens when a clan of hyenas runs into a pride of lions and clashes over a recent meal. What is a storyboard? A storyboard is what movie makers create before they film a movie. It is made up of a series of pictures that give the essence of what will happen in the movie. Each picture has a written description discussing what happens at each point.

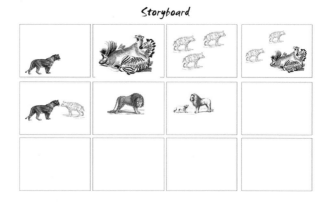

Storyboard

After completing your storyboard, choose four specific feliforms you learned about in this lesson. Draw (or find pictures of) an example of each, and list some interesting facts you learned about it. You can choose to do more than four if you like, but please do at least four.

Older Students: Spend some time researching more about the four feliforms you chose. Write down something interesting about each that is not discussed in the lesson.

Experiment
The Cougar Eats the Deer

How does the predator/prey relationship work? When a cougar cannot find enough deer to eat, what happens to the cougar population? What happens to the deer population? How does this later affect the cougar population? Let's study population growth of animals in the following experiment. You will learn why certain areas have an explosion in the deer population and what happens when the deer population is reduced.

You will need:

♦ Colored tape

♦ Cellophane tape or glue

♦ A surface on which you can mark off a 2-foot by 2-foot square with tape

♦ Several pieces of cardboard

♦ Paper

♦ Scissors

♦ A ruler

♦ Six drawings (or small pictures) of a cougar. They can all be copies of one drawing or picture.

1. Use colored tape to mark off a square 2 feet wide and 2 feet long. This represents the territory claimed by one cougar.
2. Cut the cardboard into six rectangles that are 6 inches long and 3 inches wide.
3. Tape (or glue) a picture of the cougar to each piece of cardboard.
4. Cut 20 pieces of paper, each of which should be 2 inches wide and 2 inches long. You can draw deer on them if you want, as they represent the deer that live in the cougar's territory.

This cougar will survive and produce another cougar, since it ate three deer.

In the experiment, you will stand 2 feet from the square you marked off with the colored tape, holding in your hand the cardboard piece that represents the cougar. You will then toss the cougar into the square. Every deer that it lands on (even partially) will represent a deer it has eaten. A toss of the cougar, then, represents a generation of hunting. In order for a cougar to survive in the experiment, it must eat at least three deer in one toss. That will indicate there is enough successful hunting to keep it alive for a generation.

Each deer left in the territory will produce one offspring for the next generation (the next toss of the cougar). Every time a cougar does not survive, a new one will come into the area. So, you will always have at least one cougar to toss into the territory. Every time a cougar lands on three deer, it survives the generation and produces one offspring.

5. Begin the experiment with three deer in the territory. Put them anywhere you like, but make sure they do not overlap with other deer. If the deer population ever reaches zero, add three more in the next generation.

6. Toss the cardboard cougar into the square in an effort to eat deer. If the toss is not in the territory, try again.

7. Make a table that has the following information and goes for 20 generations:

Generation	Number of Cougars in Territory	Number of Deer Eaten	Number of Deer That Survived
1.			

8. Record the number of cougars you see in the territory (for the first attempt, it will be one), the number of deer it ate, and the number of deer that survived (the ones that weren't eaten).

9. Remove any deer that have been eaten.

10. Pick up the cougar. If it landed on three deer, pick up another cougar (its offspring).

11. Now it is time to start the next generation. Count the number of deer that survived, and add that many more deer to the territory. The new deer represent the offspring of the surviving deer. Once again, just put them anywhere in the territory as long as they don't overlap with other deer.

12. Toss the cougar or cougars you have in your hand into the territory again.

13. Count the number of cougars you see in the territory, the number of deer eaten, and the number of deer that survived. Record all this in the table, on the next generation's line.

14. Remove any deer that were eaten.

15. Remove the cougars. If it ate three deer, pick up another cougar to represent its offspring. If it did not eat three deer, put it on the floor outside the territory. If you have no cougars in your hand at the end, pick up one from the floor, since a new cougar will always move into a territory not occupied by a cougar.

16. Count the number of deer left in the territory and add an equal number to the territory.

17. Repeat steps 12-16 a total of 18 more times, so that you have at least 20 generations.

Look at the data table. You should notice a pattern in the data. Do you see that the population of deer must grow before the cougar population grows? Also, do you see that as the number of cougars in the territory grows, the deer population decreases? However, once the deer population decreases enough, what happens to the cougar population? It decreases, too, doesn't it? In your notebook, explain how this pattern keeps the cougar and deer populations balanced.

Lesson 5
Marsupials

Can you imagine an animal the size of a grain of rice leaving its mother's womb before it is fully developed? Envision that hairless, pink embryo quickly scrambling up its mother's body, clinging to her fur as it finds its way into her pouch. This tiny speck attaches to its mother and begins to nurse – never letting go for months. Finally, picture the animal growing up inside this pouch, climbing in and out whenever it wishes as it matures. God created marsupial babies, called **joeys**, in this unique way.

This mother kangaroo has her joey in her marsupium.

Most mammals are **placental** (pluh sen' tuhl). This means that the baby develops inside its mother, and it gets everything it needs (food, water, oxygen, etc.) from her. Marsupials are different. God created most of them with a special pouch, called a **marsupium** (mar soo' pee uhm), in which their joeys develop and find protection.

At first, a marsupial baby develops inside its mother. However, unlike the babies of other mammals, their front legs develop ahead of the rest of the animal. They are born very early, and immediately after birth, they make the momentous climb from the birth canal to the pouch. With eyes not yet developed, these blind babies instinctively know where to go, but they only have a short time to get there. If they don't make it to the pouch quickly, they run out of energy and die. When the joey reaches the pouch, it finds one of the mother's nipples and attaches to it so it can receive milk. It will not detach again for several months. How does it keep from detaching as its mother leaps around Australia? Well, God designed the mother's nipple to swell as soon as the joey attaches, and it can't open its mouth to let loose until its jaw develops. Hidden within folds of skin that make a pouch, the joey is safe.

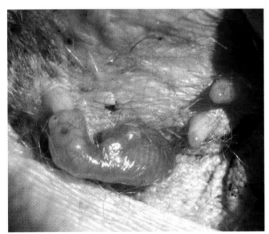
This joey only recently arrived in the pouch and is now nursing to get the energy it needs to finish developing.

With koalas, wallabies, wombats, kangaroos, and possums leading the mob, there are hundreds of species of marsupials. None live in Europe or Asia. They all live either in the Americas or in

Australia. Strangely, the majority are found only in the general area of Australia and New Zealand, although the fossil record shows us that in times past, marsupials lived all over the world.

Marsupial Migration

Sometimes people wonder how marsupials got from the ark to Australia after the Flood. Well, the explanation starts with the idea that at one time, the continents we know today were probably not separate from one another. Most scientists think that back in earth's history, there was basically one big piece of land called **Pangaea** (pan jee' uh). At some point, however, Pangaea split apart, forming the continents we see today. The illustration below shows you how this might have happened.

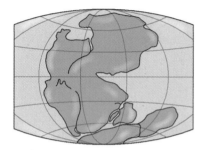

Initially, all the continents might have existed as one big piece of land: Pangaea.

At some point, the land could have split apart, and the parts could have drifted away from one another.

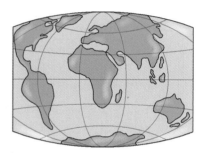

Eventually, this formed the separate continents we see today.

Most creationists think that the Flood caused Pangaea to break apart. Some think that the breakup occurred during the Flood, while others think it occurred after the Flood as a result of the stresses that built up during the Flood. Unfortunately we don't really have enough data to know for sure, so some of this is just speculation. However, if the breakup occurred after the Flood, animals could have spread throughout Pangaea and just drifted with the continents as Pangaea split apart. If it occurred during the Flood, the animals would not have been able to drift with the continents, but they still could have migrated around the world. You see, most creation scientists think that an ice age followed the Flood, which would have resulted in the oceans being shallower than they are today. That would have resulted in little trails of land (called **land bridges**) connecting the continents together. These land bridges would have been covered as the ice from the ice age melted and raised the sea levels, but they would have lasted long enough to allow animals to make their way from one continent to the other.

Of course, there is another possibility as well. The breakup of Pangaea could have *started* with the Flood, but it could have taken a while after the Flood for the breakup to be complete. Recent events in Africa indicate that this is at least a possibility. A few researchers were near the Horn of Africa in the Afar triangle and witnessed cracks forming so as to split the land. Over the next two years, more and more cracks appeared, and it is thought that eventually, water will fill those cracks, separating the land masses even more. It is possible that the Flood caused "cracks" in Pangaea, and over the next few hundred years, the continents slowly separated from one another.

Try This!

Get a copy of a world map that you can cut up. Cut out each continent so you have what look like puzzle pieces. Fit all the pieces together to make one large piece of land – Pangaea. Because the waves crashing against the coast of a continent can change the shape of the coastline (this is called "erosion"), the continents will not snugly fit together like the pieces of a real jigsaw puzzle. However, the pieces should fit together fairly well. Use the drawing on the previous page as a guide if you are having trouble putting the puzzle together.

Order Diprotodontia

Since most marsupials are in Australia, let's start our marsupial safari there. Of course, when I say "Australia," you should immediately think "kangaroo," and that's the first kind of marsupial we are going to study. While many scientists put all marsupials into a single order, called **Marsupialia**, others split them into several different orders. Since I want to spend a whole lesson on marsupials, I will take the second approach. In that system, kangaroos belong in order **Diprotodontia** (dye' proh tuh don' tee uh). Do you remember that often scientists classify animals according to their teeth? Well, this is true for the animals in order Diprotodontia. "Di"

two front teeth on lower jaw

This wallaby is showing you the two front teeth on its lower jaw, after which its order was named.

means two, "proto" means first, and "dontia" refers to teeth. So, these animals are basically called "two front teeth." That's not a very exciting name, but it's a very descriptive one. All the animals in this order, which includes kangaroos, koalas, possums, and wombats, have two front teeth that stick almost straight out from their lower jaw. Their two front teeth are so distinctive that scientists thought they should be named after them.

Creation Confirmation

Scientists have noticed that although most members of order Diprotodontia were herbivores in the past, a couple species have now started eating insects. As a result, they are now omnivores. This is a very recent development. In fact, it's so recent that it is quite a surprise to many scientists. While some scientists might find it strange that an animal group would suddenly change its diet, creationists don't find it strange at all. Creationists believe that all animals were herbivores in the very beginning, but over time some changed their diet to include meat. The observation of this occurring with members of order Diprotodontia gives us more evidence for the creationist view.

Suborder Macropodiformes

These macropods are called pademelons. The main difference between them and kangaroos is their size.

Bigfoot doesn't live in the Pacific Northwest, as many people think. Bigfoot lives in Australia! You see, a kangaroo is a **macropod**, which means "big foot," because its hind feet are very long. There are many species of macropods living all over Australia. Some prefer the plains; others prefer the forests. Some stay in rocky regions, living on boulders and cliffs, while others can climb trees and live in the rainforest areas. In addition to kangaroos, wallabies, pademelons, tree kangaroos, bettongs, and potoroos are all macropods. They are almost exactly the same in form, with size being the major difference between them. They are probably all the descendants of two kangaroo-like animals that came off the ark with Noah.

In addition to long hind feet, macropods have furry coats, long tails, thin necks, big ears, and incredible back legs that allow them to jump high and fast. How? Well, God created those legs with amazing tendons (bands of tissue that attach muscles to bones) which act like springs. When a kangaroo lands, its tendons compress, storing energy. That energy is then used as the kangaroo launches into the next hop. In other words, a kangaroo's legs act a lot like pogo sticks! Imagine what it would be like if you had springs inside your legs!

Though some macropods also move by walking on all fours, they hop when they are in a hurry. Hopping actually saves energy, because it allows their "springs" to work. Amazingly, macropods can hop at speeds of nearly 40 miles per hour. Scientists have learned that when they speed up, they don't hop more, they just make longer leaps. So, whether they are going four miles an hour or forty miles an hour, the number of hops per minute doesn't really change – the distance covered by each hop just increases. Red kangaroos can hop over 30 feet in one hop.

Try This!

Keeping your feet together, hop as far as you can. How far did you hop and still land on your feet? Try hopping like that instead of walking. It's not very easy or fast, is it? Now, imagine how much faster and easier it would be if your legs acted like springs!

When a kangaroo senses danger, its springy legs jump into action. First, it alerts fellow macropods by thumping its feet loudly on the ground. The female, called a **doe**, may make a clicking or clucking sound to call her young to her side or back into her pouch. Although kangaroos can certainly put up a good fight, they prefer to run when danger lurks.

You may know that kangaroos are great kick-boxers, even though they usually prefer not to fight with predators or people. The exception to this rule occurs during mating season. When it is time for male kangaroos, called **bucks**, to find their mates, they are ready to fight for their rights. Here's how they do it: the two bucks face each other, grab each other with their arms, and then begin kicking each other in the belly. They do this by leaning back on their muscular tail so that they can use both hind legs to kick.

Like other pack animals, you won't find kangaroos alone very often. They enjoy the company of others, forming large groups called **mobs**. Mobs hop around and eat together. They are herbivores, grazing on the dry grass that covers the desert-like regions of Australia, or consuming any other vegetation available. These creatures have a stomach that is split into chambers. First, they chew grass and swallow it. In the stomach, it forms a ball, called a cud, and comes back up for them to chew some more. We say, "They chew their cud." After chewing it a bit more, they swallow it for good. Like most Australian marsupials, they need very little water and can go for months without drinking.

To keep from getting too hot, kangaroos take naps in the afternoons, and do most of their grazing in the cool of the evening or the dark of night. But the best stay-cool secret of these creatures is the spit bath! Have you ever poured water on yourself on a hot day? Kangaroos will drool and lick saliva all over their faces and bodies to cool down!

A joey lives inside its mother's pouch for several weeks. Eventually, however, it starts to spend time out of the pouch. By the time it is 7 to 10 months old, it has left the pouch completely. It will stay at her side for up to two years. Interestingly, as soon as the joey leaves the pouch permanently, a new joey is born. Even though it is out of the pouch, a young kangaroo can still nurse by sticking its head into the pouch. God, in his infinite wisdom, created a way for the newborn joey and the joey outside the pouch to receive *different kinds of milk from the same mother at the same time*! The walking joey needs different nutrients than the one

Even though this young kangaroo is out of the pouch, it still nurses.

developing in the pouch. Thus, the milk it gets is quite different from the milk the joey outside the pouch gets. A doe can also get pregnant while she has a joey developing in her pouch, so a doe can have a joey at her heels, a joey in the pouch, and a joey waiting to be born.

Wallabies

The only real difference between a wallaby and a kangaroo is the size. If the adult male is, on average, less than 44 pounds with feet less than 10 inches long, the species is classified as a wallaby. Some wallabies are so small they look like little rabbits. In fact, there are many called hare-wallabies. Rock wallabies have special hairs on their feet that enable them to keep from slipping on the boulders and rocks they bound up every day. There are many species of wallabies, and it seems more species are forming as time goes on.

Creation Confirmation

When a scientist named John Gould studied rock wallabies in Australia in the mid 1800s, he could find only six different species. Today, there are at least 15 different species of rock wallaby. Scientists believe these species are still splitting into new species today. The formation of new species in only 100 years shows us that it does not take a long time for new species of animals to come about. There would have been plenty of time between the worldwide flood and today for all the known species of animals to form from the representative kinds kept on the ark.

Repeat all that you remember about kangaroos and wallabies.

Bettongs and Potoroos

If wallabies are small kangaroos, **bettongs** and **potoroos** are small wallabies. These little creatures are rat-sized macropods. They are usually nocturnal, spending the day sleeping in nests they

This long-nosed potoroo's scientific name is *Potorous tridactylus*.

build of grass and bark. They eat tubers (like potatoes), roots, and fungi (like mushrooms). Their faces and tails make them look like rodents. In fact, potoroos are actually called "rat kangaroos." Unfortunately, potoroos are becoming endangered in Australia. Hundreds of years ago, English people brought red foxes to Australia so that they could hunt them for sport. Now, the red foxes prey on the potoroos. Like opossums, bettongs have prehensile tails. They can be seen romping about on their springy legs, with their tail holding grass and straw they carry to their nest.

Suborder Vombatiformes

Although many people call this animal a "koala bear," the koala is not a bear.

A couple more "two front teeth" (Diprotodontia) you may know of are **koalas** and **wombats**. These animals are called **Vombatiformes** (vom' bat ih for' meez), or wombat-shaped animals. Have you ever heard someone refer to a koala as a "koala bear"? These animals have round, fuzzy ears and look cute and cuddly like a teddy bear, but they aren't bears. They are marsupials, like the kangaroo. Perhaps we refer to koalas as "bears" because their scientific name, *Phascolarctos* (fas koh' lark tuhs) *cinereus* (sin ear' ee us), comes from Greek words that mean "pouched bear." Also, when the Europeans arrived in Australia, they called the koala "the native bear." Nevertheless, koalas are not bears.

The word "koala" comes from the language of the native Australians, who are called **Aborigines** (ab' uh rij' ih neez). In their language, "koala" means "no drink." This is because, like the kangaroo, koalas don't drink much. Koalas stay up in trees, rarely coming to the ground. As a result, they usually don't drink from lakes, streams, or even puddles. Instead, they get most of their water from the leaves they eat.

If you've ever seen a koala in the zoo, it probably wasn't too exciting. Koalas hardly ever move. Why? They need to conserve energy because they eat **eucalyptus** (yoo' kuh lip' tus) leaves. These leaves are poisonous to most animals, but not to the koala. God created the koala to produce chemicals that neutralize the poisons so they can eat what virtually no other animal can. Eating the leaves isn't a problem, but digesting them is another story. The leaves are very hard to digest, so the koala doesn't get a lot of energy from them. After eating a little, they'll curl up in the fork of a tree and sleep. This helps them digest the leaves and conserve energy for when they have to eat again.

Koalas sleep up to 20 hours each day!

Sleeping all day up in a tree may seem like a precarious activity, but koalas are quite safe. In fact, they stay up there to avoid predators. From time to time, however, they must go to the ground to change trees or move to another area, and that's when they risk being eaten, usually by foxes or dingoes. Koalas aren't endangered, because they don't come down from the trees a lot. As long as there are eucalyptus trees, the koala flourishes, in a sleepy sort of way.

While a kangaroo's pouch opens at the top, a koala's pouch opens from the other side! When a newborn joey enters the rear of the pouch, however, the mother's pouch muscles tighten, closing the pouch so that the joey doesn't fall out. A koala joey stays in the pouch for about seven months, eating nothing but its mother's milk. It will then come out of the pouch, spending most of its time on its mother's back. For the next five months, it will eat eucalyptus leaves, but it will also eat special milk (called **pap**) that the mother makes. Like the kangaroo, this milk is different from the milk the joey got while in the pouch. One important thing pap contains is bacteria (a type of microscopic living thing) that will take up residence in the joey's body. These bacteria help the joey digest the hard-to-digest leaves it will eat for the rest of its life.

This is a coarse-haired wombat, which is often called a common wombat.

The other animal in this suborder, the wombat, is much like a koala that has taken to crawling and digging rather than climbing and clinging. It spends most of its time in tunnels it excavates under the Australian earth. This excavation is so extensive that a wombat's tunnel can be more than 60 feet long!

Wombats have the appearance of extremely furry pigs, ambling about on their four legs. They are short, stout herbivores that prefer night foraging. The fur of a wombat is coarse, ranging from black to grey, brown, or cream. There are only three species of wombats in the world – the **coarse-haired wombat**, the **southern hairy-nosed wombat**, and the **northern hairy-nosed wombat**.

Wombats digest their food slowly, like the koala, making them generally slow animals. They can, however, run extremely fast (about 25 miles per hour) if frightened. Their escape route is always into the tunnels. Their number one predator is...can you guess? Dingoes. These dogs will actually enter a wombat's tunnel in pursuit. The dingo doesn't always win, however. Wombats have a thick backside that isn't easy to bite. They have also been known to squeeze a dingo very tightly against the sides of the tunnel, in order to suffocate the pursuing dog.

To help you remember, explain what you have learned about koalas and wombats.

Suborder Phalangeriformes

This young brushtail possum is riding on its mother's back. Brushtails are the most common possum in Australia.

Another member of order Diprotodontia is the **possum**. Have you ever wondered whether the word was possum or **opossum**? Well, it is either possum or opossum, depending on which part of the world you are in. The original name for the American version is opossum. However, the name "possum" was given to the mostly tree-dwelling marsupials of the lands in and around Australia because they resemble the only North American marsupial, the **Virginia opossum**. Try not to get too confused as you read about possums and opossums. Although possums are similar to opossums, they are actually in different orders. You will learn about opossums in a later section of this lesson.

Possums are small animals, ranging in size from the length of a finger to about 4 feet, depending on the species. Not surprisingly, **pygmy possums** are the smallest, while **brushtail possums** and **ringtail possums** are the largest. All possums are nocturnal and omnivorous. Some possums (like the ringtail possum) have prehensile tails that can wrap around branches and other objects. Though the brushtail possum has fur on its tail, many others, such as the pygmy possum, have "naked" tails. Most possums like to live in tree holes, but some will make nests on the ground or even live in abandoned bird nests.

Depending on the species, a possum joey will stay in the pouch for four to five months. When it leaves the pouch, it will ride on its mother's back (like the young possum in the picture above) for another one or two months. During that time, it will still nurse from the pouch. In many species of possum, the tail is used for fat storage, growing wide and fat at the base when food is plentiful.

The brushtail and ringtail possums are as prevalent in Australia as squirrels are in the United States. They are also considered an Australian pest, consuming garden plants and moving into attics. Furthermore, they are dreadfully loud, awakening sleepers with their raucous sounds in the night.

Several species of possum have extra folds of loose skin between their front and back legs. This enables these special creatures to create a little parachute by spreading

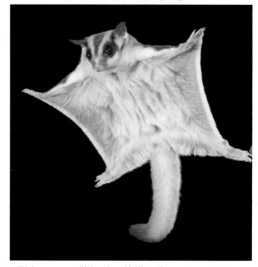

This sugar glider is gliding from tree to tree.

their legs wide. As a result, these marsupials can glide through the air as they jump from branch to branch or swoop down to the ground. One species, the **sugar glider**, can be lured to feeding places. Can you guess what they eat? Yes, you guessed it! Sugar!

Order Peramelemorphia

Now let's leave order Diprotodontia and take a peek at some other Australian marsupials. Imagine what it would be like if rats infested your yard, digging holes all over your garden and bringing with them an onslaught of ticks, which carry microscopic organisms and viruses that can cause disease. Now imagine that you aren't allowed to trap these creatures because they are a protected animal. That may be how some Australians feel about the **bandicoot** and **bilby**. These members of order **Peramelemorphia** (per uh mel ee mor' fee uh) look like rats, but they burrow holes in the ground like moles. They are also a favorite host for ticks, so the more bandicoots and bilbies you have around, the more ticks you'll have as well.

Of the two basic types of animal in this order, bandicoots look most like rats. Of course, they are not rats; they are marsupials. Their pouches open from the rear, like those of the koala. Unlike rats, bandicoots are solitary animals, living alone unless a mother has her young attached to her. They build their nests in shallow holes in the ground lined with leaf litter, or under debris. Their nests hide them from predators and protect them from rain and the sun. They are omnivorous, scratching through dirt to find insects and plant material.

Bandicoots are prey to owls and dingoes. Unfortunately, cats, dogs, and foxes that have been brought to the lands in and around Australia also prey on them. Between these "introduced predators" and the fact that they have lost some of their habitat to cities and roads, they have become endangered. Conservationists ask pet owners to keep their pets indoors at night so that the nocturnal bandicoots can forage in peace.

This bilby looks like a cross between a rat and a rabbit. Some Australians use this resemblance to sell chocolate "Easter bilbies" instead of chocolate Easter bunnies.

The other members of this order, bilbies, have long noses and long ears, making them look like a cross between a rat and a rabbit. Their name comes from an Aborigine word that means "long-nosed rat." They share most of the traits of bandicoots, but unlike bandicoots, bilbies live in tunnels they dig themselves. Generally, a bilby will dig several sets of tunnels in its territory and move from one to another as it searches for food. Like the bandicoots, it is considered endangered because of introduced predators and loss of habitat.

Order Notoryctemorphia

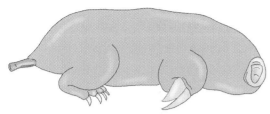

Members of order Notoryctemorphia are designed to dig.

Sometimes the scientific name for an order of animals is a perfect description. This is especially true for the little diggers we find in order **Notoryctemorphia** (noh toh rik the mor' fee uh). The name for this order comes from Greek words meaning "one who digs in the south." If you look on a globe to see where Australia is, you'll see where the "south" part of the name comes from. These southern diggers are **marsupial moles**. And you know what moles do…they dig their entire lives. In fact, they dig so much and so often, it appears that they swim through the soil, creating long tunnels and holes everywhere they go. They never build a burrow in which to stay – they just move on and on through the ground under our feet, eating grubs and worms along the way. God has given them unusual hands and feet to get the job done well. Their foreclaws look like little miniature spades. Like all moles, they are blind and don't have external ears. Their noses are covered with a horny shield to protect them as they push through the dirt, and their short, fat legs are covered with leathery skin. Their fur is silky and slides easily through the soil.

Order Dasyuromorphia

Is it a dog, a hyena, a weasel, or a devil? With its bloodcurdling, feeding-frenzied shrieks, the skinny-legged, wombat-like creature known as the **Tasmanian devil** (*Sarcophilus harrisii*) causes concern among the people of Tasmania. This member of order **Dasyuromorphia** (das ih yoor' oh mor' fee uh) has jet-black fur, which is unusual for marsupials. The fur is often marked with white on the chest and rump. They used to live on the main continent of Australia, but the dingoes are believed to have killed all those that once lived there. Today, they can only be found in Tasmania, an island south of the main continent.

The Tasmanian devil looks ferocious, but it is mostly a bluff. It will fight, but it prefers to scare its foes away.

Like most members of this order, Tasmanian devils are carnivorous, but they are mostly scavengers, feeding on whatever is available. Their genus name indicates their true nature: "Sarcophilus" comes from two Greek words meaning "flesh lover." These "devils" are scavenging scoundrels who don't mind consuming the dead carcass of any animal they find. Their bite is much more powerful than a dog's, and they'll consume every part of the animal, including the bones! Doesn't that sound like a hyena to you?

Devils are nocturnal animals, roaming the roads at night with a characteristic loping walk, seeking their next meal. When food is present, they defend it from others that might steal it, barking and hollering. They bare their teeth in a savage grimace, growing louder and louder until they reach the terrifying scream that pierces the night and gives them their reputation as devils. They also produce a foul odor when they are nervous or scared. A relaxed Tasmanian devil, however, doesn't smell bad. Although they do not form packs, they will sometimes eat with other devils, especially if a large carcass has been found. However, they defend their share of the carcass from the other devils, just as they would from any other animal.

Devils typically spend the day in a den or in the thick underbrush. They usually mate in March, during which time they do not eat at all. Like most marsupials, birth occurs rather quickly after mating – only three weeks later! The young climb up the mother into the backward-opening pouch. Up to four young are born at a time, and they stay in the pouch until about August. After that, they spend their time in the den. By December, they are independent of their mother.

The Tasmanian tiger looked like a cross between a tiger and a wolf.

The Tasmanian devil has some things in common with the **Tasmanian tiger**. Like the Tasmanian devil, the Tasmanian tiger was common in Australia, but eventually died out there. It survived in Tasmania for much longer, however. Also a fierce flesh-eater, the tiger was once hunted because it was a nuisance to farmers and people. Because of this, it went extinct in the 1930s. Devils used to be hunted also, and at one time they were threatened. Now they are a protected species, like most marsupials, and they have made a serious comeback.

Creation Confirmation

The largest of Australia's marsupials, the red kangaroo, can grow to be about 7 feet tall, but Australian marsupials used to be bigger. Fossils indicate that Australian kangaroos grew up to 10 feet tall in the past. In addition, do you remember the little wombat you studied? Well, in the past, Australia had wombats that were the size of large cows! Some people claim that the bones of these mega-marsupials are millions of years old. However, their fossils have been found near tools used by people. In fact, tests on the tools found that there is still blood on them! This suggests that these animals were around at the same time as humans, and that they were food for these people. Perhaps that's why the larger species became extinct – they were easy for hunters to find.

Order Microbiotheria

Although the majority of the world's marsupials live in Australia, you can find some in the New World as well. So let's shift our safari to North and South America and see what interesting marsupials we can find there.

This little South American marsupial is only a bit larger than a mouse.

We will start with order **Microbiotheria** (my croh bye' oh thur' ee uh). The prefix "micro" means "small," "bio" refers to living things, and "ther" usually refers to wild animals. So, animals in this order are small, living wild animals. There is only one living member of this order, and you can find it up in the mountains of Chile and Argentina. Its Spanish name is **Monito del Monte** (moh nee' toh del mahn' tay), which means "little mountain monkey." It lives in the dense, humid mountain forests, and can be found especially where Chilean bamboo is found. It makes nests in trees, hanging shrubbery, or other sheltered areas and eats mostly insects. Technically, it is omnivorous, because it also eats fruit from time to time.   It has a prehensile tail that helps it move about trees and shrubs with ease.

Order Didelphimorphia

Most of the rest of the New World marsupials are placed in order **Didelphimorphia** (dye delf' uh mor' fee uh). The term "didelphi" comes from Greek and means "two wombs." A **womb** is where an animal or human embryo grows until it is born. While these animals don't really have two wombs, the name has stuck.

Here's a quiz for you: How many species of marsupials live in North America? If you have paid very close attention, you may remember that the only marsupial in North America is the **Virginia opossum** (*Didelphis virginiana*). If you live in the United States, you have surely seen this creature, even if it was lying on the side of the road, looking quite dead. Let's learn about this amazing little animal.

Virginia Opossums

Because you have probably seen an opossum that looks dead from time to time, you might think they are not great survivors. That's not true! In fact, a Virginia opossum can survive being bitten by many poisonous snakes, including rattlesnakes, because it is immune to many poisons! It is also very resistant to most diseases. Although it is possible, for example, for an opossum to get rabies, it is very rare, because most opossums can fight off that and many other diseases. In addition, opossums can eat nearly *anything* (no matter how foul) without getting ill.

The Virginia opossum has a mousy face; coarse, grayish-brown and black fur; and a little pink nose. Its prehensile tail is used to wrap around objects and hold onto tree branches for stability. However, opossums don't usually hang upside down from trees with their tail, even though that's how artists depict them. The tails of adults are not strong enough to bear their weight. The young may hang upside-down for brief periods of time when they lose their balance, but that's it. They *do* wrap their tails around leaves and other matter so they can carry it to their den for bedding.

The Virginia opossum looks fierce, but it is generally a gentle creature that prefers to avoid fighting.

When I was a child, I was given a young opossum for a pet while I was on vacation at the beach. What a sweet, docile animal the opossum was! It never scratched or bit anyone, and it seemed to enjoy being held. I even slept with it at night. Perhaps its gentle, lovable nature was due to the fact that it spent time in its mother's pouch before entering the world. Unfortunately, there was no Internet in those days, and I couldn't figure out what to feed it. I gave it only vegetables. So after two weeks of cleaning up its watery stool, I let it go in my grandmother's backyard, hoping for the best. Had I only known that opossums are omnivorous, I could have fed it the insects it needed to be healthy. In the two weeks that I was its master, it grew from the size of a lemon to the size of a small watermelon. This rapid growth is understandable, since opossums live for only about two years.

Young opossums can be good pets, but they grow up quickly!

Opossums walk flat-footed on their paws with all their finger-like digits spread out. They can grasp quite well with their little hands, which somewhat resemble a person's hands. They are not great climbers, but they do spend time in trees, often to escape predators or to look for food. Although they are primarily nocturnal, opossums aren't at all opposed to a daytime walk around the neighborhood.

One difference between opossums and other marsupials is the pouch. The marsupium of a Virginia opossum is little more than a small fold of skin. As a result, the joey doesn't spend much time there. Typically, a joey leaves the pouch after less than two months of development. After that, it usually climbs on its mother's back and rides around until it can walk fast enough to keep up with her.

In just over a month or so, the young are independent of the mother. Also, many American opossums give birth to more young than they can nurse. Sadly, many of them don't make the journey to the pouch, which is probably why more are born than can be cared for. Unlike the possums of Australia that bear two or three joeys, eight or so are born to the Virginia opossum at a time. Producing many young obviously results in a great many more opossums; however, most Australian opossums live longer than the Virginia opossum.

The Virginia opossum has spread throughout many parts of the United States, some parts of Canada, and Mexico. This is partly because they migrate to different places looking for food, and partly because they were taken to California as a source of food during the westward expansion of the late 1800s. Even today, the Internet is full of recipes for cooking and eating opossums.

Playing Possum

When an opossum is frightened and escape is not an option, it lies down and "dies;" at least that's what it would have you believe. This, of course, is called "playing dead" or "playing possum," and it is something an opossum can do automatically. When an opossum plays dead, its lips draw back, its teeth are bared, saliva foams around its mouth, and sometimes its tongue hangs out. A foul-smelling fluid is even released from certain glands, making the opossum actually *smell* like it's dead! Additionally, its body becomes stiff, like an animal long dead. In this condition, it can be prodded, turned over, and even carried away without "waking up."

Why does the opossum do this? Well, most animals don't eat animals that are already dead. This is an instinct God gave them to avoid eating food that is spoiled. Even animals that do eat carrion will typically avoid a dead animal if it has been dead for many days. That's because the longer an animal has been dead, the more likely it is that its meat has been spoiled. So, an opossum plays dead in order to avoid being eaten!

Is this opossum dead or just playing dead? It is hard to tell.

While this is a great trick, it can have some bad consequences. Some opossums have been killed by people who find the seemingly dead animal and dispose of its "carcass." Also, if an opossum is playing dead in a road, some drivers will not bother to try to avoid it, thinking that there is no harm in hitting an already dead animal. If you find a dead opossum, the best thing to do is to leave it in a quiet place with a clear exit path. If it is only playing dead, it will eventually "come back to life" and escape quietly on its own.

Other American Opossums

This gray short-tail opossum (*Monodelphis domestica*) is a South American opossum that has no marsupium. In the picture, her young are old enough to cling to her back and side.

Heading back down to Central and South America, you'll find a whole slew of opossums: large opossums that are similar in size to the Virginia opossum, as well as tiny opossums. Many of these opossums are missing one thing that most marsupials have… a marsupium – a little pouch! They don't even have a fold of skin to keep the underdeveloped joeys warm. This is probably why they can only live in warm climates like South America. The young still crawl up and attach to the mother's belly to nurse until they are developed (which generally takes about a month). Then they crawl up and hitch a ride on their mother's back or side for a few more months. Like most marsupials, they are solitary animals that prefer to live without the company of others.

What Do You Remember?

What do most female marsupials have that other female animals do not? Where do most marsupials live? What was Pangaea? Name some of the animals that are marsupials. What are marsupial young called? What is the difference between a wallaby and a kangaroo? Do animals that are herbivores always stay herbivores? Why is it wrong to refer to the cute Australian animals as "koala bears"? What do koalas do most of the day? How is the Tasmanian devil like a hyena? How many species of marsupials live in North America? Explain the defense mechanism of the Virginia opossum. How can some marsupial joeys develop without a pouch?

Map It!

Since most marsupials live in Australia, you will be filling up that small continent with lots of pictures. Place images of kangaroos, koalas, wombats, and any other marsupial from Australia you would like to remember on the continent of Australia. Place pictures of the Virginia opossum in several places along the eastern part of the United States as well as in California. Also place it in Ontario, Canada.

Older Students: Do some research about a few South American opossums and include those on your map.

Track It!

Virginia opossum tracks are easy to tell apart from those of other creatures. In addition to their forepaws that look a bit like human hands, their back feet each have a special thumb that protrudes below the rest of the foot. If you live in Australia, you can find links to pictures of Australian marsupial tracks on the course website I told you about in the introduction.

Notebook Activities

From the information about Virginia opossums and Australian possums, create a Venn diagram to compare and contrast these two kinds of animals. Do you believe they may have come from the same two animals on the ark, or did Noah have more than one type of marsupial? Why or why not?

Create at least two notebook pages for marsupials. More than one page should be devoted to Australian marsupials, since there are so many of them. Draw (or cut out and paste pictures of) the major marsupials you learned about and write down the interesting things you have learned about them.

Project

We've studied quite a few animal tracks to this point. Now we are going to see if we can capture some animal tracks in our own backyard. We'll make cement track traps and, instead of trapping the animal, we'll trap its track on a block of wet cement. We may find the tracks of a squirrel, raccoon, an opossum, or even a rat. You may also get some bird, cat, or dog tracks as well. The way we will do this is by first placing out bait to lure an animal to your yard. Once you find your bait is being eaten every night for a couple of nights, you will make a cement slab and place your bait in the middle so that the animal will leave its tracks on the cement. It takes about a day for cement to dry (longer in cooler weather, shorter in warmer weather). You will want to wait until the evening to make your cement trap so your cement will have plenty of time before it dries. If you make the trap in the afternoon, the sun might dry the cement before an animal has a chance to leave its tracks.

You will need:
♦ Protective eyewear
♦ Breathing mask or surgical mask to protect your lungs from the cement mix
♦ Cement mix and water (amount depends on the size of your pan)
♦ A strong piece of cardboard or small piece of wood (If your parents have a cement trowel, that would be ideal.)

♦   A shallow, wide, disposable foil baking pan (available at dollar stores and grocery stores)
♦   A small disposable container, such as a margarine container or a short plastic cup
♦   Bait (such as peanut butter, peanuts, sunflower seeds, mealworms, or scraps of meat)

1. Find a spot in your yard easily accessible to wild animals.
2. Put the bait of your choice in the small plastic container, and put the container in the center of the foil pan.
3. Leave the pan, container, and bait in the place you have chosen.
4. Check back in the morning to see if the bait was taken. If not, try again the next night. If it is still not taken, try different bait.
5. Once your bait has been taken two nights in a row, wait until after dinner the next evening to make your trap. (If you make it earlier, it may dry too quickly, depending on how warm the weather is where you are.)
6. Put the protective eyewear and the breathing mask on.
7. Have a parent help you mix the cement according to the package directions.
8. Pour the mixed cement into the foil pan.
9. Smooth out the surface of the cement using a piece of cardboard or wood or a cement trowel.
10. Place your container of bait in the center, using same bait that was taken the last two nights.

   Hopefully, when you come out the next morning, you will have some tracks in the cement. Let it dry all the way, and you have a permanent record of the tracks! Try to identify the animal that left them.

   You can actually turn this into a scientific experiment if you like. Make two cement track traps and choose a variable. You can put them in two different locations and make a hypothesis about which location will attract more animals. You could also put different bait in them and make a hypothesis about which one will secure more tracks, or which animal will prefer which bait. Remember that for the experiment to be a valid science experiment, everything must be exactly the same with both traps except for one single variable.

Lesson 6
Primarily Primates

The next stops on our safari will be the jungles of South and Central America, Africa, and Asia as we search for the creatures we are about to study. You'll need to look up to spy most of them, because God designed many of them to hang up high in the trees. Can you guess what we are looking for? We're searching for **primates**. Primates come in all different shapes and sizes, from the tiny little **mouse lemur** that weighs just a bit more than a Christmas card, to the **silverback gorilla** that can weigh more than 400 pounds. Though some are significantly more intelligent than others, they are all clever creatures. So what are primates? Generally, they are monkeys and apes, but specifically, they are mammals with a few key features. Let's take a look at those features so we can better understand what primates are.

Primates have forward-facing eyes, like cats and owls. Forward-facing eyes allow for **binocular** (bye nok' yoo lur) vision, which allows an animal to judge depth. That means it can perceive how far away things are. Primates have incredible **depth perception**, and most can jump from their perch on one tree to a small branch on a distant tree with amazing accuracy. We'll do an activity at the end of this lesson to help you understand depth perception a little better.

Compare the eyes of the gorilla (left) and the antelope (right). The gorilla's eyes face forward on its head, while the antelope's eyes are on the sides of its head.

Primates also have partially or fully **opposable thumbs** and most have **opposable toes**. Remember that "opposable" means that the thumb (or toe) can turn, face, and touch the other fingers or toes on the same hand. Do you remember taping your thumb to your hand to try out life without an opposable thumb? Is your toe opposable too? Try to touch one of your toes to the rest of the toes on your foot. That's impossible, even if you happen to have long toes. Well, most primates have opposable toes! The Lord obviously intended for most primates to live in trees, so He created them with this important feature so that they can grasp limbs with both their hands and their feet!

Most primates are omnivorous. A few primates, like the **baboon** and **chimpanzee**, will even eat small mammals. Small primates are active little creatures that constantly move around very rapidly, so they need to fill up on foods that are quick and easy to digest. That's why small primates usually eat insects and fruit. The protein from the insects and the sugar from the fruits give them the energy they need to hop from tree to tree. Some primates are slow and steady, filling up on huge quantities of leaves that are hard to digest, and then sleeping on a branch for hours and hours to digest their breakfast. Does this remind you of any animal you have studied? It reminds me of the koala.

Most primates have a rather large brain for their size. This is why they exhibit higher intelligence than many creatures. We'll discuss their intelligence a bit later. Primates have nails on their fingers and toes, and except for the **spider monkey**, all primates have five fingers on each hand and five toes on each foot.

Like many animals God created, most primates form social groups. These groups, often called **troops**, are usually made of many females and one or a few adult males. You may remember that lions and some other mammals form similar social groups. As is the case with many other animal social groups, there is usually a social order in a primate troop, with one monkey at the top and all the other monkeys somewhere in the order below. Similar to other animals we have studied so far, the top male is called the **alpha male**, while the top female is called the **alpha female**.

Some troops are small, with just a few primates, while others contain several hundred primates all living together. When a male comes of age, he sometimes must leave the troop and join a group of other males. If he's strong enough, he may fight his way to the top and become the top dog (so to speak), taking over the troop. Sadly, he'll often destroy all the infants born to the former leader.

Can you tell which of these two primates is higher up in the social structure? The answer can be found in the back of the book.

A primate's position in the troop is important, because it determines things like how much food it will get, how much space it will have for itself, and whether or not it will be able to have a mate. A primate's position in the group will be determined by things like rough play, fights, and making friends with the other primates. One way primates can interact with others in the troop is by grooming one another. Typically, primates lower in the social structure will groom those that are higher. When one primate grooms another, some scientists believe it's to gain favor with the higher-up primate.

Monkeys and Man

Before we study primates in depth, it is important for you to understand there are many things primates and people have in common. In fact, there are so many things primates and people have in common that scientists actually classify human beings in order **Primates**. However, just because people are in the same order as monkeys, gorillas, and lemurs, that does not mean we are related to them in any way! It only means we have the same Creator, or, as some would say, the same Designer. Let me provide you with an illustration. If I found all the pictures you drew this year, I bet many of them would look very similar. Why? Because they have the same maker – you! Yet, just because your pictures look similar, it would be ridiculous to think that one picture actually produced another picture! Similarity between the pictures is nothing more than evidence that the same person created both pictures. In the same way, the similarities we see between people and primates just tell us that the same Creator made both.

You see, God created people last, after everything else in the world was made. And though He used many of the same chemicals and structures that gave life to the animals, God did something *very* different with man. He made us in a way that is unique. The Bible tells us, "Then God said, '**Let Us make man in Our image**, **according to Our likeness**; and let them rule over the fish of the sea and over the birds of the sky and over the cattle and over all the earth, and over every creeping thing that creeps on the earth. **God created man in His own image, in the image of God He created him; male and female He created them**" (Genesis 1:26-27, emphasis added).

Read the boldfaced words again. The Bible tells us we are very different from the animals, even though we share some features with them. Monkeys and apes were not created in the likeness of God. They are unable to pray and speak to God. They are unable to seek God with all their hearts and choose to become like Jesus. Animals cannot ponder life, build cities, or develop cures for illnesses. Animals cannot read, write, or learn about the past, nor can they dream about the future. Indeed, they have no concept of time. Animals are unable to learn to do things even a toddler can do – because a toddler has been created in the image of God, with a mind and a soul. Yes, people are very different from the animals. We are special. We are made in the likeness of God. That is a great and awesome thing. When you were born, you were born with the image of God stamped into your very being. You will always be special to God!

But what about the similarities between people and primates? These similarities cause some people to think that long ago, only primates existed, but that over time, those primates began to have offspring that looked more and more human until, eventually, humans came into being. In other words, they think that the similarities between primates and people indicate that people are *related to* primates. I know that sounds silly, but remember, creation scientists think that the different members of family Felidae (the cats) originally came from just two cat-like creatures that came off the ark with Noah. If all those different cats came from two cat-like creatures, couldn't humans have come from apes? No. The differences between the members of family Felidae are minor. It is easy to understand how the genes of two cat-like creatures from the ark could be "shuffled around" in different ways to make jaguars, lions, and even domesticated cats. However, the differences we see between primates and people are too vast to come from a rearrangement of genes. Just as a dog is too different from a cat for the two to be related, a primate is too different from a person for the two to be related.

Let's take a close look at primates and some of the features they share with people to better understand why these features are not evidence that people and primates are related. For example, both people and primates have eyes facing forward, rather than on each side of the head like some other animals. However, this is true of many other animals, such as cats, bears, and owls.

Some primates have a mouth that looks similar to ours, but inside that mouth, most have enormous canine teeth, like those of a lion. Also, primate facial expressions are different from human facial expressions. Primates "grin" when they are afraid, baring their teeth like any other mammal would when threatened. People don't bare their teeth when threatened.

The Barbary macaque on the left is a primate. While its mouth looks a bit like a person's mouth, its teeth look a lot like those of a lion (right).

Primates, like other animals, depend on their sense of smell to find food and detect danger. Though they use their sense of sight, their sense of smell is better. People are the opposite. A person's sense of sight is much better than his or her sense of smell. Also, while primates do have larger brains (given their body size) than other animals, those brains are still small when compared to human brains. A human brain, for example, is about four times larger and two to three times heavier than that of a chimpanzee.

Primates can stand upright and walk for brief periods of time, but so can bears.

Primates can sit on their rear, the way people can, with their legs out in front. In addition, they can stand on two legs and even walk for a short period of time. However, you may remember that bears are also able to do those same things. Interestingly, people are the only part of God's creation that He actually designed for walking. Our feet have an arch in the middle that acts as a shock absorber. Without it, we could not walk for very long without severe foot pain. Primate feet don't have these arches, and their legs are not designed to support them for very long when they are upright. These animals are **quadrupedal** (kwod' ruh ped' uhl), which means they walk on all fours ("quad" means "four"). We are **bipedal** (bye' ped uhl), which means we walk on two legs ("bi" means "two"). There is no other bipedal mammal in all of God's creation.

Because primates are shaped with shoulders and a wide chest, we call their front appendages arms. However, their front arms are really another set of legs. Their hands and feet serve the same function, and they can use either for any task, even eating. Although a primate's hands (and feet) are similar to human hands, they are also similar to raccoon hands. The main thing that separates the primate's hand from the raccoon's hand is the primate's nails, which are usually flat and not curved. This is not always the case, because some primates do have curved claws. Nevertheless, even considering a primate with flat nails, it is clear that a primate's hand is similar to hands other than those of people.

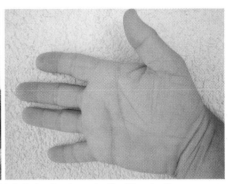

Although the primate hand (middle) has a lot of similarity to the human hand (right), it also has similarities to the raccoon hand (left).

Some primates use tools, just as people do. For example, a chimpanzee might use a shell to pry open a fruit or a clam. However, many other animals use tools in a similar manner. Some finches use a cactus spine to fish grubs out of holes in trees. Green herons fish for sea life by dropping objects in the water that attract fish. Sea otters use stones to crack open shellfish. Dolphins protect their noses with sea sponges when foraging on rocky seafloors. Hundreds of animals have been shown to use tools, including many kinds of birds, badgers, elephants, and even the naked mole rat. Some say that because primates are able to solve basic problems, this means they are related to humans. However, you may remember from Zoology 2 that even an octopus is able to solve problems, using different methods to find its way out of a trap, and "remembering" the successful method the next time.

As you can see, then, while we do share some features with the primates, many of those features are shared by other animals as well. In the end, these common feature show that primates, other animals, and people are all made by the same Creator. He used similar elements in His design throughout creation. When animals are incredibly similar (like jaguars, snow leopards, and lions), it is reasonable to think that they are related. However, the existence of a few basic similarities between living things is not reason enough to think that they are related. When living things are very different from one another, there is simply no way that they can be related.

That's the main point. If you look at primates and people, there are some similarities. However, there are many more differences. People have language. We can change our lives, create art, build cities, make music, and worship God. We can make jokes, think about the past and the future, and laugh about things that happened years ago. We have emotions, and we feel incomplete without a close relationship with God. We are people created in the image of God, with much of the wisdom, creativity, love, and joy that God Himself possesses. These are all important characteristics that animals, including primates, simply do not have. Those differences are more than enough to tell us that we are not in any way related to primates, or any other animal.

People and primates are different in so many ways, it is just not possible that they are related to one another.

Another important difference between people and primates is that some of them commit infanticide. If you remember from Lesson 4, infanticide is when an adult animal will kill the young of its species. Interestingly enough, those who think that we are related to primates also think that we are most closely related to the primates that regularly practice infanticide, such as baboons, gorillas, and chimpanzees. This horrid practice is often seen with tigers, lions, African wild dogs, squirrels, and rats. It is further evidence that apes are simply another kind of animal, with instincts like those of other animals.

If anyone tries to tell you that you are in some way related to primates, remember that you are God's special creation. You are so special that God even gave you a unique and important job to do on this earth – a purpose for your life. Ephesians 2:10 says, "For we are His workmanship, created in Christ Jesus for good works, which God prepared beforehand so that we would walk in them." You are amazingly precious to God, and you were created for a set purpose, which God prepared beforehand. Now that we've cleared up that confusion, let's jump back into our jeep and continue our safari.

Explain what you learned about people and primates in your own words.

Primate Classification

We have already talked about a lot of classification groups like orders, families, species, etc. Well, there's going to be a lot more of that in this lesson. So, I want you to keep a chart that will help you keep these groups in order in your mind. You will begin with a piece of paper with the word "Primates" written inside a box at the top of the page. As I explain how these animals are divided, you will draw lines down from that word and write the new names for the new groups below the lines in their own box. Then, as these groups are divided even further, you will draw new lines and new boxes. This will help keep all these critters straight. Here is what the start of your chart might look like:

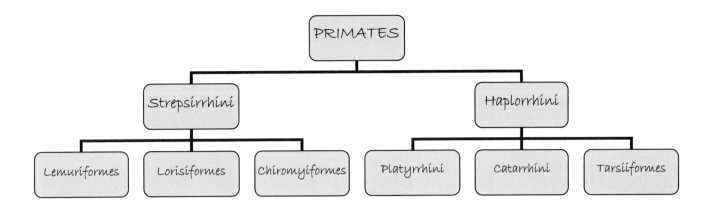

Go ahead and start your chart. Turn your page sideways so that you have a wide space in which to write. Put a box in the center at the top with the word "Primates" in it. That will represent the order Primates, which contains all the animals we will study in this lesson. Scientists have classified the order Primates into two different suborders based on, of all things, the characteristics of the nose. In Greek, "rhin" means "nose," so you'll see "rhin" in a lot of names this lesson.

The two main suborders for primates are **Strepsirrhini** (strep' sir rin ee) and **Haplorrhini** (hap' luh rin ee). Draw two boxes below the word "Primates" on your chart and write the names of the suborders, as shown above.

Suborder Strepsirrhini

In Greek, "strepho" means "curved," so members of this suborder are primates with noses that curve out from their face. Most biologists, however, refer to them as the "wet-nosed" primates, because these curved noses are usually wet, like the nose of a dog. This order contains primates known as **lemurs**, **bushbabies**, **lorises**, and **aye-ayes**. You can see pictures of these creatures below. They are all small, nocturnal, Old World primates that generally eat plants and insects. Remember that the term "Old World" refers to the continents of Europe, Asia and Africa, while "New World" refers to North and South America as well as Australia. Thus, members of this order are not found in North or South America, nor are they found in Australia (except in zoos).

Although they may not look like what you think of when you hear the word "primate," the lemur (left), bushbaby (middle), and loris (right) are all members of the order Primates, suborder Strepsirrhini.

As you can see from the pictures on the previous page, these animals have large eyes perfectly designed for a nocturnal lifestyle. It is not surprising, then, that most of them are active at night. Those large eyes also have a feature that makes them a bit frightening at night: they reflect light, even a small amount of light, like light from the moon or a flashlight. So, if you were walking in the forest of Southeast Asia or Africa, and it was dark outside, you may see a set of very large eyes staring at you out of the blackness. That would be scary. However, it would probably be just a lemur, loris, or bushbaby. You see, even though their reflecting eyes make them look frightening, these little creatures aren't a danger to anyone. They are fairly docile creatures.

This suborder is usually split into three groups: **Lemuriformes** (lee myoor' ih for meez), **Lorisiformes** (lor' ihs ih form eez), and the **Chiromyiformes** (ky' roh my' ih for meez). The ring-tailed lemur on the bottom of the previous page (left) is an example of the first group, the bushbaby (middle) and loris (right) on the bottom of the previous page are examples of the second group, and the **aye-aye** (below) is the only member of the last group. Take out your classification chart and write those three groups in three boxes below the Strepsirrhini box, as shown in the sample diagram on the previous page.

Aye-Ayes

While I don't want to spend too much time on suborder Strepsirrhini, I just have to tell you about the aye-aye! This little creature is probably the most frightening member of the Strepsirrhini crew. It's also a bit different from the rest. This black-furred creature has a face that looks a bit like a raccoon, along with a white "collar" around its neck. Its luminescent eyes can be chilling in the dark. But even worse than that are the long, bony fingers of this nocturnal troll. Of all the skeletal-looking fingers on its front legs, the one that is the oddest is the middle finger – which is thinner and longer than the rest! Why did God give this animal the genes for a long, bony finger? Well, the aye-aye sticks this handy tool finger

middle finger

into logs and branches to spear insects, like grubs, that are inside. With its highly developed ears, the aye-aye listens for the slightest noise of a wiggling grub inside a log. It then chews a little hole with its rodent-like incisor teeth, inserts its poker finger, and pulls out its meal.

Those incisor teeth are another unusual feature of this peculiar creature. In fact, they make the classification of the aye-aye a bit difficult. You see, these teeth continue to grow throughout its life, so the aye-aye has to constantly chew on wood to keep them from getting too long. Can you think of another mammal that has to do this? Rodents (like mice and rats) have the same problem. Because of this fact, the aye-aye was once classified as a rodent. However, it is considered more similar to primates than to rodents, which is why it is now classified with the other "wet-nosed" primates.

The only place where the aye-aye can be found is Madagascar. Unfortunately, they are not well-liked there. Some superstitious Malagasy people (who are native to Madagascar) think the aye-aye is a symbol of death. There is even a saying that if the aye-aye points its bony middle finger at you, you will soon die. Although many people are terrified of this little primate, the aye-aye is not afraid of them! On the contrary, this curious little animal has a habit of approaching people and even sniffing their feet. It's no wonder people dread its presence! They were once hunted and killed because they were considered a nuisance. Now, however, they are endangered, and it's against the law to kill them.

Suborder Haplorrhini

Although it doesn't look "simple," this mandrill's dry nose and some other features put it in suborder Haplorrhini.

Because these are the primates you are most likely to see (both in zoos and in the wild), I want to concentrate on the primates in suborder Haplorrhini. In Greek, "haplo" means "simple," so these are the "simple-nosed primates." Actually, biologists call them the "dry-nosed primates" to separate them from the members of suborder Strepsirrhini. They usually have round, dry nostrils that do not resemble a dog or cat's nose nearly as much as the primates you just studied. Simple-nosed primates usually have large brains (but not always), and much longer arms than legs (but not always). They have non-reflecting eyes, so you wouldn't see their big eyes staring out from the darkness on your night hikes.

The only primates living in the New World come from this suborder, but there are Old World primates found in this group as well. Scientists divide this suborder into three groups: **Platyrrhini** (plat' uh ree nee), **Catarrhini** (kat' uh ree nee) and **Tarsiiformes** (tar sih for' meez). On your classification chart, then, draw three boxes below Haplorrhini, writing the words Platyrrhini, Catarrhini, and Tarsiiformes in the boxes (see the sample on page 95).

Tarsiiformes

The primates in the Tarsiiformes group look like they belong in suborder Strepsirrhini at first. Mostly, this is because of their huge eyes. And the truth is that scientists argue over where to place these strange little creatures on their taxonomy charts. They are so odd that they don't seem to fit into any particular system. God created some unusual creatures that stump the taxonomists! Yet, God didn't create the animals for our classification system. We made our classification system in order to try to understand God's creation. God sometimes had a unique and creative plan for a species that doesn't work with our man-made structures. So, we are often confused when we try to fit an animal into the system we created.

Take a look at the **tarsier** (tar' see ur) on the right. Do you think it's nocturnal or diurnal? If you guessed nocturnal because of its giant eyes, you would be right. And, in fact, those eyes are one reason scientists think it belongs in suborder Haplorrhini. You see, they don't reflect light like the eyes of the primates from suborder Strepsirrhini. If you were walking through a forest full of tarsiers at night, your flashlight would not make their eyes shine. Also, tarsiers have a dry nose. Of course, they have many other features in common with the primates from suborder Strepsirrhini, which is why some scientists still argue about where to put them.

long tarsus

Although it looks like a primate in suborder Strepsirrhini, its dry nose and non-reflective eyes put the tarsier in suborder Haplorrhini.

Tarsiers get their name from their extremely long tarsus (ankle) bone, which gives them a strange-looking, stretched-out foot. They catch insects by lying in wait, sitting very quietly until an insect happens by. Then their long feet launch their entire body forward to catch the insect. They are tiny little creatures that could fit in the palm of your dad's hand. In fact, the smallest primate in the world is the Philippine tarsier.

Platyrrhini: The New World Monkeys

This golden lion tamarin has a flat nose with nostrils pointing out toward the sides. That makes it a member of the Platyrrhini group.

The rest of the animals in suborder Haplorrhini are the ones you usually think of when you hear the word "primate." Like most primates, they are distinguished by their noses. In Greek, "platy" means "flat," so can you guess what puts primates into this group? Their flat noses, of course! The primates in this group typically have flat noses with the nostrils pointing out toward the sides of the nose. Another thing all these primates have in common is that they are found only in the New World. As a result, they are often called **New World monkeys**.

All the little monkeys in the New World are just that…little. They are also **arboreal** (ar bor' ee uhl), which means they live and spend most of their time in trees.   They are mostly found in the depths of dense jungles, such as the Amazon rainforest. Because of this, there isn't a great deal known about them. However, we do know that members of most species choose a mate for life, and families stick together, with both the mother and the father taking care of the young.

Many New World monkeys also have a prehensile tail. Some of them have fully prehensile tails, which means they can pick up objects and do things with them using only their tail. Others have partially prehensile tails, which means they can hold onto things with their tails, but that's about it. The New World monkeys with partially prehensile tails mostly use them to hold onto a tree branch, which helps them move around the tree. Interestingly enough, it is very rare for any monkey other than a New World monkey to have a prehensile tail So next time you see a picture of a monkey with its tail wrapped around something, find out what kind it is supposed to be. If that monkey isn't supposed to be a New World monkey, the artist made a mistake in thinking that all monkeys have prehensile tails!

I want to discuss two types of New World monkeys: the **marmosets** (mar' muh setz) and **tamarins** (tam' uh rinz). They are fairly small monkeys, most reaching the size of a squirrel or a small cat. They live in the tropical rainforests of Central and South America, mainly in the Amazon rainforest. With the help of their tails, they can scurry at top speed through the trees in which they live, hunting insects and other small animals. In addition, they eat fruit and other plant parts. Many will even chew into a branch and eat the sap (gum) inside.

These little monkeys have great senses, especially their sense of smell, which helps them locate food in the jungles where they live. They live in troops, and the mothers usually have two offspring at a time. Usually one female gives birth to all the babies. She generally gives birth twice a year. Young marmosets and tamarins are dependent on their parents until they are a few months old. At that

This common marmoset is about the size of a squirrel with a very long tail.

time, they'll start catching their own insects or stealing insects from other members of the troop. When they are adults, they'll either stay with their troop or leave and start their own family. Their family unit is very important. The older siblings carry and care for the younger siblings when the parents are busy. These animals certainly have some good family values!

These cotton-topped tamarins are mates.

Marmosets and tamarins spend their nights in tangles of vines, forks of trees, inside tree hollows, or at that base of palm fronds. They are diurnal, so they spend their days looking for food and interacting with each other. They are fond of grooming others in their group, and they tend to do that whenever they have a chance to rest from their search for food. Young ones also "play" together, chasing each other around, grabbing each other, and even biting one another in a playful, gentle way.

These primates are very vocal. In fact, the best way to find them in the wild is to listen for their calls. They have several different types of calls, depending on what is going on. When one troop comes near another troop, there are usually calls to indicate whose territory is where, and which individual belongs to which group. They also have "alarm calls" that notify their troop members of predators such as large birds. They not only communicate with one another using sound, but they also have many scent glands that help communicate important messages using smells.

Although marmosets and tamarins have many similarities, there are differences between them as well. Generally, marmosets have canine teeth that are about the same size as their incisors, while tamarins have enlarged canine teeth, like those of a dog. In addition, tamarins are generally a bit larger than marmosets. While most marmoset and tamarin fathers participate in caring for the young, tamarin fathers are usually a bit more involved than marmoset fathers. For example, the young must be carried for quite some time. In tamarins, the father does most of the carrying, bringing the young to the mother only to nurse. In maramosets, the carrying is shared between mother and father.

Tell someone what you have learned about the primates in groups
Strepsirrhini, Platyrrhini and Tarsiiformes.

Catarrhini: The Old World Monkeys and Apes

In Greek, "cato" means "downward," so the primates in the Catarrhini group have downward-pointing noses with nostrils at the bottom rather than on the sides. These primates are found only in the Old World, so they are sometimes called "Old World monkeys and apes." Incidentally, scientists place humans in this group, because our noses fit those characteristics. Of course, we aren't animals, but since scientists are interested in placing all living things in their classification scheme, they need to put us somewhere. It only means that we share some characteristics with this group, so in terms of what we look like, this is where we belong.

Notice that when I referred to the primates we just studied, I called them "New World monkeys." With this group, however, I call them "old world monkeys *and apes*." That's because this group is further split into two groups: monkeys and apes. You need to add that to your chart. Draw two boxes below the box that is labeled Catarrhini, and put "Old World monkeys" in one and "apes" in the other.

So what's the difference between a monkey and an ape? Can you guess? Well, the first thing to look for is a tail. A monkey usually has a tail, even if it's very small. Apes, however, have no tail. The next thing to look for is the way the animal gets from tree to tree. Does it swing or jump? Apes have arms built for swinging, but a monkey's arms are not designed that way. Monkeys are designed for balance and stability as they jump, hop, and skitter over the tops of branches. Also, apes generally have larger brains and can (sometimes) learn new things more quickly than monkeys. Some apes have been known to use tools and solve problems. Apes also have unique

Both of these primates have downward-pointing noses, but the baboon (left) has a tail, so it is a monkey. The orangutan (right) has no tail and is an ape.

personalities, just as dogs do. Whole communities of apes may behave differently than another community of the same kind of ape. This makes apes a little more diverse than monkeys.

Old World monkeys are larger than New World monkeys. They are usually about the size of a large dog. Scientists have divided them into two groups: the **Colobinae** (kol' uh bee nay) and the **Cercopithecinae** (sir koh pith' uh sih nay). That's two more boxes to add to your chart, under the box for Old World monkeys. The main differences between these groups are that the Colobinae are mostly herbivorous, live in trees, and don't have pouches in their cheeks to store food. The Cercopithecinae are omnivorous, often use trees but are comfortable on the ground as well, and have pouches in their cheeks to store food.

I want to spend most of my "Old World monkey time" on the Cercopithecinae group, so I will just discuss one member of the Colobinae group: the **proboscis** (pro bah' skus) **monkey**, whose scientific name is *Nasalis* (nay' zal us) *larvatus* (larv' uh tus). Can you guess what makes this monkey special? Well, do you know what a proboscis is? On mammals, the proboscis is the nose. Notice the

Ask one of your parents or grandparents who Jimmy Durante was.

genus name (the first part of the scientific name). "Nasal" also refers to the nose. Now can you guess? The proboscis monkey has a *very big* nose, as you can see in the picture on the left! The males have longer noses than the females; sometimes they are so large that a male will have to push its nose out of the way to put something in its mouth!

This interesting Old World monkey lives only on the island of Borneo, which is in Southeast Asia. It lives in forests near water, such as the mangrove forests that are plentiful there. Like other members of the Colobinae group, this monkey has several compartments in its stomach. This is necessary, because it lives on hard-to-digest leaves and must have bacteria in its stomach to help the digestion process. What other animal does that sound like? The koala. Other Colobinae monkeys include colobus monkeys, langurs, and leaf monkeys.

The Cercopithecinae group includes **baboons**, **mangabeys** (man' guh bays), **mandrills**, **guenons** (guh nohnz'), **patas monkeys**, and **macaques** (muh kaks'). All these cheek-pouched monkeys live in Africa, except the macaque, which also lives in Asia. In fact, one Asian macaque, the **Japanese macaque**, is the only monkey that can endure temperatures below freezing for long periods of time. It is sometimes called the "snow monkey." Another kind of macaque, the **rhesus** (ree' sus) **macaque**, has been studied a great deal by people. This macaque, also called the "rhesus monkey," was the first primate in space! Over the years of early spaceflight, several different rhesus macaques (and other primates) were used by NASA to test the effects of space flight on living creatures, but the first one to reach space was Albert II, who flew 83 miles above the earth's surface on June 14, 1949.

Baboons and Mandrills

Of all the Cercopithecinae primates, I want to concentrate on baboons and mandrills. Baboons are easy primates to spot on your African safari, as they tend to live in very large groups. Unlike many other primate troops, baboon troops are usually made up of many adult females and males. All the males can mate with other females in the troop, but some males have a higher rank than others. Thus, male baboons often fight within the troop, trying to earn a higher position. In some cases, if a male baboon is worried about a higher-ranking male starting a fight with him, he will carry an infant, because the presence of the infant will reduce the chance of him being attacked by another baboon. Interestingly, wandering males from another troop can even become part of a new troop if they work hard to get accepted. They find acceptance into new troops slowly, usually by developing "friendships" with different females around the edge of a troop. Sometimes, they'll take care of the infants very lovingly (though they aren't related) in order to win favor with the females. They will also help defend a female and her offspring.

Depending on the particular species, female baboons give birth every one to three years to a single infant. Initially, an infant baboon is almost always by its mother's side. While it is very young, the infant is carried next to her stomach as she travels. Eventually, the infant gets old enough to ride on her back. As the young baboon gets older, the mother gives it more freedom, allowing it to interact with the other young baboons in the troop.

The brightly colored rump on this mother baboon is common among the Cercopithecinae primates.

When foraging, baboons will dig up roots, turn over rocks in search of beetles and scorpions, and even dig through elephant dung in the hopes of finding dung beetles inside. Adult males will also catch and kill small mammals to share with the troop. At night, a troop will sleep on a rock cliff or in trees for protection.

While baboons are generally brown or white with long, brown noses, mandrills have more colorful noses that are also ridged (see the picture on page 97). They are the rainforest counterparts to baboons and have a lot in common with them. However, there are differences besides their noses. While baboons are fairly common, mandrills are threatened with extinction because their habitats are being destroyed by people. Interestingly, mandrills have a less-colorful "cousin" called the **drill**. This monkey is found only in Cameroon, and while it has the same kind of nose ridges the mandrill has, its nose is black, lacking the colors that make the mandrill nose so distinctive.

Apes

When you're walking through the rainforest, you might see a stocky, tailless creature sitting in a tree or on the ground. Most likely, it is an ape. The ape might reach up with one of its long, flexible arms and grab a branch off a tree behind it without moving its body. Or it might use its arms to hold and stroke a baby ape. Or it might walk around on its knuckles while the baby climbs on its back.

Apes are divided into two groups, **great apes** and **lesser apes**. Add those two boxes beneath the box for apes on your classification chart. The great apes are generally larger than the lesser apes, which is why we call them "great." Lesser apes are also known as **gibbons**, while the great apes include **chimpanzees**, **bonobos** (buh noh' bohz), **gorillas**, and **orangutans**. They all live in Africa or Southeast Asia.

Gibbons

Can you guess how this white cheek gibbon gets its name?

Let's start our ape safari in Southeast Asia, which is where you will find the lesser apes, or gibbons, swinging from tree to tree in the rainforests. These furry apes have long fingers at the end of their long arms, a feature that enables them to reach out and grab a distant tree limb as they almost fly between the trees. With one powerful swing, they are able to propel their body into the air at a speed that allows them to accurately grasp a branch 20 feet away! Their fingers work like hooks, latching onto the branches they catch in their swing. This kind of movement is called **brachiation** (bray' kee aye shun), and gibbons are masters at it! They can move at speeds of almost 35 miles per hour this way! Swinging isn't the only way they get from tree to tree; they can also leap up to 30 feet with their powerful legs.

Gibbons grow to be only about 2 ½ to 3 feet high and weigh about 20 pounds. That's about the size of a small toddler. Though they come in many colors, they all have jet-black skin, which you can see on their bare face and on the padding found on their rear. Many primates have this type of padding on their rear. It is used as a sitting pad, like having a cushioned chair upon which to sit. As you learned in the section about baboons, many of the Cercopithecinae primates have brightly colored "cushions."

There are about twelve different species of gibbons, and in each case, individuals tend to form long-lasting relationships with their mate. They mark territories by singing a duet with their mate from the highest trees. A single ape will find a tree and sing until it finds a mate with whom to share its song, life, and territory. Their social groups consist of a mother, father, and their immature children.

Gibbons spend their day foraging for food, usually fruits, insects, and leaves. Their nights are spent sleeping in the fork of a tree, sitting upright with their back leaning against the trunk. This is comfortable because of the seat cushion God gave them. If *you* decide to sleep in the rainforest, the gibbons will not allow you a peaceful morning, because they usually awaken and greet the day with raucous calling, screaming, and hooting. This warns other gibbons that may have entered their territory and are not welcome. The **siamang** (see' uh mang), the largest and darkest species of gibbon, has an inflatable throat sac (called a gular sac). This sac can be inflated to be as big as the siamang's head. It's like an amplifier for the vocal cords, making the sounds even louder.

Though it prefers to stay high up in the canopy of the rainforest, a gibbon will walk for short distances on its two little legs, rather than on all fours, if it happens to come to the ground. Even while walking, it tries to hang onto limbs and branches overhead. These little primates have many predators that would enjoy having a gibbon for dinner. However, they are too quick to be caught and rarely become dinner for another creature.

Explain what you have learned so far about Catarrhini primates.

Chimpanzees and Bonobos

Let's hop back in our jeep, because we are leaving the rainforests of Southeast Asia and going to Africa to study the great apes. We'll start with chimpanzees and bonobos. Chimpanzees, or chimps as they are often called, are probably the most studied of all the apes. One pioneering researcher, Jane Goodall, even lived with them so she could learn about them. They live in the forests and grasslands of Africa in large groups that often break down into smaller groups. Those smaller groups might spend a long time away from the main group. They usually come back to the main group from time to time, but they can also join a new one. Scientists call this a **fusion-fission** society. The word "fusion" means "to put together," and the word "fission" means "to split apart." As you can see, then, this is a very apt description of how the troop operates.

The scientific name for the chimpanzee is *Pan troglodytes*.

Within the troop, there is generally one alpha male in charge, and each male has a certain status below him. When angry or trying to get a higher rank in the troop, chimps stand upright, swagger, stamp their feet, wave their arms, and throw things (such as branches or rocks). They also drag branches while running, screaming, and pulling back their lips to bare their teeth. Vicious fights are commonplace in chimp troops. That's not very nice behavior, but it is typical of a chimpanzee.

Subordinate (lesser) chimps in the group greet the dominant chimps with very submissive behavior. They present their back in the same way that a dog presents its tummy to a dominant dog. They also crouch, bow, or bob in front of the dominant chimp. Social grooming is probably the most important interaction they have. They groom one another constantly – usually with the inferior chimps grooming the higher-up chimps. Grooming consists of searching for and removing fleas, mites, and ticks, which are promptly eaten. Yum! Of all the apes, chimps have the most varied diet. They will eat anything, but prefer fruits and nuts and sometimes insects. They will also eat the flesh of small mammals.

Chimps have large brains and exhibit great intelligence and curiosity about the world around them. When they see something interesting, they will watch it intently. They are able to imitate behavior, as we see in the story of Curious George when he puts on the yellow hat. However, unlike Curious George, chimps don't make good pets, for they are not potty-trained easily and will often destroy the fixtures in a house. Also, they are aggressive and can hurt their owners, even after many years of care. Sadly, chimpanzees that have been kept as pets are often given up by their owner. Because they have been habituated to human life, they don't fit into chimpanzee culture and can't be released into the wild or sent to the zoo. Thus, they are often sent to animal laboratories, where they are used in experiments. Because of these issues, many states have made it illegal to own a primate.

Chimpanzees spend a lot of time in trees, but they also spend time on the ground. They move from place to place by walking on their feet and the knuckles of their hands. This is called "knuckle-walking," and it is the most common way for an ape to walk. Chimpanzees grow to be 4 to 5 feet tall and weigh more than 140 pounds.

A bonobo looks a lot like a chimpanzee.

Bonobos look very much like chimps but are just slightly smaller. Because of this, they used to be called pygmy chimpanzees. However, genetic studies show that they should be classified as a different species. Though they look like chimps, bonobos behave a bit differently. They live in a fusion-fission troop, but the male dominance is not as important as it is in a chimpanzee troop. Even when tension develops between males, it is usually followed by reassuring gestures that help the entire troop to relax. As a result, bonobos are generally considered less aggressive than chimpanzees. Also, although they knuckle-walk like any ape, they do spend more time walking upright. Both chimpanzees and bonobos are very intelligent apes, much more intelligent than gorillas, which I want to discuss now.

Gorillas

Imagine a gorilla standing over you, beating its chest. Would you be frightened by this large ape, which stands 6 feet tall and weighs over 300 pounds? The truth is, although gorillas are the largest of the primates, they are shy, docile animals that keep to themselves. A male will get aggressive when he or one of his females is threatened, or when he is challenged by a subordinate male, but those are about the only times you would see this chest-beating behavior. They aren't ferocious carnivores, but instead live on fruits, leaves, and a few insects now and again. So, if you see a gorilla, be very quiet and don't wave your arms in the air. Also, don't use a flash when taking pictures. All these things could be seen as a threat. If you keep your distance from the troop, you'll be welcome to watch them as they forage, as they groom each other, and as the infants play.

You can see why this adult male gorilla is called a silverback.

A gorilla troop is made up of several females and young with one male over them. The lead male is usually called a **silverback gorilla**, because it develops gray hair on its back at about twelve years of age. Silverbacks also grow long canines at maturity, making them look rather fierce. Silverback leaders are always the center of the troop's attention, making all the decisions, involved in every fight, guiding the troop to feeding grounds, and taking responsibility for every other animal in the troop. When a male is born to the troop, it is allowed to stay until it is about eleven years old. Then it must leave, joining a bachelor group until it finds a mate and starts its own troop. If a male is able to challenge the leader and win, it will take over the troop. If a new silverback comes into power, it will often commit the horrid practice of infanticide, killing all the infants in the troop. This ensures that all the females will be devoted to the new male so that they can have more of his babies.

Gorillas inhabit the jungles and forests of western Africa where they knuckle-walk along the ground. They spend more time on the ground than any other primate. However, in the evening, the females and young of a troop will make nests to sleep in, and those nests are often in trees. Every single night they build a new nest to sleep in, even if it's only a foot away from the nest they slept in the night before. Each gorilla builds its own nest, with the exception of the very young. They sleep with anyone who will take them. Tree nests are usually built in the forks of a tree, using a lot of branches and leaves to support a gorilla's hefty weight. Ground nests are built by pulling vegetation and securing it together.

The only real predator for the gorilla is the leopard. When gorillas feel threatened, they gather close together in a group. The male defends his troop against any threat by beating his chest and charging the threatening creature.

Though gorillas have the largest brain of all the primates, they are thought to be less intelligent than other apes. Unlike chimpanzees, for example, gorillas don't often use tools in the wild. In studies conducted by researchers, they also don't imitate behavior like chimpanzees or appear to be as curious as chimpanzees. Nevertheless, they are considered more intelligent than most non-primates.

Orangutans

Orangutans are very intelligent and are the world's largest arboreal animal.

Moving our safari back to Southeast Asia, we will find orangutans in the trees of Sumatra and Borneo. Their faces are long and sad-looking, and their bowed legs support big, bulky bodies. The name "orangutan" may sound like it comes from the orange coloring of these creatures, but it actually comes from Malay words that mean "man of the forest." Perhaps that is what people thought of when they saw these very intelligent creatures sitting for long hours, staring down intently with their deep-set eyes.

Many scientists consider orangutans the most intelligent of all the apes, which in turn means they are the most intelligent animal in the world. Even though the chimpanzee is very intelligent, some studies indicate that the orangutan has better problem-solving skills and can use more complex tools. They hold leafy branches over their heads to shade themselves and protect themselves from the rain. They even fashion nests with a roof for protection against the rain. I guess these smart creatures aren't too fond of the rain in their rainforest home!

The adult male can be recognized by its cheek flaps, which increase in size as it ages. These cheek flaps get so large that they almost cover the eyes. These giants can grow to be almost 200 pounds. That's a big ape, but only half the size of a gorilla. They claim huge territories, which they defend against other males while allowing females to come in.

The cheek flaps you see on this male orangutan are made of fat and grow larger as the ape gets older.

Unlike other apes, the orangutan is highly arboreal. It spends most of its life in trees, foraging for food by day and sleeping in a self-made nest by night. Like the gibbon, young orangutans are masters at brachiation, easily swinging from tree to tree. However, older orangutans tend to move through the trees slowly, using all four of their limbs. They mostly prefer eating fruits, nuts, and leaves, which is one reason they spend so much time in trees. However, from time to time they will also eat tree bark, small animals, and even dirt!

Unlike other apes, orangutans are loners. In the wild, the only time you will see orangutans together is when you find a mother with her young one or a few orangutans sharing a large tree because fruit is plentiful there. It takes a long time for a mother to raise her young one. Typically, a young orangutan doesn't leave its mother until it is 7 to 10 years old. After that, though, it goes out on its own and doesn't enjoy the company of others, except to mate.

Well, that completes our study of primates. You have learned a great deal and even learned to identify them like an expert. If you want to research more about some of the New World and Old World monkeys we didn't discuss, check out some books from the library or go to the course website I told you about in the introduction to the book.

What Do You Remember?

How are primates different from people? Explain how primates are similar to other wild animals. Are most primates social or solitary? What single feature is used to classify the major groups of primates? Name a New World monkey. Name an Old World monkey. What is the difference between monkeys and apes? Which animal is considered a lesser ape? Tell someone a little bit about some of the animals you have studied in this lesson.

Map It!

In the following locations on your map, put drawings or pictures of the animals you studied:

Africa – Bushbabies, chimpanzees, gorillas, lorises, baboons, mandrills, guenons, macaques
Southeast Asia – Lorises, gibbons, macaques, orangutans, proboscis monkeys
South and Central America – Marmosets, tamarins
Madagascar – Aye-ayes, many kinds of lemurs

Notebook Activities

Today you are going to create a travel brochure for a person going on an African safari to observe primates. In the brochure, you should have drawings or pictures of some of the primates a person might see, descriptions of them, and interesting bits of information about each one.

You also need to complete your classification chart by adding to the bottom boxes you currently have. For each specific type of primate you studied, add a box connected to the classification group to which it belongs. For example, bushbabies are part of the Lorisiformes group, so connect a box labeled "bushbabies" to the Lorisiformes box. In the same way, gibbons are lesser apes, so connect a box labeled "gibbons" to the lesser apes box.

Experiment
Depth Perception

Do you remember that primates have **depth perception**? That means they can judge how far away an object is. This is an important skill for a primate jumping from one branch to another that might be a long way off. How well can you do this? Can you estimate how far away something is? Let's see.

You will need:
♦ A measuring device (like a tape measure or a ruler)
♦ Pencil and paper

1. Go outside and choose a few objects like trees, large stones, a lamppost, etc.
2. Measure the distance between some of those objects. This will help you get a feel for measuring distances.
3. Stand in a particular place and mark where you are standing.
4. Try to guess the distance between you and each of the objects you chose earlier. Make a chart like the one below to record your results. Write down the object and your guess as to how far from you it is.
5. Keeping the place where you were standing marked, measure the actual distance from where you were standing to each object. Write down that measurement as the actual distance in your chart.
6. When you are done, look at your guess and the actual distance for each object. Determine the difference between the two.
7. Do this for a few more objects, both near and far.

Sample Chart

OBJECT	GUESSED DISTANCE	ACTUAL DISTANCE	DIFFERENCE
Rosebush	2 feet	1 foot, 4 inches	8 inches
Maple Tree	6 feet, 6 inches	7 feet, 1 inch	7 inches

You may begin to see a pattern. Do you usually judge a distant as too close, too far, or are you usually on target? Realize that while primates and some other animals can make judgments like this, most animals cannot. So, while a primate could tell that the maple tree in the chart above is much farther from it than the rosebush, most animals could not.

Lesson 7
Rodentia and the Rest

We'll spend the rest of our time on wild animals studying the common and not-so-common creatures found in God's animal kingdom. We'll begin by studying order **Rodentia** (roh den' tee uh). Can you guess what that is? Remove the last two letters and look at the root word. What do you see? Rodent! You may think this only covers rats and mice; however, you might be surprised at some of the other animals classified as rodents. After exploring rodents, we'll study animals that are often mistakenly thought to be rodents, as well as a few strange, oddball animals. I think you'll find this lesson to be quite interesting!

Rodentia

Rodents have thrived everywhere on this planet except in Antarctica. There are more rodent species than any other mammal, with more than 2,000 species on every continent – again, with the exception of Antarctica, of course. Indeed, rodents make up about 40 percent of all the mammals in the world. So, even though we are only devoting a small space to rodents in this book, they would take up a rather large space compared to all the other animals if we collected them.

Most rodents are rather small, like mice and rats. One kind, the teeny-tiny pygmy jerboa, is less than 2 inches long when it's fully grown. That's smaller than your dad's pinky finger! However, some rodents aren't small at all. When I was a child, I heard terrible stories about giant rodents the size of dogs walking through restaurants in South America. That thought struck fear in my heart and convinced me that I didn't want to travel down there. As fictitious as it sounds, there actually is a rodent that grows to that size in South America. It's the 100 pound, 4-foot

The capybara (*Hydrochaeris hydrochaeris*) is the largest rodent living on the planet.

long capybara. Little did I know that there was a very large rodent living in my own state (Texas)! Perhaps you are unaware that the beaver is a rodent!

Have you ever wondered just which creatures are rodents and which aren't? Look at the following list and see if you can pick out the rodents correctly: mice, porcupines, lemmings, hedgehogs, gerbils, rabbits, squirrels, chinchillas, moles, shrews, groundhogs, prairie dogs, badgers, bats, chipmunks, hares, and beavers. I'll give you a hint: seven are not rodents. The animals above that are rodents are: porcupines, lemmings, mice, gerbils, squirrels, chinchillas, groundhogs, prairie dogs, chipmunks, and beavers. Were you surprised by any of these animals? Well, let's find out why some are rodents and some are not.

What makes a rodent a rodent? Let's begin with the word "rodent." The Latin word "rodere" means "to gnaw," and "dent" refers to "tooth." Put those words together and you get "rodent," or gnaw-tooth. Rodents are characterized by teeth that need to gnaw. Have you ever read Aesop's fable about the rodent who freed a lion caught in a net? If you have, you know that rodents are notorious for gnawing. Why? Well, in the front of a rodent's mouth are four long, sharp incisor teeth: two on the top and two on the bottom. These teeth never stop growing, and a rodent must gnaw on wood and trees to keep them from getting too long. In other words, they nibble and chew to wear down their incisors. They chew holes in trees, houses, churches, etc. to make a home for themselves. Squirrels, rats, mice, and many other creatures are notorious for chewing holes in people's homes. Of course, not all rodents chew holes in buildings. Beavers chew down trees to build their homes.

Though they enjoy chewing on anything, most rodents eat plant material, with some exceptions. A few will eat fish or insects, and squirrels have been known to eat the eggs of nesting birds. Many (like prairie dogs) are extremely social animals, often forming huge colonies. Other rodent colonies are smaller, and new members are kicked out of the group when they become mature. Some rodents (like porcupines) are loners.

Prairie dogs are very social rodents, living in colonies (called "towns") that can have thousands of members.

Smaller rodents have a short lifespan of only a few years, but they make up for this by having many young before they die, sometimes reproducing 300 new rodents before they depart from the earth. Because they reproduce a lot, these rodents spread throughout regions very quickly. Larger rodents, like beavers, bear only a few young every year, but they usually live for several years.

Rodents have varied lifestyles and habitats, ranging from burrowing gophers and mole rats to arboreal squirrels and "flying" squirrels. There are aquatic rodents (like beavers and muskrats) and desert-dwellers such as kangaroo rats and jerboas. Some are nocturnal, like mice and rats, whereas others are diurnal, like beavers and squirrels.

Though there are many differences among rodents, there are also many similarities. Not only do they all have the gnawing teeth I told you about earlier, but also none have canine teeth. In addition, most rodents have similar body plans. They are squat, with short limbs, and most are plantigrade walkers. Most rodents have a long tail, except a few, like hamsters and capybaras, which only have a little stub of a tail. Many rodents use their tails for specific purposes. A beaver, for example, uses its flat tail to help it swim. Hopping rodents have long tails with a tuft on the end that help them balance. Some have prehensile tails that can wrap around objects like a fifth arm. The flying squirrel has a bushy tail that fans out and functions a bit like the tail of an airplane.

Rodents provide food for many wild animals. If there were fewer rodents, there wouldn't be enough food for many other animals. Rodents are also important for seed dispersal. Not only do squirrels bury acorns that sprout into trees, but the seeds released in their droppings sometimes sprout into new plants as well. Rodents, such as rats, are used by humans for many things, such as testing fields for explosive mines. They are also used in science laboratories. Because of the help of laboratory rats, we have medicines that can cure (or help with) many diseases. You might be alive today because of a lab rat!

Many scientists find it useful to split rodents into three main groups: **mouse-like rodents**, **squirrel-like rodents**, and **cavy-like rodents**. What is a cavy? It is a rodent that has a chubby body, short legs, a large head, and short ears. The capybara I mentioned earlier is a cavy-like rodent, as are guinea pigs and, of course, cavies. Beavers, squirrels, and springhares are squirrel-like rodents, while voles, lemmings, rats, mice, gophers, and dormice are mouse-like rodents. Now that you know some basics about these interesting creatures, hop in your jeep, because we're heading into rodent territory.

Mouse-Like Rodents

The most common examples of mouse-like rodents are, of course, mice and rats. Although laboratory rats have helped us cure disease, they have also caused people problems. You see, rats often make their home with people, feeding off our crumbs and trash. Because rats are notorious for carrying parasites that spread diseases, this has caused some big problems.

In the 1300s, for example, rats spread the **black plague**, which caused the death of an estimated *75 million people*! How did rats spread the plague? Well, during that time in history, cities were often filthy and overrun with flea-infested rats. When a rat was infected, its fleas would get the germ that

Like primates, rats are very intelligent mammals and have even demonstrated problem-solving skills. Unfortunately, they can cause disease and even famine.

caused the disease by biting the rat. When the infected rat died, its fleas would hop off and find somewhere else to live. Often, that was a person or another rat. When the flea bit the rat or person, it would spread the disease. So the rats gave the disease to fleas, and the fleas carried it to people and other rats.

Rats are also detrimental to mankind because they eat crops. If a farm becomes home to a rat colony, the rats can destroy large portions of the farm's crop. Even after the remaining crop is harvested, rats can continue to consume what is in storage. In fact, rats can eat so many crops that in 2005, they caused a famine (called the "rat famine") in northeast Nicaragua.

Although we use the words "mouse" and "rat" a lot, you have to realize these words refer to many different animals. There are lots of different species of rodents referred to as rats, and there are even more species of rodents referred to as mice. One obvious difference between rats and mice is size. While mice typically are less than 4 inches long (not including the tail), adult rats are generally longer than 6 inches (once again, not including the tail). While mouse-like rodents (and cavy-like rodents) are very interesting, I simply cannot discuss all rodents in detail in this book. As a result, I have chosen to concentrate on the squirrel-like rodents.

Special Squirrels

Squirrels are at home in the high branches of trees.

What better animal to introduce the squirrel-like rodents than the squirrel itself? Most people don't appreciate squirrels. They can empty a bird feeder quickly, they are prolific, and they sometimes eat newborn songbirds. Their ability to safely run along narrow tree branches, jumping from one tree to another while grasping only the tiniest twig with perfect accuracy, is nothing short of amazing. They are most active in the late winter and early spring, when the mating season begins. They chase their potential mate through the tree tops at lightning speed while performing amazing acrobatic feats.

Have you ever looked up and seen large piles of leaves stuck up in your trees? Believe it or not, that mess is actually a well-designed squirrel nest, called a **drey**. Though the outside may look rough and shoddy, the inside of the drey is cozy, lined with any soft material the squirrel could find on the ground. Did you leave a mitten, sock, or other soft item outside? Perhaps it's in a squirrel drey now. If a squirrel's nest becomes over-infested with fleas or other parasites, it will move out and build a new nest. That's why there may be more nests than squirrels in your area.

There are many species of squirrels, and while most of them are herbivores, eating seeds, nuts, and flowers, they will eat bird eggs, young birds still in the nest, and frogs if food is scarce. This is not very common, however, because squirrels are industrious and gather up food in preparation for the winter. They collect nuts and bury them in specific locations they remember by sight and smell. When they run out of food, they will go to one of those places and dig up their stores. Since they usually bury more than they eat, some of those nuts germinate and grow. In a way, then, squirrels act as farmers, planting and spreading seeds so that new plants will grow.

Flying Squirrels

One type of squirrel you might not be familiar with is the **flying squirrel**. Like the sugar glider you learned about previously, these squirrels are designed with extra skin flaps, which, when stretched out, can be used like an umbrella to glide from one tree to another. They don't really fly; they just use their "parachute" to glide as they fall. However, they can launch themselves into such a powerful glide that they can reach a tree many yards away. They can even turn a corner while they glide, steering with a flick of their wrist bones. To an untrained eye, this looks like flying. Do you remember what the only flying mammal is? If you did Zoology 1, you know it's a bat. The flying squirrel, however, is a beautiful picture of our creative God. How wonderful to see a mammal designed with special features that are delightful to our eyes!

There are many flying squirrels all over North America, from Canada to Mexico. They can also be found in Asia and northern

You can see the flaps of skin that form the parachutes these flying squirrels use to glide through the air.

Europe. Scientists refer to the many different species of flying squirrels as **Pteromyini** (tare' uh mee nee). They typically live for five years or so in the wild, but they are often kept as pets. Pet flying squirrels can live much longer.

Beavers

If the river running past your home slows down and becomes a stream (or if a stream becomes a pond), it may be the work of a **beaver**. Though their habit of felling trees to build dams may seem like a destructive force and an inconvenience to landowners, the work of the beaver is actually an important contribution to nature. You see, the dam creates a wetland environment, generating a habitat for hundreds of different species that may not have survived otherwise. Almost half the endangered species depend on wetlands, which are in short supply. This makes beavers a **keystone species** – many animals depend upon them.

Beavers are well designed for life in the water. Their fur keeps water off their skin, and they can hold their breath for 15 minutes!

Like people, beavers are among the few living things that can actually change the entire landscape of North America and Europe, where they live. And beavers can do it much more quickly and without the cost we would incur if we were to change the landscape ourselves. They consistently preserve wetlands, and even purify the water downstream. You see, toxins are broken down in the **silt** (tiny grains of dirt and mud) that collects upstream of beaver dams. As a result, the water downstream is cleaner. Beavers are quite beneficial, wouldn't you say?

Beavers, of course, build **dams**. The largest known beaver dam was discovered near Three Forks, Montana. It was 2,140 feet long, 14 feet high, and 23 feet thick at the base! Many people mistakenly think that beavers live in their dams, but they typically do not. Beavers live in a **lodge** they build for their family. Beavers build dams to raise the water level so they can live more comfortably in the area where they have built their lodge. The drawing below should help you see the difference:

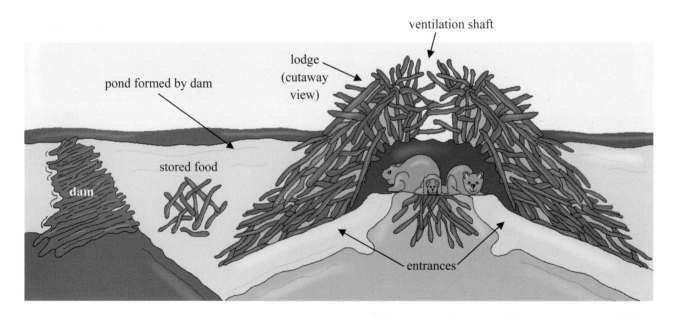

So you can see that a beaver dam is just a long structure that slows down a river's flow so that a pond develops. The beaver family actually lives in the lodge, a teepee-shaped pile of logs. All adult family members chew down trees to make the dam and lodge. As

As you can see, a beaver dam (left) is very different from a beaver lodge (right).

shown in the drawing on the previous page, most beaver lodges have more than one entrance, and the beavers actually live in the dry area above the water level. The lodge is mostly waterproof, because the spaces in between the sticks are sealed with mud. However, there is usually an unsealed area that allows air to pass in and out of the lodge. It is called the **ventilation shaft**.

You might think that beavers chew on wood just to make their dams, but that is not true. They eat the wood as well. As herbivores, beavers eat only plants. They really like green plants, especially water lilies, but in the winter, those are hard to find. As a result, they also eat wood. They tend to eat the bark and the soft wood right underneath the bark. In fact, beavers store wood underwater so that they have a ready supply of food whenever they need it.

Beavers form strong family bonds, with a pair of beavers becoming partners for life, which is 10 to 20 years. A beaver mother generally has two to four young, called **kits**, every spring, and both parents care for them. The young stay with their parents for two years, and yearlings act as babysitters for the new litter. Beavers weigh about 40 pounds when they are fully grown.

Beavers are equipped with valves that close their ears and noses when they are underwater. In addition, a skin flap seals the mouth, and clear covers close over their eyes. These covers act like "swimming goggles," keeping debris out of their eyes while still allowing them to see. They also have webbed hind feet for easy swimming. If you've ever worn flippers in the water, you know how much faster you can swim with webbed feet. Their enormous front incisors are perfect for cutting into wood. The most prominent identifier of a beaver, though, is its flat, hairless tail, which it uses as a rudder in the water. On land, its tail is a prop when the beaver sits upright to feed on bark. When a beaver is threatened, it swims rapidly away, slapping its tail on the surface of the water to create a loud smack, which can be heard for miles around. This serves to warn all surrounding beavers of the danger. Unlike what you may have seen in cartoons, beavers do not use their tails to "pat down" mud or anything else. The beaver has long been hunted for its warm, waterproof fur. In fact, entire fur trades were set up to collect beaver pelts, and they nearly became extinct as a result. In Europe, there are only small pockets of beaver populations remaining, while in North America, their population has rebounded so that they are no longer endangered.

Though beavers are important for ecology, they are often a nuisance to man because they tend to reshape the land, flooding bridges and railroad tracks as well as crops. They can also limit a city's water supply with their dams. Thus, there are many books and websites dedicated to teaching people how to remove beavers and their dams. It's actually not easy to do. You see, if you destroy their dam, a beaver family can rebuild it in a day!

Order Insectivora

While I would love to spend a lot more time on the rodents in God's creation, there are just so many more interesting animals that we must keep this jeep moving if we are to ever get done. Our next stop, then, is order **Insectivora** (in sek' tiv or uh). This order is where taxonomists put animals that usually eat insects and can't be put in any other order. This includes hedgehogs, moles, shrews, solenodons, and tenrecs. While some biologists have stopped using this order and now split its members into several different orders, it is a nice grouping for our purposes. Most of its members are small; shrews, for example, are one of the smallest mammals. They usually rely more on their senses of hearing, smell, and touch than on vision, and they often have tiny eyes. Some (like certain moles) are even blind!

Hedgehogs

If you are in Europe, Africa, or Asia and happen to see a small, spiny ball on the ground, it might be a **hedgehog**. In Europe, they are an especially common site in people's gardens. They range from the size a small mouse to that of a rabbit.

A hedgehog is born with quills coming out of its body, but initially they are soft. In a short time, however, they harden into sharp "needles" that effectively protect the hedgehog from predators. When it feels threatened, it will roll up into a ball so that only its spines are visible. Most predators will simply avoid the sharp, prickly ball.

Although they mostly eat insects, they will supplement their diet with other small animals (like frogs, snails, and snakes) from time to time. In addition, although they do not actually eat plants, they do chew on them from time to time. You see, hedgehogs are immune

Although hedgehog spines can be prickly, these animals are often kept as pets.

to many poisons. As a result, a hedgehog can chew on poisonous plants, making a froth of poisonous saliva in its mouth. It can then lick that saliva onto its spines, making them even more irritating to a would-be predator.

Shrews

Although it looks cute, this northern short-tailed shrew (*Blarina brevicauda*) is poisonous.

Shrews have long been considered evil creatures. In fact, the word "shrew" means an ill-tempered person. Early writings lament the fact that shrews seem innocent and cute, but when touched, they turn into vicious terrors, biting deeply. Some species even have a poisonous bite, putting them among the very few poisonous mammals. People are only bitten when they try to handle a shrew, however. Thankfully, a shrew's poison is not lethal to humans, but it does cause several days of pain.

Shrews are small, secretive creatures that look a lot like mice. They forage on the ground, under leaf litter, and in rotting wood. They eat mostly insects, but they do eat other small animals, like reptiles and amphibians, from time to time. The poisonous ones are especially more likely to eat something other than insects. Some shrews can climb trees, others can burrow under the ground, and many are aquatic, able to swim quite well.

Shrews are amazingly abundant, which may surprise you if you've never seen one. That's because, as I mentioned, they are secretive creatures that depend on their hearing and smell more than their vision. They can hear you coming from a long way off. Shrews can be found on every continent except Australia and Antarctica. They are ravenously hungry all the time, so they spend a lot of time foraging in order to satisfy their constant craving for food.

There is a shrew-like mammal called the **solenodon** (suh len' uh don) that is also poisonous. The two species of solenodons are found in Cuba and Haiti and look like large, fat shrews. Of course, when I say "large," I mean "large by shrew standards." They are typically less than a foot long, not including the tail. Although they sometimes eat plants, they mostly eat small animals, including insects. Solenodons are nocturnal and tend to live in forests or brush. Oddly, solenodons walk with an awkward gait that causes them to zigzag all over the place. They rarely walk in a straight path.

Treeshrews

A while ago, a group of shrew-like creatures were accused of being primates and were removed from order Insectivora. Although these animals (an example of which is pictured on the next page) don't really look like primates, there are certain internal similarities. After many years of study, the little creatures were cleared of all charges and taken out of order Primates. Instead of being returned to order Insectivora, they were given their own order, **Scandentia** (skan' den tee uh).

So what is a **treeshrew**? Well, even though it has the word "shrew" in its name, it is not a shrew. In fact, even though it has the word "tree" in its name, most species are not arboreal, either. However, they do look a bit like squirrels that have a long, pointy nose. These creatures live mostly in Southeast Asia and India. They eat insects and fruit, holding the food between their hands while they eat, like squirrels and raccoons. They are very territorial, marking their territory with scents from special glands.

Although they look nothing like primates, treeshrews were once classified in that order.

Order Lagomorpha

In order to get the most from their food, members of order Lagomorpha actually eat their own feces.

For many years, rabbits were considered rodents. As scientists learned more about them, however, they were given their own order, called **Lagomorpha** (lag' uh mor fuh). This order name comes from the Greek word "lagos," which means "hare," and "morph," which means "shape." These, then, are the "hare-shaped" animals.

Like rodents, the front incisor teeth of lagomorphs are constantly growing. However, they also have a second set of smaller incisors behind their front ones, which is what separates them from rodents. They eat a lot of plant material, and in order to get the most nutrients from their food, they often process it through their system twice. They do this by *eating their own feces*! This is how it works: they produce a special kind of wet feces that they know they can eat. Once these feces are eaten, more nutrients are absorbed, and they produce dry, inedible feces. The lagomorphs can tell the difference between the two and they don't eat the dry feces.

Scientists usually split the members of this order into two groups: **rabbits** (which includes **hares**) and **pikas**. Rabbits and hares have long legs for running over open ground. Their ears are long, their nose protrudes outward in an egg shape, their tail usually has white fur underneath, and they are generally quiet. Pikas, however, are much smaller, with short legs for running over the rocky areas where they live. They have short, round ears and no tail. Also, they tend to be more vocal than rabbits and hares.

This is an American pika (*Ochotona princes*).

Pikas live in parts of western North America, and they can also be found in central and northern Asia. They love cold temperatures and are not designed to tolerate very high temperatures. Like all members of this order, pikas don't hibernate, which makes them a year-round meal for many animals. They live on rocks, or dig burrows in open meadows, depending on the species. They can often be seen sitting out in the open on rock piles, resembling a big ball of fluff.

Although it is easy to tell a pika from a rabbit or hare, telling the difference between a rabbit and a hare is a bit tricky. In general, hares are larger than rabbits, and their legs are usually longer than those of rabbits. Also, hares have longer ears than rabbits, and they are often tipped in black. The most important difference, however, is that newborn hares are **precocial**, while newborn rabbits are not. Do you remember that term from Zoology 1? It means that they are born much more developed than rabbits. They have fur, for example, and their eyes are open. Rabbits are born rather undeveloped (no fur and their eyes are closed), so we say they are **altricial**.

Notice the longer legs and ears that mark this lagomorph as a hare rather than a rabbit.

There are differences in the ways rabbits and hares live as well. First, rabbits are social mammals, while hares tend to be solitary. Second, rabbits tend to live in burrows underground. Hares, on the other hand, just make shallow depressions in the ground, forming a crude "nest." They even have their young in those crude nests. Of course, since hares give birth to precocial young, they don't need as much protection as young rabbits, which are kept safer in their underground burrow.

Try This!

Using what you just learned, determine whether each animal pictured below is a hare, rabbit, or pika. The answers can be found with the "Answers to the Narrative Questions" at the back of the book.

Order Dermoptera

The flying membrane of a colugo is much bigger than that of a flying squirrel (see picture on page 115).

As we trek through the forests of Southeast Asia, we may see giant, furry, winged animals zipping from tree to tree above our heads. They may be the size of cats and have the face of a dog, but they aren't cats or dogs. They are called flying lemurs, although, ironically, they are not lemurs and they do not actually fly. Like flying squirrels, they are gliding mammals belonging to the order **Dermoptera** (dur mop' tuh ruh), which means "skin wings." They are called **colugos** (kuh loo' gohz), and only two species are known to exist in the world.

The colugo's most distinctive feature is its gliding membrane, the skin that it can stretch out like a parachute. Called a **patagium** (puh tay' jee uhm), it stretches from the colugo's shoulders to the tips of its fingers, down to the tips of its toes, continuing on down to the very tip of its rather long tail. No other gliding mammal has such an extensive patagium. In addition, their feet are webbed, which gives them even more of a "parachute." The colugos actually resemble a kite with a head when they are sailing through the rainforest. Their ability to glide is highly developed, and their body is so specifically designed for this that they are rather clumsy climbers and crawlers. Like primates, they have depth perception, which allows them to determine just where they want to land.

When a colugo lands on a tree, its sharp claws anchor it to the bark. To further secure itself to the tree, it often "hugs" the branch it is on. It eats leaves, flowers, and fruits from the trees it visits. Colugos are nocturnal, and if you look at the picture on page 122 again, you will see that its eyes glow when they are hit by the light. Can you remember other nocturnal animals with this trait?

When the female colugo gives birth, the underdeveloped baby crawls onto her stomach and clings there until it is weaned. The mother carries the baby around everywhere, even when she glides from tree to tree. The patagium can be folded into a warm pouch for carrying the young.

Order Monotremata

Do you remember when I told you that sometimes an animal just doesn't fit into the nice, orderly charts that scientists have created to classify the animals? Well, the discovery of two creatures in order **Monotremata** (mon' uh trem' ah ta) really caused scientists to pause and ponder, wondering what on earth to do with these creatures. You see, both of these types of animals have hair and feed their young with milk they produce themselves, yet they lay eggs! This posed a dilemma for scientists: before the discovery of these two creatures, only animals like birds, amphibians, reptiles, and arthropods were known to be egg layers! Remember what we call such animals? In Zoology 2, you learned that we call them **oviparous** (oh vip' ur us). Mammals, on the other hand, are **viviparous** (vye vip' ur us), giving birth to living young. How could these animals be mammals if they laid eggs? Well, in the end, the members of this order, the **platypus** (plat ih' puhs) and the **spiny anteater**, are classified with mammals.

Platypuses

The platypus looks like cross between a beaver and a duck.

When the first specimen of a dead platypus was brought to English scientists from Australia, it was thought to be a fake. They thought someone had sewn a duck's bill and a beaver's tail to a mammal, adding some strange creature's legs and feet. No animal in creation looked anything like this oddity. They even tried to cut off the bill to see if it was authentic. Eventually, however, a live specimen was brought to England. At that point, then, scientists had to admit that it was a real animal. Even after that, however, the platypus was still not accepted as a mammal because scientists had determined that it lays eggs. However, when it was learned that the platypus nursed its young with its own milk, scientists created a new place in their mammal charts for the platypus.

The platypus is designed for water, possessing a thick coat of waterproof fur that covers its entire body except its feet and bill. Its tail is large and flat, like a beaver's, and its bill has nostrils on top so that it can easily breathe as it swims at the surface of the water. Its bill is not hard like a duck's bill, however; it's soft and leathery. Adults lack teeth but have horny plates on their jaws for chewing.

Male platypuses have an interesting weapon – a small, hard, hollow spur connected to a gland that makes poison. If you were stuck by this spur, you would experience extreme pain as the venom worked its way through your body. When the female is ready to bear young, she usually lays two sticky eggs in a special nursery chamber of her burrow, and she waits there without eating until they hatch. In about ten days, the newborns burst out of their shells, ready to eat. While the mother does nurse its young, they don't latch onto her like most mammal babies. Instead, the mother's milk glands drip milk onto her fur, and the young lap it up from there.

Creation Confirmation

The amazing bill of the platypus is a testament to the fact that it was created by God. Early on, scientists who studied the platypus noticed that it hunts underwater with its eyes and ears *shut*. They assumed it poked through the mud of a river or lake with its bill, grabbing anything it happened to hit. As they learned more, however, they found that the platypus did not blunder around trying to find food. Instead, special nerves on the platypus's bill are so sophisticated that they can actually detect *weak electric fields*. The prey it loves to eat – mostly things like shrimp, worms, and insect larvae – produce electric fields underwater. The platypus bill detects those fields, even when the animals that make them are under mud and rocks. This amazing bill is more efficient than the best electric field sensor human science can produce! It is a stirring testament to the fact that the platypus was created by an awesome Designer!

Echidnas

The other strange egg-laying member of order Monotremata is the **echidna** (ih kid' nuh). It looks like a cross between a bird, an anteater, and a hedgehog. These cat-sized creatures have a thin beak, spines all over their back, and an appetite for ants (as well as other insects and small animals).

Echidnas come in two different forms: short-beaked (found in Australia) and long-beaked (found in New Guinea). The main difference is the size of the nose. The one pictured on the right is a short-beaked echidna. Both types can curl into a ball for protection, or, if the ground is wet and soft, they can dig in the dirt and hunker down, with only their spines sticking above ground.

Can you see why this odd animal is often called a spiny anteater?

One interesting feature of the echidna is its pouch. Yes! Like a marsupial, the echidna keeps its newborn in a pouch. Of course, unlike the marsupial, the newborn hatches from an egg that the mother lays in the pouch. The echidna only gives birth to one baby at a time, which stays in its mother's pouch until it begins to get those prickly spines. Then, it's not really welcome in the pouch any longer.

Order Edentata

Let's continue our safari by studying order **Edentata** (ee den' tah tuh), which holds the **sloths**, **anteaters**, and **armadillos**. The word "edentata" actually means "no teeth," but that's not really true of all these animals. Some of them have a few teeth, but they all lack incisors and canine teeth. Many biologists no longer use this order, splitting sloths and anteaters into order Pilosa and armadillos into order Cingulata, but this grouping works well for our purposes. Let's start our discussion of the Edentata with sloths.

Sloths

This is a two-toed sloth. Notice that its front paw (the one on top) has two claws, but the rear paw (underneath) has three.

Graceful and serene, the sloths move through trees in the Central and South American rainforests in which they live. They spend 99 percent of their time in trees, often hanging upside down. They sleep about fifteen hours a day and spend the rest of their time eating and searching for juicy leaves and buds. Their lazy lifestyle gives them their name, because "sloth" can mean "inactivity" or "apathy." Sloths don't have to drink water, as they get all they need from the water found in their food. As a result, the only time they come to the ground is to defecate (expel solid waste).

Sloths are equipped with long, tough nails, which they use to help them cling to and climb through trees. They can also use them in defense if they need to. In fact, their nails are used to separate them into two groups: **two-toed sloths** and **three-toed sloths**. Can you guess the difference? Two-toed sloths have two nails on their front feet, while three-toed sloths have three. Both kinds of sloths have three nails on their back feet. Also, two-toed sloths are a bit faster than three-toed sloths, but both are pretty slow!

One very interesting thing about the sloth is that it has a **symbiotic** relationship with algae. Do you remember learning about symbiosis in Zoology 2? It is when two or more creatures live together in a close relationship. Well, algae (microscopic green creatures) live in the sloth's fur. The sloth provides a nice home for the algae, and the algae give the sloth's fur a green tinge. This helps camouflage it in the trees where it lives. That's a good thing, because the sloth moves so slowly that its only chance is to hide from predators, which include ocelots, jaguars, and snakes. Though sloths now grow to be about 2 feet long, there are fossil remains of sloths that were the size of elephants!

Anteaters

Anteaters are true edentates, because they have no teeth. As their name implies, they love to eat ants, although they also eat termites. In a pinch, they will eat grubs (beetle larvae) and even fruit. Captive anteaters rarely get any ants to eat and are fed mostly fruit and protein-rich foods, like eggs and ground beef. Anteaters are often called ant bears because they look a lot like bears with a long nose and long tail. They can even get large like bears, with some species growing to be about 8 feet long from tip to tail. Also like bears, some are great at climbing trees, where they sometimes go to find certain species of ants.

This giant anteater gives you some idea why they are sometimes called "ant bears."

Anteaters are mainly found in South and Central America, but a few have been found in Mexico. Have you ever seen a sign that says "deer crossing" while traveling down a country road? Well, in South America the anteaters are so numerous, you can see signs warning of anteater crossings. If an anteater crosses the road in front of you, you might notice that it's a knuckle-walker. It tucks its claws under its palms and walks on its knuckles, like an ape!

The anteater locates its prey in the wild using its excellent sense of smell. Once an anteater has found an appealing dining area, it uses its powerful forelegs and sharp claws to rip open an ant or termite hill, which can be almost as hard as concrete. It's careful not to destroy the whole nest, so that the ants can rebuild it, providing another meal at a later date.

After ripping open the nest, the anteater uses its long snout and 2-foot-long tongue to scoop out termites and ants from their nests. Do you know how long 2 feet is? Get out a tape measure or ruler and see how long it is. Now that's a long tongue! Anteaters produce a sticky goo they use to coat this long tongue, and insects stick to the goo, making it very easy for the anteater to catch its prey.

Anteaters must like fast food, because they can eat up to 30,000 insects each day! One reason an anteater can eat so quickly is that its tongue can be flicked in and out of its mouth about 150 times each minute!

Try This!

See if you can flick your tongue in and out of your mouth as quickly as an anteater. Set a timer (or have someone watch a clock) and begin flicking your tongue in and out of your mouth. Stick it out as far as you can each time (as the anteater does), and make sure it goes all the way back in. Do it as quickly as you can, and count how many you can do in a minute. How many can you do? I know I wouldn't make a good anteater. My tongue is pretty slow.

Like some other animals you have studied, anteaters carry their young around on their back or tail. If a young anteater falls off its mother's back, it will grunt until she picks it back up again. Unless they have young, they are solitary animals that prefer to live alone. Anteaters are diurnal when they live far from civilization and nocturnal when they live close to people. When it's time for bed, anteaters find a secluded spot and curl up to sleep, with their long, bushy tail covering their head and body.

Armadillos

Although it will eat ants, an armadillo is not an anteater.

With a hard shell covering all but its underside (and in some species, the tail), the armadillo is well protected from danger. One kind, the three-banded armadillo, can even roll itself into a ball. None of the others can, but they are moderately fast runners and diggers, which help them escape danger. Though they can't see well, they have an amazing sense of smell and can use it to detect predators coming from a long way off. This allows them to get away long before the predator comes close enough to eat them.

Like anteaters, armadillos love to eat ants, and they have a long, sticky tongue for lapping them up. However, these armored critters will eat a lot of other kinds of insects, and they will even eat plants. They aren't too picky, and will even eat carrion if it's available.

There are about twenty species of armadillo living in South and Central America. In addition, one species, the nine-banded armadillo (shown above), can be found in the United States. While many of the other species of armadillo are declining or endangered, the nine-banded armadillo is increasing in population and moving northward and eastward. Some have even been spotted as far north as

Illinois and southwestern Indiana. However, like all edentates, they can't tolerate extremely cold weather, so they are not likely to hit Canada.

Armadillos are great swimmers. They dog-paddle long distances across wide rivers and lakes. They can even walk along the bottom of streams and ponds because they can hold their breath for up to six minutes at a time! Because their hard shell makes it hard for them to float, they gulp in air to make themselves more buoyant. Their ability to swim long distances is one reason their population has been able to spread so rapidly across several states.

Nine-banded armadillos usually give birth to four identical young. All four young have the same genetic makeup so, in effect, all four baby armadillos are clones of one another! They are the only mammal known to do this. You can find recipes for eating armadillos all over the Internet. During the Depression, people ate armadillos regularly. However, it's not advisable to eat them, as they sometimes carry leprosy. Although it is not clear whether or not people can get leprosy from armadillos, it is probably not worth the risk.

Order Tubulidentata

This is the Old World counterpart to the anteater.

There is an anteater lookalike in the heart of the African savanna that is not actually an anteater. It is an **aardvark** (ard' vark), and it is the Old World counterpart to the anteater. An aardvark's strong claws are almost like hooves, and it uses them to dig into ant and termite hills, just as an anteater does. In fact, the aardvark loves to eat ants and termites just as much as an anteater does. It is a nocturnal, solitary animal. About the only time you see more than one is when they are mating or a mother is raising her young. Aardvarks also have the same general shape as an anteater: a long snout, a thick torso, and a long tail. There are differences, however. The aardvark is smaller than most anteaters, its hair is not as thick, and its snout is flattened, like that of a pig. In fact, in Afrikaans (a language in South Africa), "aardvark" means "earth pig."

It is obvious that the anteater and the aardvark are very similar, and they used to be classified in the same order. However, scientists have argued over classifying the aardvark with animals like elephants, because it has a very thick epidermis. In fact, its skin is so thick that the bites of ants can't hurt it. Nevertheless, scientists have decided to place it in its own order, **Tubulidentata** (tuh boo' luh den tah' tuh), which means "tube-shaped teeth." That, of course, is another difference between aardvarks and anteaters: aardvarks have teeth, while anteaters do not.

What Do You Remember?

What is the main thing that makes an animal a rodent? How are rodents helpful to the world? How are they destructive? Into what three groups do many scientists divide rodents? Name three members of order Insectivora. Which mammals are poisonous? What are the differences among rabbits, hares, and pikas? Why are animals like the platypus and echidna difficult to classify as mammals? How is the echidna like a marsupial? Which animal in order Edentata really has no teeth? What disease do armadillos sometimes carry? How is an aardvark similar to an anteater? Describe some differences between the two animals.

Map It!
Include these animals on your map:

Rats – All continents except Antarctica
Flying squirrels – North America, Asia, and northern Europe
Shrews – Everywhere except Australia and Antarctica
Beavers – Europe and North America
Hedgehogs – Europe

Sloths and anteaters – South and Central America
Armadillos – South and Central America and the central and southern United States
Aardvarks – Africa
Treeshrews and **colugos** – Southeast Asia
Platypuses – Australia
Echidnas – Australia and New Guinea

Track It!
Here are the tracks of some of the animals you studied in this lesson:

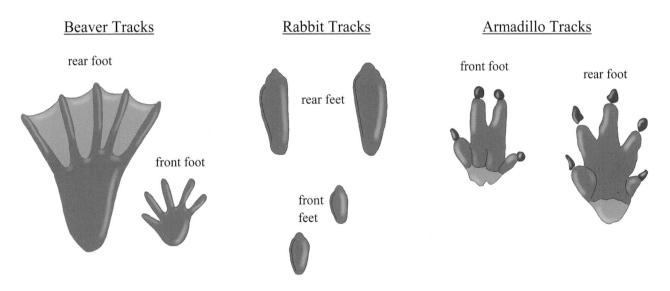

Beaver Tracks — rear foot — front foot

Rabbit Tracks — rear feet — front feet

Armadillo Tracks — front foot — rear foot

Notebook Activities

For your notebook, draw or cut out a picture of each animal you studied and write down one or two interesting facts about that creature. Once you are done with that, I want you to think about the platypus. This animal seems to have parts from many different animals. If you were going to combine different animal parts to create a new animal, which parts would you use? What purpose would each part serve for the creature? Draw your animal creation for your notebook.

Experiment

After an owl swallows a rodent, strong acids in the owl's stomach begin to digest the rodent's muscle and other soft parts. The owl can't digest the bones and fur that come along with the meal, however, so the owl forms these indigestible materials into tight packages called **owl pellets**. Several hours after a meal, an owl will vomit these pellets onto the ground. By carefully sifting through such a pellet, you can find the bones of the animals the owl ate. Usually you will find rodent bones, so this experiment will give you a chance to examine the actual bones of a rodent!

You will need:
♦ Owl pellets (You can buy these at science supply houses. The course website, discussed in the introduction to the book, has links to several places that will send them to you in the mail. If you need to wait for them to arrive, you can move on to the next lesson.)
♦ Paper plate
♦ Bamboo skewer or toothpick
♦ A blank sheet of paper
♦ Tweezers
♦ Latex or rubber gloves

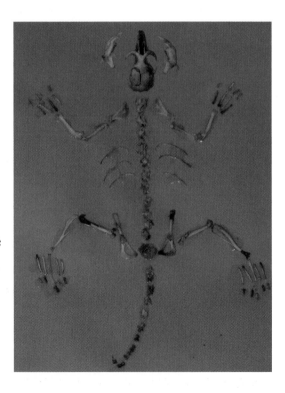

1. Put on the gloves.
2. Place the owl pellet on the paper plate.
3. Carefully pull apart the owl pellet with your hands while holding it above the paper plate.
4. Sift through the pellet, separating the bones and other fragments with a skewer or toothpick.
5. As you find bones, pick them up with the tweezers and examine them. Place them on the sheet of paper.
6. Using the picture to the right as a guide, see if you can assemble an entire rodent skeleton. You might not have all the bones, but you will probably have many of them. If you need more guidance, check the course website I told you about in the introduction to the book.
7. Once you have as much of the skeleton as you can find, you can keep it by gluing the bones onto the paper.

Lesson 8
Ungulates

In addition to all the creatures that swing in trees, dig burrows under the ground, chase after prey, and do all the other actions associated with wild animals, God created beasts of burden. These animals help people with their work or give them food. We call them **livestock**. One thing that is common among most livestock is that they have hooves. We call these hoofed creatures **ungulates** (un' gyoo litz). Some animals in the wild are also ungulates, so we'll include them in this discussion. Can you think of some animals that might be ungulates? The list includes horses, giraffes, deer, cows, goats, sheep, pigs, camels, llamas, rhinos, and many more.

Ungulates are divided into several different groups. Elephants have their own order, as do hyraxes. Most of the rest are split between two other orders. How would you go about grouping these animals? Some animals (like rodents) are grouped by their teeth, while others (like primates) are grouped by their nose. Well, many ungulates are grouped by their toes. Those with an odd number of toes are put in one order, while those with an even number of toes are put in a different order. You will learn about all the major orders of ungulates in this and the next lesson.

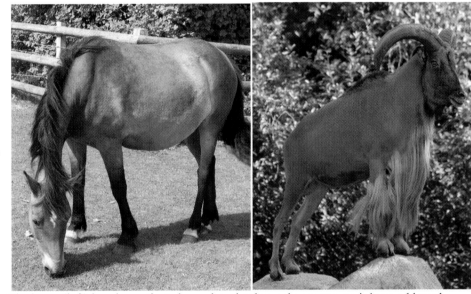

The horse (left) is a domesticated ungulate that has only one toe, so it is an odd-toed ungulate. The Barbary sheep (right) is a wild ungulate that has two toes, so it is an even-toed ungulate.

As I mentioned, many ungulates have been domesticated, but there are plenty of ungulates in the wild as well. Many live in open habitats, such as fields, where they can race away from predators at top speed. Some ungulates, such as mountain goats, live on steep cliffs, where their feet provide stability and balance as they search for food. Deer are forest ungulates, while the fearsome hippopotamus lives in rivers and small lakes.

In this section of our mammal study, our jeep will take us from the jungles to the forests, and then down home to the farm. Hop in, because we're starting our study in Africa and Southeast Asia, two places we have been before. First we'll stalk wild elephants, and then we'll travel back in time to study the wooly mammoth and mastodon, which became extinct some time ago. We'll end our journey studying ungulates with an odd number of toes.

Order Proboscidea

This is an African bush elephant, which was once thought to be the same species as the African forest elephant. Genetic testing showed that the two elephants really are difference species.

In Africa and Asia there are three different species of elephants. Elephants are enormously large, with thick, wrinkly, almost hairless skin. It's no wonder these creatures are called **pachyderms** (pak' ih durmz), which comes from two Greek words meaning "thick-skinned." With a long trunk (called a proboscis) that serves as nose and upper lip, elephants are quite distinct creatures in God's animal kingdom. The Lord designed the elephant's trunk to be very versatile. Elephants use it to inhale water, which they then spray into their mouth for a drink or onto their bodies to cool off. They also use it for picking things up, breaking branches, or even to scratch. The African elephant's trunk is like an arm with two pincher-like fingers at the tip. These two fingers are so specialized and sensitive that an elephant could easily pick a tiny flower from a field, yet its trunk is so powerful that it can easily move a large fallen tree out of its path.

When two elephants meet in the forest they "shake hands" by intertwining their trunks. The elephant also tears up food with its trunk before putting the food in its mouth. Amazingly, this special appendage can also smell. The elephant can actually raise its trunk up high to catch a waft of air telling it where other elephants, predators, or food may be. In addition to these kindly uses, the elephant will use its trunk to defend itself, slapping a predator or intruder with incredible force.

In addition to their proboscis, elephants have another tool to help them retrieve food and defend themselves: their **tusks**. The tusks are used to dig for water, salt, or roots. They are also used to peel the bark from trees so the elephant can get at the tasty pulp inside. They can even be used to move logs and brush from the elephant's path. Are you right-handed or left-handed? Well, an elephant is either right-tusked or left-tusked. You can usually tell which it is just by looking at it. The most used tusk is the dominant tusk, and because of use, it's often shorter and less sharp than the other tusk. Aren't you glad the hand you use the most doesn't get worn out and shorter? However, don't feel too sorry about the smaller tusk – elephant tusks are enormous; they can grow up to 10 feet long and weigh more than 200 pounds!

Elephant tusks, which are really overgrown incisor teeth, are ivory, which is made of calcium phosphate and several other minerals. At one time, people could buy ivory at any store. It was used to make boxes, piano keys, jewelry, statues, and other decorative items. This ivory came from one source – elephants. The demand for ivory and the price that the elephant hunters were paid for the ivory caused a serious decline in the elephant population. As a result, elephants are endangered. Even though it is now against the law to kill an elephant, poachers can still be found in the African plains and jungles slaying elephants for their prized tusks.

There are two species of African elephants. The first is the **African bush elephant** (*Loxodonta Africana*), which lives on the plains of Africa. This is an easy elephant to see on your safari. A male African bush elephant is usually about 12 feet high. Do you have a tape measure so you can see how tall that is? You will probably have to go outside, since most homes don't have a ceiling that high. The other African elephant is the **African forest elephant** (*Loxodonta cyclotis*), which lives…guess where? The forest, of course! The forest elephant is a bit smaller than the bush elephant, but in appearance, that is the only real difference. The male African forest elephant grows about 9 feet high.

There is only one species of Asian elephant. Its name is very easy to remember. It is called...the **Asian elephant** (*Elephas maximus*). The Asian elephant is smaller than the African elephant. It can be as small as 7 feet high when it is fully grown. Though similar in behavior, the Asian elephant looks quite different from its African brother. Not only is its body smaller, but its ears and tusks are also

The elephant on the left is an Asian elephant. Notice that its ears and tusks are smaller than those of the African bush elephant on the right. Also, notice that its head has more hair.

smaller. In fact, while both male and female African elephants usually have tusks, only male Asian elephants have them. The Asian elephant is also more hairy than the African elephant, and its proboscis ends in only one finger-like flap of skin at the tip, rather than the two that the African elephant has. Thus, the Asian elephant can't use its trunk like tweezers.

An adult African elephant eats anywhere from 220 to 660 pounds of food and drinks 50 gallons of water each day! Elephants eat mostly wood, leaves, grass, and fruit, and their eating habits can change the very environment in which they live. In an effort to get their daily intake, elephants can uproot small trees and demolish bushes, turning forests into grasslands! In addition to all that food, elephants need salt in their diets. They instinctively know where salt is located underground, and they use their tusks to dig it up. In fact, elephants have been known to make caves in their effort to find salt!

This elephant is giving herself and her young one a dust bath.

Do you remember that elephants drink by drawing water up with their trunk and then spraying it into their mouths? They also use their trunks to spray that water on themselves. Well, water isn't the only thing an elephant sprays on itself. It also sprays itself with dust. Why does it do that? The dust covers its skin, acting like a sunscreen and an insect repellent all in one. For an elephant, a dust bath is as important as a water bath. In fact, they often mix the two, making a mud bath.

An elephant is family-oriented, but only if it's a calf or a female. Usually, the only adult elephants in a herd are females. At the head of every elephant herd is the oldest and most experienced female. She may be up to seventy years old. This old lady is called the **matriarch** (by scientists, not by other elephants). The matriarch rules over the rest of the herd. Elephant calves are protected from all threats by every female in the herd. If danger lurks, the females will form a circle, facing outward, placing the calves in the center for protection. Males only join the herd when it's time to mate. Otherwise the males are solitary loners, or they live in bachelor groups with other males.

Elephants are extremely intelligent and are known to communicate with one another quite extensively. They speak to one another in voices below the range human ears are able to hear. They also communicate with their body posture, by touching, and by foot stamping. All these things mean something very clear and unmistakable to the other elephants in the herd.

In countries where elephants are common, they are domesticated and used to carry people around and help them in their work. Elephants can be used to fell trees, move heavy logs, clear paths through the forest, carry loads, and transport people. Long ago, elephants in Asia were trained for warfare and used like horses to carry soldiers into battle and to trample the enemy. An elephant army was quite a frightening sight. The elephants were even equipped with armor, just like their riders.

Share some of the things you have learned about elephants today.

Wooly Mammoths

When artists make drawings of wooly mammoths, they often mistakenly render them as much larger than elephants, when the truth is that these creatures were usually about the size of an African elephant. They had two features that distinguished them from other elephants: their tusks curled upward, and they were covered with long hair.

Although no wooly mammoths exist today, remains from these creatures have been found in North America, Europe, Africa, and Asia. So many mammoth skeletons and bones have been found in the Russian province of Siberia, it has been estimated that there are millions of mammoths buried in that area alone. Sometimes, special frozen finds reveal entire specimens. Contrary to what you may have seen on television, these "frozen mammoths" are not encased in ice. They are frozen solid, like a turkey that has been left in the freezer.

© 2001 S.W. Clyde
http://www.byways.org

This mammoth skeleton was on display at the College of Eastern Utah Prehistoric Museum.

Why are so many wooly mammoths found in such a hostile place as Siberia? If you aren't familiar with the land of Siberia, you need to understand that it is one of the most frozen places on earth, aside from the North and South poles. Though people live there, it's very difficult for animals to survive there in the wild – especially a giant like the wooly mammoth. Mammoths need so much food to survive that it would be close to impossible for them to find it in Siberia. Siberia is nothing but a frozen tundra – an ice desert in Russia. So, what are mammoth remains doing in Siberia? Another puzzling question is why on earth are all these creatures frozen together?

When investigating this mystery, scientists discovered some interesting clues. Because the mammoth's entire body was frozen, scientists could dissect them and examine the content of their stomach; they could tell what they ate before they had died. Interestingly, such things as grass and flowers were found inside these mammoth's stomachs, and long grass was found in their teeth. But the kinds of grass and flowers found are not currently found in Siberia! These warm-weather plants must have once grown in that region. Perhaps Siberia was not always as cold as it is today.

Creation Confirmation

Old Faithful in Yellowstone National Park gets its name because hot steam spews out of it at such regular intervals that each eruption can be predicted.

The answer to the puzzle of why so many mammoths can be found in Siberia comes when we understand what the world was probably like shortly after the worldwide flood discussed in the Bible. You see, Genesis 7:11 tells us, "In the six hundredth year of Noah's life, in the second month, on the seventeenth day of the month, on the same day all the fountains of the great deep burst open, and the floodgates of the sky were opened." Do you know what the Bible means when it refers to the "fountains of the great deep?" You can get an idea from looking at a **geyser** (guy' zur). Do you know what that is? It's a place where an opening allows water from deep under the earth to spew up onto the earth's surface. The interior of the earth is very hot, so the water is steaming hot. One famous geyser is Old Faithful in Wyoming.

If God released the fountains of the deep, the earth would have literally cracked open with huge geysers like Old Faithful, spewing hot water vapors and volcanic emissions into the air. All that hot water would pour directly onto the earth and flow into the oceans, raising the temperature of the ocean waters. Do you know what happens when water gets hot? Think about it. If you heated up water in a pan for a long time, what would happen? If you aren't sure, ask your mother to show you.

Hot water evaporates faster than cool water. Thus, the warmer oceans would evaporate more quickly, which would cause more clouds to form. This would cause more snow and rain. In addition, the dust coming from the volcanic eruptions would partially block the sunlight, cooling the earth. This would result in what is called an **ice age** – a time when the entire earth is, on average, cooler than normal. Wooly mammoths would have been perfectly suited for the ice age. Even though they could not stand ridiculously cold temperatures, their wooly coat would still offer quite a bit of protection from the cold.

So how does all this explain the number of wooly mammoths in Siberia? Well, even though the *average* temperature of the earth would have been cooler in the ice age, certain parts of the earth (like Siberia) would have been warmer, because the warm ocean water so near to them would have heated up the area. Thus, wooly mammoths would find plenty of food in Siberia while it continued to be warmed by the ocean water. Over time, however, the oceans would cool, and the climate in Siberia would begin to change. Eventually, it would end up becoming the cold wasteland we see today, and that would lead to the demise of the wooly mammoths.

There is a lot of evidence that the ice age happened, and even scientists who do not believe the Bible's account of a worldwide flood think that the ice age existed. In fact, they think that *many* ice ages existed in the past. However, without the worldwide flood account as given by the Bible, the *cause* of the ice age is a complete mystery. In fact, in 1997, *U.S. News and World Report* listed 18 "great mysteries" in science, and "What causes ice ages?" was one of them. You see, to have an ice age, you need cooler-than-average temperatures, but more rain and snow than normal. This seems to be a contradiction, because a cooler earth should have cooler oceans, which would produce *fewer* clouds and *less* rain and snow. Of course, the biblical account of the Flood tells us exactly what caused the ice age: a warmer-than-normal ocean caused by the fountains of the great deep and a cooler-than-normal earth caused by volcanic dust in the air. It also explains why wooly mammoths used to live in Siberia!

Mastodons

When the ark landed, God told Noah to bring out all the living creatures so they could multiply and increase in number. As the animals followed God's instructions, they also spread out to find new feeding grounds. As they spread out, natural selection began working on the genetic information God had given them, allowing them to specialize into different types of elephants. The wooly mammoths became adapted to live in one type of environment, African elephants adapted to another, Asian elephants adapted to another, and **mastodons** adapted to still another environment.

If you were able to see a wooly mammoth and a mastodon standing next to one another, you would not see many differences. Skeletal remains tell us that mastodons were shorter and stouter than mammoths. However, if you could open their mouths and look at their teeth, you would see the main difference between them. While mammoth molars were flat with tiny ridges, mastodon molars were jagged. This tells us that while mammoths specialized to live on the open plains, grazing on grasses and flowers, mastodons specialized to

While mastodons like the one drawn here looked much like mammoths, they lived in the forests rather than the plains.

live in the forest, eating mostly twigs and leaves. One other difference is that *some* mastodons had a second pair of tusks that came out of the lower jaw. Those mastodons, then, had *four* tusks!

Although the mastodon is now extinct, Native American history has many legends and stories about hunts for these creatures. Evidence from a mastodon fossil shows flint marks on the bones of the creature, indicating that people used knives to cut the flesh from the bone, showing these tales to be true. Mastodons were a big source of food for some Native Americans. The question is – how and when did these creatures become extinct? It is possible that they were hunted to extinction by the Native Americans, but that is rather unlikely. Scientists found evidence of tuberculosis in many remains and believe that the entire population may have been wiped out by this disease. If a disease spreads through a whole population of animals, it can make them extinct.

Explain in your own words what you have learned about wooly mammoths and mastodons. How does the Flood account in the Bible explain both the ice age and why wooly mammoths lived in Siberia?

Order Perissodactyla

The animals in order **Perissodactyla** (puh' ris uh' dak tuh luh) – **horses**, **donkeys**, **rhinos**, and **tapirs** – have a large middle toe that defines the center of the foot. Like others you have studied, these animals are digitigrades, which means they walk on their toes. Most have three toes on the hind feet, and some have four toes on the front feet. Some (like horses) have only one functional toe. Let's start our discussion there.

Family Equidae

Do you know anyone who is consumed with all things equestrian? The word "equestrian," by the way, comes from the name of the horse family: **Equidae** (ek' wuh day). Many people love horses because God designed them with such beauty. They have powerfully built, sleek bodies, and they can be as friendly as a puppy and as loyal as an old dog. For thousands of years, horses have secured the respect and admiration of humankind. From Alexander the Great, who named a city after his beloved horse, Bucephalus, to Roy Rogers and his horse, Trigger, people throughout history have been devoted to their horses. Before cars were invented, horses were the main source of transportation. Today, they are ridden for fun and sport.

Horses aren't the only members of this family. Donkeys, **zebras**, and animals called **kulans** and **kiangs** are also included. Of these, donkeys and horses are the ones that have been truly domesticated. Over the years, horses have been bred for different tasks and purposes. There are work horses, riding horses, and race horses. Just like horses, donkeys have also been bred into many varieties.

Although this looks like the colt of horse, it is actually a young kulan, which is a different species.

Horse History

How long have horses been domestic? Well, evidence shows that they were a friend to man for quite some time. The Book of Job, thought to have been written around 2,000 - 1,500 B.C., discusses a horse and its rider pursuing an ostrich in a hunt. We know the Egyptians pursued the children of Israel up to the Red Sea with their horse-drawn chariots. That's a story with a sad ending for the horses, but a happy one for you and me – since Jesus was born because of the survival of the Jews. Later, Jesus entered Jerusalem on a donkey. So although we don't know for sure how long horses have been serving people, we know it has been for a very long time.

Today, there are wild horses that roam in herds all over the western part of the United States. These wild horses are actually descended from **feral** horses, meaning that their ancestors were originally domesticated but turned wild. Their ancestors belonged to the Spanish, Native Americans, or early settlers. The wild mustangs that still roam across the western United States have been wild for so long that the original horses that escaped or were let loose are long dead. Eventually the free horses formed herds. These herds were probably small at first, but eventually grew larger as more and more horses escaped or were born from the herd. In the American West, many people tried to catch these wild horses. Occasionally a few were caught and tamed.

The wild horses that roam the American West are descendants of domesticated horses that went feral.

Horse Care

Horses are easy to feed but very difficult to care for. Because they are herbivores, they can eat any herbs, including grass and hay. They love sweet fruits and vegetables and are sometimes fed sugar cubes for treats. They need about 10 to 15 gallons of water per day. So, if you have lots of water and plenty of food, you're off to a good start.

However, caring for a horse is very complex because of the way the animal is built. Though a horse has powerful thigh muscles that enable it to run at top speeds, they have absolutely no muscles below their knees. Remember, the horse is a digitigrade, so it runs around on its toes! Can you imagine what it would feel like to run around on your toes all the time? That's a bit what it is like for a horse! It's so important to take care of the horse's feet that many horses have horseshoes placed on their feet by a professional farrier. The horse's hooves are like fingernails that need to be cut constantly, and new shoes must be put on every time. If a horse's shoes are too big or his hooves are too large, he'll trip when he walks.

Horses need protection from disease through vaccinations, dental exams, and regular visits to the veterinarian. If they are kept inside in a barn, they must have daily exercise to stay healthy and happy. So, if you decide that you want a horse, you have to remember that it requires a lot of money and work to take care of it.

Horse Sense

A horse's first response to threat is to momentarily startle (to see what's happening) and then to flee. Yet, if it is unable to escape or thinks its offspring are threatened, it will rear up on its hind legs and kick at the threatening creature with its powerful legs. As a result, horses are very aware of their surroundings. They have excellent night vision, and because of where their eyes are located, horses can see almost all the way around their bodies. Each eye can also focus on a different thing! Interestingly enough, that also means horses cannot see things that are closer than 4 feet *and* directly in front of their nose.

Horses have excellent senses of smell and hearing.

God gave horses excellent hearing. They can hear a wider range of sounds than people, and they can turn their little ears around to determine the place from where the sounds come. Their sense of smell is equivalent to that of an ape, which means it's better than ours. They are also very sensitive to touch in the head, leg, and belly regions.

Like many of the animals we have studied, horses are social animals that form herds, generally made up of a dominant male, several females, and their offspring. They form strong attachments to each other. Outside of a herd, they form attachments to their owners and to other animals they spend a lot of time with. Horses that are left alone for too long begin to act strange, chewing wood, kicking the walls, rocking back and forth, and so on. It's important for horses to have daily contact with others.

Horses communicate with each other using different methods: by nickering or whinnying, mutual grooming, and through body language. Horses are able to pick up cues from people, as well as other horses, which tell them about the other's mood. Horses also "speak" to one another with their ears, using a form of horse sign language! If a horse's ears are forward and pricked up, it is happy and interested in what's going on. If its ears are flickering, the horse is listening carefully. If its ears are flat back against its head, the horse is unhappy and annoyed. If its ears are lowered down to the sides, it might be bored, relaxed, or sick.

Although they can sleep standing up, horses will also lie down, especially when they are at ease.

Horses can sleep standing up because their legs are locked into a standing position when their muscles are relaxed. That's not the case with people, as we use our muscles to stay standing. Because of this, some horses might go a month without lying down. However, it depends a lot on the individual. Contrary to what you might have heard, it is not necessarily a sign of sickness for a horse to lie down to sleep. It is only a sign of sickness if the horse lies down more than usual.

Horse Breeds

Because horses have been bred for so many years, specific personalities and characteristics have developed in different breeds. Often, horse breeds are labeled as being **hot-blooded**, **warm-blooded**, or **cold-blooded**. While *all* horses are warm-blooded mammals, these terms mean something different. Larger, gentler horses that have been bred for working and hauling are often called cold-blooded horses. These include draft horses and Clydesdales. Horses are considered hot-blooded if they are smaller and built for speed. They make excellent racehorses and include such breeds as Arabians and thoroughbreds. However, because of their breeding, they are sometimes temperamental and intolerant. Warm-blooded horses are somewhere in between hot- and cold-blooded horses, with the athletic skill of the hot-bloods and the gentler personality of the cold-bloods. They are medium-sized horses: large enough for farm work but small enough to be ridden. They are the favorite for horse riding competitions and shows and include quarter horses and paints. Now please understand that even though different horse breeds can be thought of in these terms, each horse is an individual with its own personality. It is easy to find individual quarter horses, for example, that are more temperamental than individual Arabians.

The Gait

The way in which a horse walks is often called a **gait.** There tend to be four basic gaits: **walk**, **trot**, **canter**, and **gallop**. Some horse breeds have others, but these four are the common ones.

Walk: This is the slowest and steadiest gait, with the horse keeping two or three hooves on the ground at all times. If you hear a horse walking, you should hear four distinct footfalls. As a result, this is called a **four-beat gait**, as there are four beats for every full sequence. It can start with any leg, but assuming it starts with its right hind leg, the order is (1) right hind, (2) right fore, (3) left hind, (4) left fore. The order refers to when the hoof hits the ground. The little drawing to the right illustrates the walk, as if you are looking down at the horse from above. The numbers tell you the order in which the hooves hit the ground.

Trot: During a trot, the horse is suspended in the air for a moment in every stride. The horse springs up in the air, with the fore foot on one side and the hind foot on the other side moving together. The other two hooves hit the ground when the horse lands. This, then, is a **two-beat gait**, as there are only two beats in a sequence: (1) the right fore/left hind hooves hit the ground and (2) the left fore/right hind hooves hit the ground. While this is a faster gait than the walk, it still conserves energy for the horse. A very slow trot is sometimes called a **jog**. If you are riding a trotting horse, it is best for you to rise up in the saddle on one beat and come down on the next beat. This is called **posting**.

Canter: This **three-beat gait** is faster than a trot. The horse spends time suspended in the air in this gait, but only at the end of the sequence. A canter starts with a hind hoof hitting the ground. If it is the left hind hoof, it is called a **right-lead canter**, because the right foreleg will be the most extended of the horse's legs. There are three beats to this stride, because two of the diagonal legs hit the ground at the same time. For a right-lead canter (illustrated on the right), the hooves hit the ground in this order: (1) left hind, (2) right hind/left fore, (3) right fore. A left-lead canter starts with the right hind hoof hitting, then the left hind/right fore hit together, followed by the left fore leg. In a canter, there is a pause between the third beat of one sequence and the first beat of the next, because that's when the horse is in the air.

Gallop: The gallop is the fastest of the standard gaits, and like the walk, it is a **four-beat** movement. The gallop feels just like a fast canter, because the only real difference is that rather than the two diagonal legs hitting together, the hind foot on the diagonal hits the ground a split second before the fore foot. Once again a gallop is left-lead or right-lead, depending on which hind hoof hits the ground first. The drawing, then, illustrates a right-lead gallop. Even though this is a **four-beat gait**, it doesn't sound like a walk, because the beats aren't evenly spaced. Beats two and three are in rapid succession, and there is a pause between four and one, because that's when the horse is in the air.

If you are having trouble understanding this discussion, the course website I told you about in the introduction has links to videos that show horses using these gaits.

Growing Horses

This Shetland pony can pull twice its own weight. A good draft horse can usually pull only a bit more than its own weight.

An ancient way to measure things was by the length of a person's foot or hand. Today, the term "foot" means 12 inches. You may be surprised to learn that we also still use the term "hand" as a way of measuring things – a hand is 4 inches. We talk about how tall a horse is by saying how many hands could be placed from the ground to its shoulders. If a horse is 15 hands high, how high is that? Multiply 4 by 15, and you have 60 inches high. That's 5 feet high. Which is actually pretty small for a horse, but it's still considered a horse if it's 15 hands high. Generally, the difference between a horse and a **pony** has to do with how tall it is. If an equine is less than 14.2 hands tall, it is usually considered a pony. However, there are other differences as well. Ponies have thicker hair as well as thicker manes and tails. They also tend to be stockier than horses, and for their size, they are generally stronger than horses.

We have developed different names for horses based on their level of development. A **foal** is any horse that isn't a year old yet. A **yearling** is any horse that is between one and two years old. A **filly** is a female horse that isn't fully grown, while a male horse that isn't fully grown is called a **colt**. A **mare** is a fully grown female, and a **stallion** is a fully grown male. A **gelding** is an adult male horse that has been neutered (sex organs surgically altered) to make it calmer and more obedient.

You may have heard the phrase, "Don't look a gift horse in the mouth." That means that when you get a gift, you shouldn't complain that it's not exactly what you wanted. This phrase came about because you can tell how old a horse is by looking at its teeth. When people went to buy a horse, they would look at its teeth to determine the horse's age and decide whether or not they wanted to buy it. So the phrase is saying that if someone gives you a horse, don't determine how old it is; just be happy with the gift. Telling a horse's age by looking at its teeth takes some practice, but if you want to learn how to do it, check out the course website I told you about in the introduction to the book. There, you will find links to articles that show you how it can be done.

How much can you remember about horses?

Donkeys

Donkeys are generally smaller than horses, with larger ears, a loud voice, and a much less compliant personality. Their mane is stiff and upright, and the hair is coarse. A donkey's tail is more like a cow's tail, covered with short body hair for most of the length, and ending in a tasseled switch. The donkey is very vocal, braying with a raspy Aw-EE, Aw-EE sound. A donkey might be called a burro, ass, jack, jennet, miniature donkey, mammoth, jackstock, standard, or a Mexican burro. These are all names for different donkeys. A male donkey is usually called a jack.

Note the mane and tail, which indicate this is a donkey, not a horse.

You may wonder, "What is the difference between a mule and a donkey?" Well, if a female horse mates with a male donkey, the horse gives birth to a **mule**. Mules usually cannot reproduce. Also, if a female donkey mates with a male horse and the donkey gives birth, its offspring is called a **hinney**. Hinneys also cannot reproduce.

Although donkeys have long been considered ignorant, they are actually quite intelligent creatures. They are not as easy to train as horses, because they seem to have a mind of their own and will not do anything that doesn't seem like a good idea to them. They prefer to do things that are good for the donkey, which may not necessarily be good for the person who owns the donkey.

Donkeys are unique beasts of burden because they can easily carry unusually heavy loads. They can carry something that weighs 30 percent of their own weight, and thus were a big help to travelers and farmers in days gone by. Donkeys and mules are mentioned throughout the Bible. Samson killed a thousand Philistines with the jawbone of a donkey, Balaam's donkey spoke, and Jesus even rode into Jerusalem on a young donkey.

Though wild donkeys still roam northern Africa and the Arabian peninsula, all the wild donkeys in America are feral donkeys – pets that got loose or were abandoned, which later formed groups that ran wild. Of course, there is another member of this family that has never been domesticated. Let's go to Africa to find out about this interesting equine.

Zebras

The zebra foal in this picture is standing behind its mother. Notice its stripe pattern is completely different from its mother's.

Have you ever heard that you have fingerprints that are different from every other person's in the world? You have a unique fingerprint that God gave just to you. Even twins have different fingerprints! Animals often have distinguishing marks that allow you to tell one individual from another as well. Every zebra, for example, has its own stripe pattern that is totally different from every other zebra. Some scientists think that zebras use stripe patterns to tell each other apart.

Zebras are similar to horses and donkeys. They look like a striped donkey, with their smaller, stockier frame, a thick, coarse mane that stands up straight, and rather large ears. Like donkeys, zebras have a powerful kick with their hind legs, as well as a fierce bite. This helps them deal with their main predators: jaguars, leopards, lions, hyenas, and African wild dogs. In fact, a zebra can kill a leopard with one well-placed kick. Like most horses and donkeys, they usually try to outrun predators, though, and don't resort to combat unless they are trapped. A fleeing zebra zigzags from side to side, looking over its shoulder to see if its predator is still in pursuit. If it can escape within the first 100 yards, it's usually home free. When zebras stand together in the wild, they usually stand side to side, facing opposite directions. This way, they can scan every inch of horizon for possible predators.

Zebras tend to live in herds, just as horses do, and like horses, the leader of a zebra herd is a stallion. They are usually attached to the other members of the herd and will even risk their own lives to rescue a hurt or injured member. If one zebra gets separated from the group, all the zebras in the herd will search for it until it's found, calling with their loud braying voices. Like donkeys, zebras are noisy and are often braying and barking at one another. Like horses, zebras groom each other as a means of communication. Mothers especially love to groom their foals, and the whole herd watches over the young. When they run as a herd, the young are kept in the center of the group for maximum protection.

There are three different kinds of zebras: **plains zebras** (also called Burchell's zebras), **mountain zebras**, and **Grevy's zebras**. Plains zebras, which live in the open grasslands and near the deserts all over Africa, are the most numerous of the three groups. The mountain zebras live in the stony mountains of southern Africa, while Grevy's zebras live in the dry deserts of eastern Africa. Several other species of zebra have become extinct because they were hunted and their territories were made too small. When a zebra lives in a small territory, it's hard for it to stay far away from predators. Today, though, the African government and wildlife groups have set up nature preserves, where zebras can live without being hunted and without having their land turned into cities or farms.

Describe what you have learned about donkeys and zebras today.

Rhinos

The rhinoceros might look a bit like a dinosaur, but it is not. It is a mammal and a three-toed member of order Perissodactyla. We'll actually study dinosaurs in depth in Lesson 12, so let's not worry about them for right now. Instead, let's study this odd-toed ungulate.

Depending on the species, rhinos can grow to be 14 feet long and weigh as much as 4 tons. That's about the size of a minivan! They aren't as

This young rhinoceros is staying close to its mother.

tall as a minivan, though. They grow to be about 5 to 6 feet high at the shoulders. Their lumpy, bumpy skin makes up a lot of that weight, as it's almost an inch thick in some places. Although you might think they have plates in their skin, that's not true. Their skin has folds that make it look a bit like armor. The Asian rhino probably has the most obvious folds in its skin, giving it the appearance of being covered in plates. Rhinos have a symbiotic relationship with **oxpeckers**, sometimes called **tick birds**. The oxpeckers eat parasites like ticks and other parasites that live on the rhinos' skin. These birds also warn rhinos if danger (like a lion, tiger, or hyena) lurks nearby.

There are five species of rhinoceroses currently alive. The **black rhino** and **white rhino** live in Africa. They have two horns, the longer of which is in front. Black and white rhinos are actually the same color – gray. It is not clear why white rhinos are called "white." One thought is that the lips of a white rhino are wider than those of a black rhino, and Dutch settlers in Africa used the Dutch word "*wijde*" to refer to the white rhino's wide lips. It's possible that this word was misunderstood by others who were not Dutch and, over time, it got replaced by the word "white." Whatever the reason, you cannot tell the difference between these species by looking at their color. The white rhino is the second-largest terrestrial (land-living) mammal, next to the elephant. The largest land mammal that ever lived was a rhinoceros that was 18 feet tall and weighed about 20,000 pounds! Of course, that species of rhino is now extinct.

The **Indian rhino** lives in India and Nepal, and the **Javan rhino** lives in Indonesia and Vietnam. Both of them have one horn. The small, hairy **Sumatran rhino** has two horns. It lives in the dense rainforests and mountains of Southeast Asia and eats many things, including bamboo.

Rhinos must consume a huge amount of vegetation in order to feed their massive bodies. They are timid and shy, yet they will charge an intruder at speeds over 30 miles per hour when frightened, just to scare them off. That's faster than a man can run! The truth is, with their tiny little eyes, rhinos can't see well, so they sometimes charge objects like trees and rocks, mistaking them as threats. Although they don't have eagle eyes, rhinos have keen senses of smell and hearing. In actuality, most of their charges are bluffs, but these colossal beasts are still dangerous, even if they do only eat grass.

Like most mammals, the males are territorial. They mark their territory with their droppings and urine. They don't usually run in groups, but females share territory with the males. Sometimes males will herd females into their territory. They are not very aggressive creatures, and will bathe together without fighting. When they do occasionally fight, it usually doesn't end until one rhino is dead. If it isn't eaten by a crocodile or other common predators, a rhinoceros can live for about 30 to 35 years, giving birth to young every two to four years. Though they can be quite ferocious when threatened, they are actually gentle and kind, especially to their young, which live with them for two years, learning how to survive in the wild.

Rhino horns are made of the same material found in hair and fingernails – a chemical called keratin (kair' uh tin).

All rhinos have at least one horn. The horns are worth their weight in gold and have cost many rhinos their life. You see, the Chinese grind up their horns and use it as medicine, and the people of Yemen use it to make handles for their knives. So, they are hunted and killed for those precious horns. As a result, they are now an endangered species. Some conservationists try to save rhinos by sawing off their horns, thinking that no poacher would want to kill a rhino if it doesn't have a horn! You may wonder if this hurts the poor creature. Some creatures have sensitive horns, but not the rhino; it doesn't hurt at all! Does it hurt when someone cuts your hair? Well, a rhino's horns are made of the same material that your hair is made of! Don't be fooled, though. Its horn is as tough as nails and can gore another animal right through. However, it's not a sensitive horn. So, it's a bit like getting a haircut for the rhino – only much harder for the "hair dresser," who has to tromp through the jungle or bush and shoot the rhino with a tranquilizer in order to slow it down, then walk over and saw off the huge horn. Of course, because the horns are made of the same substance as hair, they also grow like hair does. So, every few years, the conservationist has to head back out, chase down the same rhino, and cut off the horn that grew in its place.

Tapirs

The last family of odd-toed ungulates contains tapirs. Though they are shaped like large pigs, with a short, stout body, they have that special elephantine quality. God equipped tapirs with a proboscis, just like an elephant. Interestingly enough, many tapirs love the water, and they actually use their proboscis as a snorkel! They stay underwater and stick their nose up into the air in order to breathe! Unlike elephants, however, tapirs are covered with hair. A baby tapir is born with a speckled coat that camouflages it in the forest. Generally, the coat turns brown or black (often with white markings) as the tapir grows into adulthood.

A tapir looks a bit like a cross between a pig and an elephant.

Most tapirs live in the rainforests of Central and South America, though one kind of tapir, called the Malayan tapir, lives in Southeast Asia. They all have egg-shaped, white-tipped ears and a pig-shaped body with a stubby tail. Their hoofed feet are splayed for walking on soft, muddy ground. They have four toes on their front feet, but they are odd-toed ungulates because they have three toes on their hind feet. Their short proboscis is amazingly flexible; it can move in all directions, allowing the animals to grab leaves and other herbivorous fare that might otherwise be out of reach. The length of the proboscis varies according to species.

Although many tapirs live in dry regions, a tapir that does happen to live near a river will spend most of its time there. It will walk into the river, sink to the bottom, and walk along the riverbed with its proboscis protruding above the water. If there is no river nearby, a tapir will try to find a mud hole and wallow in it like a pig for hours to keep cool.

Tapirs are generally shy, but when they are scared they can defend themselves with their very powerful jaws. They have been known to attack people when threatened.

What Do You Remember?

What are the different uses for an elephant's proboscis? Why do elephants blow dust? How are mammoths like elephants? How are they different? How do mammoths help us understand how the ice age might have happened? What kind of habitat did the mastodon live in? How are horses and ponies different? What does it mean when a horse is labeled hot-, cold-, or warm-blooded? Identify the following: filly, colt, foal, stallion, mare, and yearling. Explain the main differences between donkeys and horses. How are zebra stripes like your fingerprints? How are zebras like donkeys? Why are rhinoceroses endangered? What is a rhino's horn made of? How are tapirs like elephants? How are they like pigs?

Map It!

Asia – Asian elephants, wooly mammoths, mastodons, tapirs
Africa – African elephants, donkeys, zebras, black and white rhinos
Central and South America as well as Southeast Asia – Tapirs

Track It!

Fore Hoof
(no shoes)

Hind Hoof
(no shoes)

Fore Hoof
(no shoes and ground is perfect for prints)

Horse and donkey tracks are the odd-toed ungulate tracks you are most likely to find. If the horse is shoed, of course, you will see a horseshoe imprint on the ground. However, if it is "barefoot," the track you see will generally be a circle with a slightly flattened end. The fore hooves are usually rounder than the hind hooves. If the ground has the right consistency, you can even see details of the hoof.

Notebook Activities

For your notebook, make a page about each animal type I discussed. Include drawings (or pictures) and facts about each. Also, make a true/false quiz about odd-toed ungulates. For example, one question could be, "Rhinoceros horns are made of bone." The answer, of course, would be "false." Put the answers on a separate page, and give the quiz to family and friends.

Review Game

Now you are going to create a board game that will help you review all the animals you have learned about so far. It will be an exciting and fun way to lock the information you learned into your brain.

You will need:

♦ A folder or poster board for the game board
♦ Cutouts of every continent (except Antarctica)
♦ Index cards
♦ Facts you have learned from the book to date
♦ Beads in different colors (Use a color for each player. You need several beads of each color.)

1. Glue the continents onto your game board in the same basic pattern as they appear on a world map.
2. Create questions about the animals you have learned so far. On each card, write a question in the middle of the card.
3. Write the answer upside down, really small, on the bottom of the card.
4. On the other side of the card, glue a small cutout of the continent on which that animal lives. Animals from Southeast Asia will have the entire continent of Asia on the back of their card. If an animal is from more than one continent, make at least one card for each continent.

How to Play:

The purpose of the game is to become the ruler of as many continents as you can by answering questions correctly about animals that live on the continent. Every correct answer allows you to place one bead on the continent. Whoever has the most beads on a continent wins that continent.

Make a stack of cards for each continent. There will be an Africa stack, an Australia stack, and so on. Then, have each player choose a bead color and gather all the beads of that color. Every player should begin with the same number of beads.

Begin play with the youngest player and go clockwise to each player in turn. The first player chooses which stack they want a question from. The next player picks the card up from that stack and asks that person the question on the card (being careful not to show the card, since the answer is on the bottom). When the player answers the question correctly, the player will be allowed to place one of his or her beads on the continent. If the player answers incorrectly, he or she does not get to place a bead on a continent. When one player runs out of beads, continue the round until everyone has had the same number of turns. Then, the game is over. Whoever has the most beads on a continent wins that continent.

Lesson 9
Order Artiodactyla

Although there were only a few species in the odd-toed ungulate order, that's not so with the even-toed ungulate order called **Artiodactyla** (ar' tee uh dak' til uh). There are more than 200 species in this order, and most of them are thriving, both on the farm and in the wild. Because this order is so diverse, there is really only one thing you can say about all these animals – they don't have a middle toe. That's why they are called even-toed ungulates. Think about it. If you have an odd number of toes, one of your toes will be the middle toe. If you have an even number of toes, the middle of your foot will be between your toes. That's the case for all animals in this order.

Although it is hard to come up with traits common to *all* members of this order, many of them have a special way of eating. Imagine chewing your food and swallowing it, only to have it come back up your throat and into your mouth to be chewed and swallowed again. This is what many animals in this order do! This is a process called **rumination** (roo' muh nay' shun) and the animals that do this are called **ruminants** (roo' muh nuhntz).

A ruminant has three or four chambers in its stomach, whereas you and I have only one. Each chamber processes the food in a different way. Since most ruminants have a four-chambered stomach, that's the one I will describe. The first time a ruminant chews its food, the animal chews quickly. It then swallows the food, which goes to the first two chambers of the stomach. There, it gets softened and partially digested, forming a little ball, called a **cud**. The cud is then sent back to the mouth,

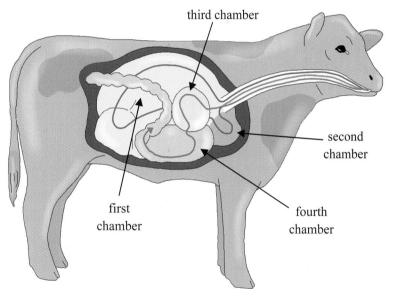

The food a cow swallows (blue line) initially goes to the first and second chambers of the stomach. It then goes back up to the mouth (green line) as cud. Once the cud has been chewed a long time, it is swallowed again so that it can go through the third and fourth chamber for complete digestion (red line).

where the ruminating creature chews it some more. This time, it chews for a long time to break down the food and thoroughly mix it with saliva. The cud then goes down into the stomach, where it travels to the third chamber for special processing. It then moves to the fourth chamber for the final portion of digestion before it's sent to the intestines. This method allows the animal to get the most benefit from the food it eats. When you see a ruminant lying on the ground and chewing, it is probably working on its cud. Cattle, goats, sheep, llamas, giraffes, bison, buffalo, deer, wildebeests, and antelopes are all ruminants. Although pigs and hippos are also in order Artiodactyla, they are not ruminants.

Family Bovidae

Let's start our study of the even-toed ungulates by putting on our cowboy boots and rustling up some **cattle**! Have you ever seen a cow up close? Was it chewing? When we think of an animal that chews its cud, the one that comes immediately to mind can be found on farms and ranches all over the world: cows, or cattle to be more precise. **Cows** are the females, whereas the term "cattle" refers to both males and females. Do you know what the males are called? **Bulls**!

Cattle are in family **Bovidae** (boh' vuh dee). However, so are antelopes, gazelles, goats, and sheep! That's a pretty interesting mix of animals to put in one family. Some are completely domestic, like goats, sheep, and cattle. These animals have been farm animals throughout history. In fact, the word "chattel," which means "property," comes from the same root word as does "cattle." Can you think of why people associate property with cattle? Today, we measure wealth by the amount of money you have. Many years ago, however, before everyone started using money, wealth was measured in livestock. People with a lot of livestock (cattle) were rich, while people without a lot of livestock were poor.

The horns and two toes on this bull tell you it is in family Bovidae.

Although many members of this family are domesticated, others (like **gazelles**, **antelopes**, and **mountain goats**) are wild. Some of these animals form herds, while others are solitary. So, what makes all these animals similar? Well, the first thing similar among all **bovids** (the term used for members of this family) is the structure of their feet. They carry all their weight on two toes. They all eat grass and chew the cud. All the males (and sometimes the females) have twin horns made of bone on either side of their head. Sometimes the horns are straight; other times they are curved. However, they never branch like a deer's antlers.

Most wild bovids live in Africa, with a few living in North America, Europe, and Asia. Domestic bovids, like cattle, are found all over the world. Since you probably have the least experience with wild bovids, I want to spend most of the time in this lesson on them.

Antelopes, Gazelles, and Impalas

Do you know what an **antelope** is? Most people imagine it is a large deer living in North America. However, there are no antelopes **indigenous** (in dij' uh nuhs) to North America. Do you know what that word means? It means "native to." So, there are no antelopes native to North America. If they are in North America, they were brought there. Elk are indigenous to North America, but they are deer. You'll learn about them in a moment. Most antelopes live in Africa, along with very similar animals called gazelles and **impalas**. All these creatures have long legs and can run like the wind. They are all ruminants.

This blackbuck (*Antilope cervicapra*) is an example of an antelope.

There are several species of gazelles. They are particularly fast and have great endurance. Endurance is the ability to keep going and going and going, even when it's really hard. People who run marathons, for example, have a lot of endurance. A gazelle can run for a long time without getting tired. Some of their predators, like cheetahs and lions, try to tire out these animals by chasing them, but they usually give up long before the gazelle does.

What the impala lacks in speed and endurance, it makes up for with an amazing ability to jump.

Impalas are common ruminants of the African plains, and boy, can they jump! They lack the speed and endurance of gazelles, but when they are frightened or startled, the whole herd starts leaping about in all directions. Scientists think this confuses their predators. They can spring more than 8 feet into the air and land more than 30 feet from where they started. That's an amazing jumper! In spite of their incredible acrobatics, impalas are the favorite target of almost every African predator.

Wildebeests

Huge **wildebeest** herds are one of the most common sights on the eastern and southern African plains. These large, dark ungulates have horns with no ridges and a mane. There are actually two species of wildebeest, but the wild one is the **blue wildebeest**. The other species, the black wildebeest, was hunted to near extinction and can now be found only in protected game farms in the southern parts of Africa. Blue wildebeests are constantly on the lookout for fresh water and good grazing grounds. As a result, they tend to migrate throughout parts of Africa.

The migration of wildebeests is quite fascinating. All year long, over a million wildebeests, and about 200,000 gazelles and zebras, move in a basically clockwise pattern over 1,800 miles of territory. There is no beginning or end to the migration, as it continues round and round the Tanzanian plains and Kenya's Masai Mara. Many people travel to Africa just to see the unbelievable site of a sea of wildebeests roaming, grazing, and stampeding through the African plains.

This herd of wildebeests is resting during the warmth of the African afternoon.

Bovines

Farms and ranches throughout the world are peppered with large, slow grazers called **bovines**. Can you think of which animals this group might include? Cattle, **buffalo**, **bison** and **yaks** are the most common animals in this group. Throughout the world, they are used as sources of milk, meat, and hides. In the Unites States, their meat is the most common kind served on the kitchen table.

Cattle were some of the first domestic farm animals in the entire world. There are several breeds of cattle kept on farms. Each breed is used for a specific purpose, whether for its milk, meat, or hides. Cattle hides are used to make leather, which is used in clothing and furniture. One interesting breed is the **zebu cattle**, which can be easily recognized by the hump on its back. These cattle, native to India, are able to tolerate heat and insects, resist parasites, and survive in droughts better than most other cattle. This is because over the centuries, they have been exposed to famines, insects,

The hump tells you this is a zebu.

parasites, and extreme weather in India. Because of this, only those that had characteristics allowing them to deal with such problems were able to survive. These characteristics include loose, oily skin and the ability to sweat profusely. The sweating helps them to tolerate extreme heat. Also, zebu cattle can walk long distances to water, which is scarce in some areas of India. These special cattle are such good survivors that they have been cross-bred with other cattle to produce a similar breed called the **Braham cattle**, which can be found in many parts of the world.

Sadly, in India, where the zebu cattle thrive, many people are hungry. Men, women, and children die of starvation each day in India. These cattle walk freely throughout India, among these starving people. Hinduism, the dominant religion in India, teaches people that the cattle are sacred and should never be eaten. India has more cattle than any other country, as well as the highest number of people that die of starvation. Can you imagine what it would be like if your family was dying of starvation, yet you would be sent to jail if you killed the most readily available food source?

Try This!

There are many organizations that are dedicated to feeding the hungry children in India. Go to the course website I told you about in the introduction to this book to find links to websites of these organizations.

Bison and Buffalo

Although they are called buffalo, bison are not buffalo. Buffalo are in the same family, but are in different genera.

When Lewis and Clark were exploring North America, they tried counting the **bison** as they went. When they reached the areas where bison were plentiful, however, they wrote, "…if it be not impossible to calculate the moving multitude, that darkened the whole plains, we are convinced that twenty thousand would not be an exaggeration." Indeed, there was a time when bison were so numerous in the United States that no one would have believed that they could ever become near extinction. Yet, that's exactly what happened. Though bison originally numbered in the tens of millions, by the 1900s there were fewer than 1,000 left. They became an endangered species and were finally protected.

What happened to bring the bison to near extinction? Well, Native Americans killed bison for their hides, meat, and bones. Some would hunt bison by surrounding a herd and moving them towards a cliff. They would then start a stampede. Bison cannot see very well, so if one startles and begins to run, the whole herd goes with it – just in case! In the end, they would stampede right off the cliff and die. Once horses arrived with the Europeans, Native Americans (and the European newcomers) used them to help them hunt bison.

Many years after Europeans arrived in North America, the bison hide trade became big business. With shotguns available, huge numbers of bison were killed for their hide, by both Native Americans and the new arrivals. Sadly, whereas the Native Americans would use the entire bison – skin, meat, and bones – the trade in hides caused many bison to be butchered for their hide alone. No other part of the bison was used. It seemed like a big waste of the animal to both the Native Americans and conservationists.

Because of over-hunting, the bison population was almost wiped out. However, small herds were preserved with new laws and were able to replenish their numbers. Today, bison populations are strong once again, and they are no longer endangered! You can even get bison meat (often incorrectly called "buffalo meat") in the store and at certain restaurants. Of course, this meat does not come from wild bison. It comes from bison that are raised on a farm specifically for their meat. Maybe you could try it sometime!

Wild bison are typically found in colder areas, like Colorado, Montana, and Canada. With their warm coats, they are able to survive cold winters quite well. They can even find food where other animals wouldn't be able to, because they use their heads as shovels to dig through snow to uncover the grasses beneath. In the spring, bison shed their heavy winter coats. To help this shedding process, they forcefully rub against large stones and trees. Pretty soon, all the bison are walking around with tattered winter coats hanging off their shoulders. In spite of their great size and bulk, bison are quite fast. They can run at speeds of up to 30 miles per hour!

As mentioned under the picture on the previous page, bison are not really buffalo. Buffalo are a part of family Bovidae, but they are different animals. Water buffalo are typically found in Asia, and African buffalo are, of course, from Africa. As you can see from the picture of the African buffalo on the right, they are quite different in appearance from bison.

This African buffalo is a true buffalo, not a bison.

Before we study any more creatures, tell someone what you have learned about how ruminants eat and what you know about family Bovidae.

Caprines

When my sister was young, my father gave her a present. It was a baby goat, called a **kid**. She nurtured and fed her kid, developing a close relationship with it. They were inseparable. In fact, it often followed her to school, much like Mary's little lamb. However, one day, she came home from school, and her goat was nowhere to be found. My father neglected to tell her one very important thing. He had purchased the goat not as a pet, but as a meal. My sister didn't eat dinner that night. **Goats**, **sheep**, **duikers** (dye' kurz), **chamois**, and a few other animals are part of a special group in family Bovidae called **caprines** (kap' rynz). These tasty creatures are raised domestically for their milk and meat. In addition, sheep provide wool. There are also many caprines that roam in the wild.

Caprines are usually stocky, well-built creatures. They can be very large like the musk ox, or quite small like the gorals, which are generally only about 3 feet long. The male is usually larger than the female and always has horns. Many sport beards as well! A male caprine is called a **buck** or **billy**, and a female is called a **doe** or **nanny**.

These North American wild sheep are not in peril; they are at home on rocky cliffs.

While goats and sheep are the typical examples of caprines, this is a very diverse group of animals indeed. In fact, even the word "sheep" describes some rather different creatures. Did you know that the animals pictured on the left are sheep? They aren't the wooly, cuddly creatures you probably think of when you think of sheep, but they are **North American wild sheep**, often called **bighorn sheep**. These sheep are so good on their feet that they are at home on steep mountain ledges.

Duikers give you another idea of how diverse caprines can be. These deer-like animals get their name from the Afrikaans word for "diver," because these secretive creatures dive for cover whenever anyone is around. In other words, these caprines are shy creatures native to Africa. Their body is especially suited to slip into the dense thicket, with short front legs and long back legs. They never stray too far from their hiding places, in case they need to make a quick escape into the brush. They don't run around in big groups, either, preferring the company of only two or three other duikers. Though duikers pick around on bushes for seeds and fruit, they are one of the few bovids that will eat other animals, typically insects.

A few species of duiker are threatened because of the **bushmeat** trade. The forests and plains of Africa are often called "the bush," and the meat of the wild animals that live there is often called bushmeat. Bush animals killed for their meat are part of the bushmeat trade. Apparently, certain duikers have especially delicious meat highly prized in Africa, so they have been overhunted by those who trade in bushmeat. But how does one catch an elusive, secretive creature like a duiker? Interestingly, they are hunted at night using bright lights. When a bright light is flashed into their eyes at night, they are blinded and too confused to run, which allows time for the hunter to shoot them.

Many duikers look like deer, even though they are caprines.

In addition to the bushmeat trade, duikers are threatened by the loss of monkeys in certain regions of Africa. Duikers often eat the fruits that monkeys dislodge from high in the trees. Without the monkeys to knock down fruits for them, some duikers have a hard time finding enough to eat.

Try This!

A great story in the Bible shows how easily caprines can develop specific features. Jacob tricked his father-in-law by breeding the sheep and goats in such a way as to produce certain features. Read the story now! It's found in Genesis 30:25-47. In only a short while, Jacob was able to breed his sheep and goats in such a way as to give them the characteristics he wanted. If Jacob could do this in only a few years, we can see how easily the earth could be filled with so many different species of caprines in the few thousand years since the original animal kinds left the ark. Today, there is a breed of sheep called Jacob's sheep that are supposed to be similar to the sheep Jacob bred.

Family Camelidae

Though there are many other interesting animals in family Bovidae, we simply must move on if we are going to get through the rest of order Artiodactyla! So let's head into the desert to study a special creature created for life in the hot, sandy parts of the world. I am talking, of course, about **camels**. In the Middle East, camels have been an important part of human transportation for a long time. In fact, if you were to talk to someone from the Middle East about riding on animals, he would assume you were talking about camels, not horses! Camels are a part of family **Camelidae** (kam el' uh dee), which also includes **llamas** and **vicugnas**. Animals in this family are called **camelids**.

The Bactrian camel has two humps, while the dromedary camel has only one.

Camels are known for their humps. What is the greatest number of humps a camel can have? Can you take a guess? Although the popular children's song has a camel with many humps, camels can only have one or two humps. In fact, only one camel has two humps – the bactrian camel that lives in Asia. The more common species of camel, the **dromedary** (drahm' ih duh' ree), has only one hump. Have you ever wondered what those humps were filled with? What do you think? I was told all my life that they were filled with water, and guess what? That's not true. *They are filled with fat.* Fat is stored in the humps so it can be used when other food is not available. Their humps enable camels to survive during times of famine or on long treks through the hot desert. The longer a camel goes without eating, the smaller and flabbier its humps become. The other animals in this family have no humps.

Camels are designed for life in a desert. They can survive for a long time with no water, and when they finally find a watering hole, they can drink 20 or more gallons of water at one time! Their big eyes are equipped with long lashes that keep out dust; and their nostrils are mere slits that can close up during a dust storm. Also, their two-toed feet are wide to provide more padding and stability when walking on shifting sand. If you ever meet a camel, you should be nice to it. Why? Well, because camels make a point of spitting large amounts of saliva on unfriendly people or unfriendly camels. In fact, all members of this family spit at animals they are not happy with.

Camelids have been domesticated for thousands of years. They provide not only transportation, but milk and clothing as well. The llama, for example, is shaved like a sheep, and its hair is used to make clothing and other items. Llamas have been domesticated for so long that no wild llamas exist anymore, unless they are feral. These specific camelids have been designed for life in the mountains. They actually have special

Llamas have no hump, but they do spit like camels when they are upset.

blood that allows them to deal with the lower levels of oxygen found in such high places.

Deer

This buck still has velvet on his antlers.

Although you might think that deer belong in family Bovidae with the antelopes, they are different enough from other members of order Artiodactyla to merit their own family – **Cervidae** (sir' vuh dee). These cud-chewers are found over most of the world. One thing that separates deer from other ungulates is their antlers. Bucks (male deer) grow a beautiful new set of antlers every single year. During the late winter or early spring, a buck's antlers actually fall off. Soon after that, a new set begins to emerge, usually bigger than the set before. The growing antlers are made of bone covered by a layer of velvety skin. They are also very sensitive. Growing antlers requires a lot of nutrients, so bucks eat a lot during the spring. The horns harden once they are fully grown, which is usually in the summer. At that point, the velvet dries, cracks, and begins to fall off. The buck rubs its new set of prized antlers on tree trunks and other structures to help scrape off the velvet. The tree sap often stains the antlers dark. If you find yourself hiking in the forest in the winter, be sure to look for the discarded antlers of the bucks in that area.

So what are the antlers for? Bucks mostly use them to attract females (does). A nice pair of antlers tells a doe that the buck is strong and has the ability to find nutritious food. Bucks often spar with other bucks to determine who is the strongest. They begin sparring when they are young. Once their horns are grown, they lock them in clashes that look quite dangerous. However, deer rarely resort to bloodshed. They usually just lock horns, pushing and shoving for a while. Then the weaker one unlocks and runs off. Generally, bucks fight either for territory or for the right to mate with a doe.

Although they look fierce, buck fights rarely include bloodshed.

There are more than 40 different species of deer currently living in God's creation, and they each have their own special characteristics. **Musk deer**, for example, is a collection of several species of deer that produce an extremely powerful scent. Their scent, called **musk**, has been used for hundreds of years in making perfumes and in natural medicine. Thus, these deer have been hunted for their musk, which sells for about $1,000 a pound. **Moose** are also part of family Cervidae, and they represent its largest members.

These reindeer are looking for grass underneath the snow.

Of course, the most famous deer of all would have to be Rudolph the red-nosed **reindeer**. In North America, reindeer are often called **caribou**. They are the only deer species in which females also have antlers. As you may have guessed, they can be found in freezing cold climates in the northernmost regions of the world. They are equipped with a furry nose (unlike other deer) for foraging in the snow. They have been given a powerful homing instinct that helps them to find their way home, even through blinding blizzards.

Stop a moment and explain everything you have learned about sheep, goats, camels, and deer.

Family Giraffidae

If you were to look across the African savanna, you might see something in the distance that looked like heads without bodies, floating above the tree line. That's because **giraffes** are so tall that they tower above the African plains where they live. In fact, they are the tallest of all God's creatures alive today. They can grow up to 18 feet tall. It's hard to be impressed with that number unless you can actually see how tall 18 feet is. If you have a tape measure, measure out 18 feet along the ground. Now imagine something standing that high!

Creation Confirmation

God created giraffes with unusual body proportions – a small head on top of a long neck on top of a stout body on top of long, skinny legs. This body design would be a problem, if it hadn't been crafted by a Master! You see, a giraffe's tall neck means that its heart must be *very strong* and produce a high **blood pressure**. Why? You will do an experiment at the end of this lesson to see, but essentially, the higher the blood must be pumped, the more pressure it takes to get the blood up there. As a result, giraffes have the highest blood pressure of any mammal in God's creation!

These giraffes' brains don't explode when they bend for a drink because of complicated systems that are unique to giraffes.

So why does this present a problem? Well, giraffes must bend over to drink water. They also bend over to eat particularly tasty plants growing from the ground. When they bend over, the blood no longer has to travel *up* to get to the head, so it is much easier for the blood to get there. As a result, the high-pressure blood *should* just shoot towards the head, filling the brain so fast with blood that it would just explode! Obviously, that doesn't happen. Why?

Well, the short answer is that there are several specific features unique to giraffes that reduce the blood flow to the brain as the giraffe bends down. However, some of these features are so complicated that scientists to this day don't fully understand how they all work! That's not the end of the story, however. You see, as the giraffe raises its head, the blood pressure must come back, or not enough blood will make it to the brain. Have you ever been bent over for a while and then raised back up to a standing position suddenly? What happened? Did you get dizzy? Most people do. Why?

Well, like a giraffe, your body can reduce its blood pressure when you are bent over so that your brain doesn't get too full of blood. It can't do this as well as a giraffe's body, because you don't have the complicated systems the giraffe has. Nevertheless, it can do so a bit. When you raise back up, if your blood pressure doesn't increase quickly enough, not enough blood gets to your brain, and you get dizzy. Since a giraffe's head is so much higher than yours, the problem is much, much bigger for a giraffe. Thus, its complicated systems must not only lower the blood pressure in the brain while the giraffe is bent down, but they must also increase the blood pressure quickly as the giraffe raises its head again. Imagine that! The giraffe has systems that can do all of that, and they do it so well that scientists can't even figure out exactly how they work! Only a Master Craftsman could have put together such an amazing system!

Leaf Lovers

The size of this adult's hand gives you an idea of just how long a giraffe's tongue is!

Giraffes feed on all kinds of plant material. Because they are such big creatures, they must eat a great deal. As a result, God gave them long necks so they could reach the tops of trees to find the food they need. If there is a drought, they can even eat twigs and dried leaves. Their favorite food is flowers, which they enjoy in the spring. Because there are so many thorns on the trees in Africa, especially near the flowers they love, God gave giraffes a long tongue that is more like an arm. It can reach around the thorns to grasp the leaves!

Like cattle, giraffes chew their cud. When it's time for the food to go back into the mouth for more chewing, a big mass moves from the stomach, up the long neck, and back into the mouth. You can actually see the cud moving up the neck, sort of like an elevator rising up a skyscraper. It's an interesting sight to see.

On top of the giraffe's head are two little horns that, unlike most animal horns, are covered with hair. The males develop extra little bumps that form from built-up calcium. As a male ages, these growths sometimes begin to look like additional horns. There are usually two in the back and one in the middle, so it can look like the giraffe has five horns.

Like bovines, giraffe males are called bulls, females are called cows, and young ones are called calves. The bulls fight by trying to throw their competitors off balance. They might bump the back legs of their foe with their neck or head

Giraffes eat all manner of plant material, including leaves from the tops of trees.

to make him fall. Sometimes they use their head like a club and swing it at their enemy. Sometimes, they engage in "necking" contests where they entwine their necks and wrestle with each other until one is brought down to the ground. It's a lot like arm-wrestling. Have you ever arm-wrestled? Sit across the table from someone and join your right hand with his right hand. Place both of your right elbows on the table. Now try to force his hand to the table, while he does the same to yours. This is arm-wrestling, which is a bit like giraffe necking. Sometimes, young males have necking contests for fun.

Puzzling Spots

The stripes of a tiger are similar to the stripes of a zebra, and the spots on a cheetah resemble the spots on a newborn fawn. But the markings on a giraffe are not repeated anywhere in the animal kingdom. Their ginger- and sand-colored markings blend well with the African woodlands, so part of their purpose is camouflage. However, there is at least a bit more to them than that. You see, every giraffe has its own unique pattern of spots. Researchers who study giraffes can tell them apart by their markings, especially on the neck. Do you remember another African creature that can be identified by its markings? The zebra.

The giraffe on the left is a Masai giraffe, while the one on the right is a reticulated giraffe.

There is only one species of giraffe, but they are divided into subspecies based on the shape of their spots. **Masai** (mah' sye) giraffes, from Kenya, have spots with jagged edges, while **reticulated** (rih tik' yuh lay ted) giraffes have spots shaped a lot like rectangles. Their colors vary from light tan to almost black.

You may have been told that giraffes don't make any noise. That's not true. Although it is rare for them to make vocal sounds, they have been known to bellow or snort when extremely frightened. The calves also bleat when looking for their mother. When a predator is near, all giraffes stand facing the predator with their eyes and ears forward, and they will fight with deadly kicks if necessary. Their main predator is the lion. A large lion can bring down even the largest of giraffes, and the pride can feed off it for days.

A giraffe paces. This doesn't mean it walks back and forth. We say that an animal walks with a pace when two legs on one side of the body move at the same time. So, the front and back legs on the right side move forward simultaneously, and then the front and back legs on the left side move forward.

When a baby giraffe is born, the calf falls 6 feet to the ground with a big splat! The surprise of the impact causes the baby to take a huge breath of air. Within an hour it gets up to walk. Though it is just a newborn baby calf, it is about 6 feet tall! That's taller than most adult men! When it gets older, the mother giraffe often leaves it with a group of other calves in a nursery. One mother is left behind to babysit everyone else's calf. When the calf is 4 months old, it stops nursing and begins to eat solid foods. Then, the calf doesn't have to stay in the nursery anymore; it can go out in search of food with its mom.

Okapis

Deep in the rainforest lives the other member of family Giraffidae, the **okapi** (oh kop' ee). This animal's features are similar to those of a giraffe. It has an extended neck (but not as long as a giraffe's); furry horns; upright ears; a long, black, arm-like tongue; and a tufted tail. They are also usually silent like the giraffe. The okapi is much shorter than the giraffe, however. Its smaller size enables it to walk through the forest much more easily than a giraffe could.

An okapi looks like a cross between a giraffe and a zebra.

Besides its size, there are other differences between the okapi and the giraffe. First, its markings are strange. Most of its body is solid and usually dark brown, but there are zebra stripes on the rear and legs. Second, while the giraffe lives in a herd, the okapi is a solitary animal. Also, while the okapi has excellent hearing, its eyesight is not very good. Giraffes have better eyesight than okapis and worse hearing.

Okapis have special features that help them live in the rainforest. Only the males have horns, and the horns are short and slant backward so that they don't get caught in the thick foliage of the jungle. Okapis also have a layer of oil over their entire coat, which makes the rain slide right off them. This is important since it rains a lot in the rainforest. If you ever get a chance to touch an okapi – which isn't likely unless you work in the zoo – you will notice that its skin is so velvety, your handprint is visible on its fur even after you remove it. If your mom has some velvet on hand, try leaving your handprint on it. It's not an okapi, but it will give you an idea of what an okapi's fur feels like.

Before we move on, try to recall all you have learned about ruminating ungulates so far.

Family Suidae

Have you ever heard farmers call to their pigs saying, "Soooey, soooey"? Well, perhaps this came from their family name: **Suidae** (soo' uh dee). This family includes more than the domesticated pigs with which you are familiar. It also includes **warthogs** and **forest hogs**. Members of this family are often called swine, which is a term that also refers to a bad person. This might be because pigs, though they can be sweet and gentle, can behave badly when penned up. If you fall into a pigpen, a **sow** (female pig) may attack you as a threat to her piglets. The rest of the pigs will usually join in. They'll bite with their sharp teeth and gore you with their tusks, if they have any.

Pigs were created to be forest dwellers, where they clean up the forest by eating everything they find. Wild pigs are still found in forest and grasslands throughout Europe, Asia, and Africa. These thick-skinned creatures have coarse hair, and some even have a mane that runs down their back. Their tail is usually thin and can curl around in a twist. They are also equipped with two toes and a long snout. The snout is probably the swine's most famous feature. It ends in a round disk at the tip. Some use this tough snout to forage and dig for roots under the ground. Most wild pigs also have two teeth protruding out of their mouths in front of their nose. These two teeth are the canines, which form tusks that curl upward. They use them to defend themselves, and **boars** (male pigs) use them to fight off other boars infringing on their territory or their females.

The mother pig doesn't always get a chance to lie down when her piglets want to nurse.

In the wild, pigs live in groups of sows and their offspring. These groups are called **sounders**. Boars are generally solitary. Unlike many ungulates, a sow gives birth to a litter of pigs, rather than just one or two. She nurses the litter much like a cat, lying down with each piglet attached to a nipple. Sometimes the piglets even nurse while mother walks about! Wild piglets are generally spotted or striped. These markings provide camouflage in the forest, where they hide under shrubs while the mother goes in search of food. The markings often fade with age.

When someone unkindly calls someone else "a pig," it implies that the other person eats too much. However, pigs don't eat too much, though they will eat pretty much anything. A pig is like a trash compactor and will eat many things, including fungi, snails, worms, small birds, dead animal flesh, and decaying vegetables.

There are many species in family Suidae besides the pigs with which you are familiar. The warthog, which became famous as a result of the Disney movie *The Lion King*, is also in this family. It is typically found on the outskirts of forests in Africa. Like their domesticated family members, they deal with Africa's heat by wallowing in the mud. If it gets cold, they huddle together and share each others' warmth. Interestingly enough, warthogs often sleep in aardvark holes!

Warthogs have manes, much like horses and wildebeests.

This is a red river hog. While it has some features in common with a pig, it is clearly different from a pig.

There is a lot of confusion in the terminology used to refer to the members of family Suidae. As I already told you, male pigs are called "boars." However, there is one species of pig, *Sus scrofa*, that is also called "wild boar." This is unfortunate, because females of that species are called "wild boars," even though they are sows. In addition, there is a lot of confusion between the words "hog" and "pig." In the United States, "hog" is used to refer to a pig that weighs more than 120 pounds. However, from a scientific point of view, hogs are not pigs. Hogs are really their own group within family Suidae. The red river hog pictured above, for example, is a hog. The ears alone tell you that it is not a pig.

Creation Confirmation

Though pigs were domesticated and kept for food for thousands of years, one group of people were told by God never to eat pigs: the Israelites. In Leviticus 11:7, God tells them, "and the pig, for though it divides the hoof, thus making a split hoof, it does not chew cud, it is unclean to you." Why would God tell the Israelites that pig meat is unclean?

It turns out that pig meat (pork) can be home to many things that cause disease for people. For example, there is a kind of worm that infests pork and causes a disease called **trichinosis** (trik' uh noh' sis) that can be fatal. To completely rid pork of this worm, the meat must be frozen at 5 degrees for 21 days or -22 degrees for 25 hours. Clearly, such processing was not available to the people of Old Testament times; thus, God decided to protect His people from trichinosis by simply forbidding them to eat pork. Even with today's rigid inspection standards that exist for meat products, undercooked pork can still cause trichinosis.

Now it is important to understand that the Israelites did not know about trichinosis or other disease-causing things in pork. Because God knew, however, He prohibited His people from eating pigs in order to keep them safe. To some people, it may have seemed like a silly, religious rule to not let them eat the meat that other cultures ate. However, it was a rule that helped keep God's people safe. In fact, scientists who study the dietary regulations set forth in the Old Testament generally agree that following such a diet would have made the Israelites much healthier than the other tribes that lived during Old Testament times. This might be the reason why the Jewish race is still alive and well today, despite the fact that most of the other races mentioned in the Old Testament (like the Hittites) are not. We can always trust that God has our best interests at heart, even if His rules seem too strict. Christians are no longer bound by the dietary rules in the Old Testament, however, because God told Peter he could eat the animals that were previously declared unclean (Acts 10:9-16).

Family Tayassuidae

This is a collared peccary, also called a javelina.

Peccaries (pek' uh reez) form another family of even-toed ungulates called **Tayassuidae** (tay yuh soo' uh dee). Take out the "tayas" part, and you have the name for the family that contains pigs. These creatures are much like pigs, with a few differences. Peccaries have long, thin legs, and tend to be smaller and thinner than pigs. Their tusks are also different from those of a pig. While a pig's tusks curl away from the face, a peccary's tusks grow straight down. Also, peccaries live in herds that include the males. Peccaries also have a powerful musk gland on the top of the rump. Basically…they really stink. Their odor is always present and gets worse when they are mad or excited. You'll probably know that a peccary is nearby *before* you see it.

Another difference between pigs and peccaries is where they are indigenous. Pigs are indigenous to the Old World, while peccaries are indigenous to the New World. Now, of course, domesticated pigs are found everywhere today, but the only wild pigs in the New World are once-domesticated pigs that went feral. They are often called **razorbacks**. Peccaries, however, are truly wild pigs that are native to the New World. You can find them in the southwestern United States, Central America, and South America.

Peccaries have a spirit of **altruism** (al' troo iz' uhm). Do you know what that means? It's when someone behaves with unselfish concern for others. How do we know this about peccaries? Well, when a herd is attacked by a predator, one single peccary sometimes sacrifices himself for the good of others. He'll confront the attacker, allowing the herd to escape. In other words, he dies so that all the others may live. Who does this remind you of? It reminds me of Christ, who suffered the wages of sin so that we wouldn't have to.

The **javelina** (hah vuh lee' nuh) pictured above can be found throughout Texas. If you ever saw the movie *Old Yeller*, you've seen how they treat dogs that bark at them. The name comes from the Spanish word for "javelin" or "sword." This refers to its razor-sharp tusks, which it uses to defend itself and attack its prey. One favorite prey for javelinas is rattlesnakes, although their best-loved food is cactus. The cactus prickles don't hurt their thick snouts. They're hunted for their meat in the winter, but it's against the law to hunt them at any other time.

Family Hippopotamidae

What do you think is the most feared animal in Africa? The fierce lion? The huge elephant? Actually, it's the **hippopotamus**! With its enormous, gaping mouth and long, tusk-like canines, it can snap a boat in half, not to mention a person. Even worse, these fearsome creatures attack even when they are not provoked. These beasts have killed many more people than Africa's lions have. Violent, unpredictable, and utterly unafraid of humans, they will knock over boats and crush the

Hippos are violent animals that even attack when unprovoked.

passengers with their powerful jaws. Most deaths happen when the victim gets in the hippo's way as it is trotting to deeper water, or when the victim gets between a mother and her calf. While the lion will slaughter a human for food, the herbivorous hippo doesn't have any reason to do so, other than to harm the human. So instead of hungry, hungry hippos, as the board game suggests, they are simply angry, angry hippos.

Not only are they dangerous in the water, but they are also quite frightful out of the water. This massive, 11-foot long, 5,000-pound creature is a sight to behold when it charges at full speed, bellowing boisterously and swinging its giant head like a sledgehammer. If you think you could outrun the hippopotamus, think again; hippos can run at speeds greater than 20 miles per hour, which is faster than most humans can run. Not quite the docile creatures you imagined, are they?

The hippopotamus was named from the Greek words "hippos" (meaning "horse") and "potamos" (meaning "river"). As big as these creatures are, they are designed with a special ability to both float in the water and sink down to the bottom, depending on how they are breathing and their body position. When they sink to the bottom of a body of water, they can walk around or rest for up to five minutes at a time. God designed them to live in the water quite easily, with webbed toes, as well as eyes, ears, and nostrils located at the top of their head. Their nostrils and ears have valves that close when they sink in the water. Under the water, they appear graceful and pleasant as they trot around with surprising ease.

If you've ever spent a long time in the water on a hot, sunny day, you know that water plus sun equals sunburn. Well, that is also true for the hippopotamus, with its exposed skin. Wouldn't it be great, though, if your body just squeezed sunscreen out of its pores onto your skin? That would save you a lot of time. Well, that's exactly how God designed the water-loving hippo. Its skin puts out a reddish-brown fluid that acts as both a sunscreen and a kind of antibiotic ointment, giving it protection from microscopic creatures that could cause it to get sick.

What Do You Remember?

What is rumination? Are deer a part of the antelope group? Which animals migrate with wildebeests? What do impalas do when they are frightened or startled? Where are zebu cattle found? Tell the basic history of bison. What special features do camels have that enable them to survive in the desert? Why might you find a set of antlers with no deer attached? How do giraffes give evidence for our Creator? How did God protect the Israelites by telling them not to eat pig meat? How are peccaries different from pigs? Which is the most dangerous animal in Africa?

Map It!

Africa – Gazelles, wildebeests, impalas, duikers, giraffes, okapis, hippopotamuses, wild pigs
Asia – Water buffalo, bactrian camels, wild pigs
Middle East – Dromedary camels
North America – Bison, javelinas (just in the southwestern United States)
South America – Peccaries
You can also put deer in many parts of your map, as you can find them over most of the world.

Track It!

Deer Tracks   **Cattle Tracks**

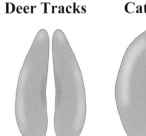 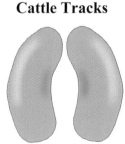

The most likely Artiodactyla tracks for you to find are those of deer and cattle. They look very similar, but deer tracks are generally slender and long, while cattle tracks are a bit wider and more circular. An adult deer's tracks are usually a bit more than 2 inches to a bit more than 3 inches long, while adult cattle tracks are usually longer.

Notebook Activity

Have you ever been to the zoo? Each zoo is designed differently. Some group the animals by types, others by continents. Some have walking trails and special exhibits that look like an animal's natural habitat. Some exhibits are simply animals in a cage. They usually have bathrooms, gift shops, and places to eat. If you were going to design a zoo, what would it look like? How would you group the animals? What kind of exhibits would you have? Today, you are going to design a zoo using the animals you have studied so far. Think it through before you begin. Write down all the animals you will have in your zoo. Make notes about what kind of habitats you will create for them. Will there be a train that takes visitors from one side to the other? What about a gondola? After you have planned your zoo, tape several pieces of paper together to make a large square or rectangle and begin mapping out your zoo. In your notebook, write down the information you will include on each of the even-toed ungulates in your zoo. If you wish, you can even make a model of your zoo. You may want to build it on a large piece of foam board, or a piece of wood so that you can move it around. To create exhibits and walkways, you could use clay, Popsicle sticks, bamboo skewers, paper plates, small boxes, colored paper, toilet paper tubes, or anything you think will work. Be creative and have fun!

Experiment

Do you remember that a giraffe has the highest blood pressure of any animal? In this experiment, you will learn why it needs such a high blood pressure. ***Do this over a sink.***

You will need:

♦ A small plastic bottle (like the kind drinking water comes in)
♦ A pin
♦ A balloon
♦ Water

1. Take the lid off the bottle and fill it so that it is nearly (but not completely) full of water.
2. Put water in the uninflated balloon. Do not add water under pressure so that the balloon expands. Just fill it with whatever water will fit in the uninflated balloon.
3. Put the opening of the balloon around the opening of the bottle so that it forms a tight seal.
4. Turn the bottle upside down, holding the bottle with one hand and the balloon with another.
5. Use the pin to poke a small hole in the bottle about an inch below the water level.
6. Watch how the water leaks out of the hole. Most likely, it will just dribble out.
7. While you are watching the hole, use the hand that is holding the balloon to squeeze it. What happens? The water squirts out in a long stream, doesn't it? That's because by squeezing the balloon, you added pressure. Squeeze the balloon a little and then a lot and note the difference.
8. Take the balloon off the bottle and empty about half the water out of the bottle. Do not pour out the water in the balloon.
9. Put the opening of the balloon back on the opening of the bottle as before, and once again, turn the bottle upside down, using one hand to hold the bottle and the other to hold the balloon.
10. Once again, use the hand holding the balloon to squeeze the balloon, and look what happens to the water in the bottle. What does it do? It rises, doesn't it?

What does this experiment tell you? It tells you that for a fluid (like blood or water) to rise, it must be under pressure. Remember, squeezing the balloon increased the pressure, and that caused the water to rise in the bottle. The harder you squeezed the balloon, the more the pressure, and the higher the water rose. Now do you understand why a giraffe needs high blood pressure?

Lesson 10
Orders Squamata and Rhynchocephalia

What is your reaction when you see this lizard, which is called a bearded dragon?

When people see a monkey in the zoo, they generally don't have a strong emotional reaction. Why, then, do people have such strong emotions when it comes to snakes and lizards? Why do they either shiver in fear or jump with excitement at the thought of a snake? Few people feel nothing at all. It's either fear or fascination. Which is it for you? Which is it for your parents? Well, however you feel about them, they are special and important creatures made by God.

You have studied reptiles before in Zoology 2, so you already know what makes a reptile a reptile. You learned about how they reproduce, how they breathe, their skin, and all the other features that make these creeping creatures, known as **herps**, unique. Yet, we studied only the reptiles that spend most or all of their lives in the water. In this lesson, we'll discuss the herps that live on the land.

Reptiles

Class **Reptilia** contains lizards, turtles, snakes, and the like. It comes from a Latin word that means "to creep." That's quite fitting, since we're now on the part of the book where we study the creeping things. Most reptiles creep or slither, and most can swim. Because they're **ectothermic** (cold-blooded), most reptiles warm themselves by basking in the sun. They are covered with thick, scaly skin from head to toe. This keeps them from drying out as they catch some rays. In fact, the scales are what separate them from other animals. Unlike the scales of a fish, a reptile's scales can't be removed one by one. They all grow as one whole piece. They don't stretch, so a reptile must **molt** in order to grow bigger. Their skin basically dries up and peels off – either in one piece or in flakes. Once the skin has peeled, the new skin stretches into place. Ah! That feels better! I'm sure if our skin got tighter and tighter as we grew, we'd enjoy a good molt now and then.

There are four different orders of reptiles that are currently living in God's creation: **Squamata** (sqwah mah' tuh), **Testudines** (test uh deen' eez), **Crocodilia** (crok uh dil' ee uh), and **Rhynchocephalia** (ring' koh suh fail' ee uh). Squamata contains lizards and snakes, Testudines contains turtles and tortoises, Crocodilia contains alligators and crocodiles, and Rhynchocephalia contains the lonely tuatara. We'll cover orders Squamata and Rhynchocephalia in this lesson. In the next lesson, we'll cover orders Crocodilia and Testudines, and we'll also squeeze in their slimy friends, the amphibians.

Snakes

The word "Squamata" comes from the Latin "squama," which means "scale," so it is no surprise that order Squamata contains lizards and snakes, which are often called **squamates** (sqwah' maytz). Let's begin our discussion of this order with the most unlikable kind of squamate – the snake. Has anyone ever stared at you without blinking? It gets a bit creepy after a while, doesn't it? When we were children, we often played a game to see who would blink first in a staring contest. Well, if you played that game with a snake, the snake would win, because snakes don't blink. You see, rather than eyelids, snakes just have a transparent layer of skin over their eyes. This layer sheds when the squamate molts.

This is the skin from a snake after it molted.

Have you ever seen a snake's skin without the snake inside? The way a snake molts is quite fascinating. First, the new skin begins to grow under the old skin. The old skin starts to get dull in color – even the eye coverings cloud over, causing the snake to be nearly blind. Well, as you may have guessed, this makes the snake vulnerable to predators. So, it usually hides somewhere to do its molting – somewhere wet is preferred because moisture makes the molt go faster. Then, after the eyes cloud over, the skin around the lips loosens and is slowly forced back over the head, neck and body. The snake crawls through narrow crevices and over anything rough in an attempt to crawl out of the old skin. Once the old skin is gone, the snake must feel wonderful because its new skin is shiny, its colors are bright, and most important of all…its eyes have returned to their usual unblinking, sharp-seeing state. Most adult snakes molt two to five times a year. Juveniles molt more often because they grow more quickly.

The fangs on this snake's upper jaw are hollow so they can inject venom into its prey.

Because they are ectothermic, snakes may bask in the sun to warm up or crawl under the ground or under leaf litter to cool down. Some snakes rest in water to cool off on hot summer days, because most every snake can swim.

Unlike turtles, all snakes have teeth. Usually, they are thin, needle-like teeth in their upper and lower jaws that point backward. Can you think of any reason that a snake's teeth would point that way? This design makes it difficult for captured prey to escape once it has been bitten. Some snakes have hollow fangs in the front of the mouth that are used to inject venom (poison). You may remember from Zoology 2 that snake venom is either a **neurotoxin** (noor oh tahk' sin), that makes the muscles (including those that control breathing) stop working, or a **hemotoxin** (hee muh tahk' sin), which interferes with an animal's blood flow. In the United States, there are only four types of venomous snakes: **rattlesnakes**, **copperheads**, **cottonmouths**, and **coral snakes**. Australia, on the other hand, has at least 21 species of venomous snakes, including the much-feared death adders.

The truth is, many snakes are non-venomous and, though they may bite if you pick them up, their bite won't do any lasting harm to you. How do you feel about snakes? Do you think the earth would be a better place without them? Well, aside from the serpent in the Garden of Eden, the earth really needs snakes. You see, the rat population would quickly take over the world if we had no snakes. Snakes help keep the populations of insects and rodents under control. In fact, snakes such as the black rat snake are called the "farmer's friend" because of the rat control they provide.

Snakes have the same senses as other vertebrates, but they can't hear sounds the way mammals do. This is because they do not have ear openings. Instead, they detect vibrations that travel through the ground or water. As you study more science, you will learn that sound really is just a series of vibrations that travel through air, walls, ground, etc., so when a snake detects vibrations, it is detecting sound. As a result, it's difficult to surprise a snake. Of course, snakes will generally try to hide or slither away if they hear you coming.

What if you could stick out your tongue and taste the food Mom was making in the kitchen? A snake's sense of taste and smell combine so that it can do just that! A snake flicks its forked tongue out into the air to gather odor and dust particles from the environment. The tongue moves these particles to the roof of its mouth, where they are collected by the **Jacobson's organ**. This organ tells the snake what's out there. So, like the Bible says would happen to the serpent, snakes eat dust! However, this is a good thing for the snake, for it is often how the snake finds its dinner.

Some snakes, called **pit vipers**, have another special sense. They can actually sense heat. Remember, warm-blooded animals have body temperatures usually higher than the temperature of

Snakes "taste the air" with their tongues.

their surroundings. It is impossible for us to see this without very complicated equipment, but pit vipers have special sensory organs (pits) in their head between their eyes and nostrils. These organs are considered by some to be the most sensitive heat detectors in the world. This means that even in total darkness, a pit viper can detect and pinpoint anything with a temperature different from its surroundings. As a result, pit vipers tend to hunt for prey at night. After all, they have no problem finding their prey with their heat-sensing pits, but their prey will have a hard time seeing them coming.

All snakes are carnivorous, but most would not be interested in eating you. Small snakes eat insects, spiders, and earthworms, while large snakes eat rabbits, birds, mice, rats, and frogs. Giant snakes eat even bigger things, like kangaroos and other large creatures. They eat by swallowing their prey whole. Many simply bite their prey and open wide their mouth to begin eating the struggling creature. The creature is caught in the backward-facing teeth, while muscles in the neck produce waves that move the creature down into the snake. Others kill their prey with their poison and then swallow. Some snakes are **constrictors**. After striking, the snake loops its body once or more around its prey and tightens the coils each time the animal exhales. The animal eventually cannot breathe and dies from suffocation.

You can see the ligament that makes it possible for the snake to open its mouth so wide.

Snakes are able to eat prey wider than their own body. This is because their lower jaw is loosely attached to their skull with connective tissue called **ligament** (lig' uh munt). This allows the mouth to open much wider than is possible with other animals. In this way, a large animal can be swallowed by a medium-sized snake. However, a large meal makes a snake vulnerable, since digesting a large creature makes moving difficult. Also, the digestion process is slow, and it is possible for parts of the dead animal to rot before it is digested! Nevertheless, most snakes eat large enough prey that they go several days or even a few months between meals.

Most snakes track their prey by sight and smell. Pit vipers also use their ability to detect heat. Herpetologists (scientists who study snakes) sometimes classify snakes into two categories based on how they hunt their prey. **Ambush predators**, such as rattlesnakes, lie motionless for hours, waiting for prey to pass within striking distance. **Active hunters**, on the other hand, go in search of prey using their senses to find and track the animals they want to eat.

Snake Defense

Although snakes are predators, they are also prey. Almost every carnivorous animal will eat a snake. Birds, cats, raccoons, and alligators are examples of snake predators. In fact, many snakes prey on other snakes! A snake's number one defense against predators is escape. Snakes are more afraid of you than you are of them, and if they can escape, they will. If they can't slink away, they will often try to lie motionless, hoping you don't see them. Yet, if they are discovered, they try to scare you away. Generally, they attack only as a last resort.

Many snakes try to trick you into thinking they are much bigger than they really are. They'll flatten their neck to make their head look wider and their body look bigger. Harmless water snakes do this, making themselves look like venomous cottonmouths. **Cobras** are also famous for doing this. They raise themselves up and stretch out their hood – the skin near the head. This makes them look bigger to scare off any animal thinking of attacking. Of course, if the animal decides to attack, cobras can cause a lot of harm. Their venom is a powerful neurotoxin that can even kill a person. So, if you see a cobra stretch out its hood, you need to get away. The good news is that you can run a lot faster than any snake. However, if a snake is in striking distance, you don't want to move quickly because it will get scared and strike you. Although you can outrun a snake, you most likely aren't fast enough to avoid its quick strike! Move slowly and carefully until there is lot of distance between you, and then run. Spitting cobras can spit venom on a predator from a long way off. The venom is dangerous if it gets into an eye, but it's harmless if it only gets on the skin.

This cobra is trying to make itself look bigger because it feels threatened.

Some snakes try to scare off threatening animals by hissing. They do this by forcing air out of the lungs through the throat. Can you do that? Try it and see if you are able to hiss as well. Other snakes release a foul odor. This often discourages predators that don't like eating smelly animals. Other snakes open their mouth wide to reveal their teeth. The cottonmouth, for example, gapes its mouth open, showing its cotton-white mouth. Some snakes even pretend to be dead. The hognose snake will roll over on its back, hang its tongue out of its mouth, and emit a foul odor.

The last resort, of course, is to bite. If the snake is not venomous, the bite is usually like getting a cut or a scratch and only requires a little soap and water to clean it up. A bite from a pit viper or a coral snake can be a serious thing and requires immediate treatment at a hospital with antivenin. Interestingly enough, however, a venomous snake will not always inject venom when it bites. Such "dry bites" are thought to be another way to scare away threatening creatures.

What have you learned so far about snakes?

Baby Snakes

Most snakes lay eggs. When a female snake is about to lay eggs, her tail gets very fat. She lays a clutch of leathery eggs in a hole, under a log, or in some other hiding place. Some snakes, such as mud snakes and rainbow snakes, stay with their eggs until they hatch. King cobras are known to be

The white point at the center of this baby snake's mouth is its egg tooth.

especially good parents, with both the male and the female watching over the eggs. You may remember this from the story of Rikki-Tikki-Tavi. Another good parent is the python. Mother pythons wrap their bodies around their eggs to keep them from getting too warm or too cold while they develop. Others snakes might remain a few days and then depart, leaving the eggs to chance.

Like most animals that hatch from eggs, snake hatchlings have an **egg tooth** designed to tear open the shell so that the baby snake can get out of the egg when ready. When the young hatch, they look just like their mom and dad, except for the egg tooth. The first time they shed their skin, the egg tooth disappears. Now please understand that not *all* snakes lay eggs. Some mother snakes keep their eggs inside their body until they hatch, and the young then come out of their mother's body. This is not the same as mammals. A mammal mother provides nourishment for her young as it develops. A snake that keeps her eggs inside her body does not nourish the developing babies. They get their nourishment from the egg. If you remember from Zoology 2, we call such animals ovoviviparous (oh voh vye vip' ur us).

Slithering Snakes

How does a snake move without legs? Well, it has special scales on its belly called **scutes** (skootz). These scales can actually grip the ground and push the snake forward. Larger snakes that are fairly heavy will simply lift their scutes forward, grip the ground with them, and then push the ground with them. This pushes the snake forward in a straight line, and is called **rectilinear** (rek' tuh lin' ee ur) **motion**.

scutes

Notice that the scales (scutes) on the underside of this rat snake are quite different from the scales on top of its body.

Most snakes, however, aren't heavy enough for this to be an effective way to move. As a result, snakes also move by **lateral undulation** (un' juh lay' shun). In this motion, the snake shapes its body into an "S," and the muscles push against tiny irregularities in the surface, such as pebbles, twigs, and plants. This is the "slithering" motion that most people associate with snakes.

Snakes might also use **concertina** (kon sur tee' nuh) **motion**. This is when the snake anchors the back of its body with its scutes and then extends the front part of its body forward. Then, it anchors the front part of its body with its scutes, releases the back scutes, and pulls the back of the body forward. They do this to move forward in tight spaces or to climb trees. Other snakes use a **sidewinding** motion, especially when trying to move on smooth surfaces that have little to hold onto. In this motion, a snake lifts its head off the ground and pushes it in the direction of travel. When the head lands, it picks up the next section of its body and pushes it in the same direction, leaving the rest of its body in contact with the ground. It continues to do this over and over. This process is called sidewinding because the snake travels sideways rather than in the direction the body is pointing. If you are having trouble visualizing this kind of motion, go to the course website I told you about in the introduction. You will find links to diagrams of how these kinds of motion work.

Though snakes are quite good at moving forward, they are pretty slow. Most snakes travel at 1 to 3 miles per hour. If it can't hide, you could easily catch it. The fastest snake on earth, the black mamba, has a maximum speed of under 13 miles an hour, and it can only do that for a short amount of time. These "speed demons" live in the tropical regions of Africa.

Harmless or Venomous?

Since a few thousand people in the United States get bitten by venomous snakes every year, it is a good idea to be able to recognize the venomous snakes that are out there. In the United States, it is fairly easy to tell which snakes are venomous, because three of the kinds of venomous snakes (rattlesnakes, copperheads, and cottonmouths) are pit vipers. They are easy to identify because they have pits between their eyes and nostrils. That's where they detect heat. The other kind of poisonous snake in the United States is the coral snake, and it has pretty red, black and yellow patterns on its skin. Some non-venomous stakes have the same basic colors, but you can identify the coral snake by remembering this simple rhyme: "Red on black, poison lack. Red on yellow kills a fellow." In other words, if the red markings are next to the yellow markings, you have a coral snake that is venomous. Otherwise, you have a non-venomous snake, like the king snake.

The snake on the left is a pit viper, which is venomous. You can tell this by the pit between its eye and nostril. The middle one is a venomous coral snake (yellow touches red). The right one is a non-venomous king snake (red touches black).

There are other methods for trying to identify venomous from non-venomous snakes, but they are either difficult to employ or not always reliable. For example, the scutes of a non-venomous snake usually form a single row over the entire underside of the snake, while the scutes of venomous snakes often split into two rows near the tail. This, of course, is often hard to see, because snakes don't usually show their undersides. It is also not always true. In the same way, the pupils of many non-venomous snakes are often round (like a person's pupils), while the pupils of venomous snakes are often more oval, like a cat's. However, snake eyes are small, so their pupils are hard to see from a distance, and once again, this is not always true. A coral snake's pupils, for example, are rounded.

There are many misconceptions about identifying harmless and venomous snakes. For example, some have said that if the snake shakes its tail in the air, it's venomous. That's because some venomous snakes, like the **rattlesnake**, do that. A rattlesnake has modified scales on the end of its tail that bang against each other when it shakes its tail, making a rattling sound. However, many harmless snakes vibrate their tails when confronted. In dry leaves, this could even make a rattling sound. Another misconception is that a large, triangular head means a snake

The venomous rattlesnake "warns" you that it is thinking about striking by shaking its rattle.

is venomous. While this is often true, it is not *always* true. Many harmless water snakes flatten and expand their head when frightened, causing them to resemble the dangerous cottonmouth.

There are even those who think that any snake that is in water is venomous. That is not true. While all sea snakes (snakes that live in the *oceans*) are venomous, few snakes that swim in freshwater are. In the United States, the cottonmouth (also known as the **water moccasin**) is the only poisonous water snake. It is a pit viper, however, so it can be identified by the pits between its eyes and nostrils. It also has a white mouth. This particular snake is quite aggressive and will often stand its ground instead of trying to escape.

Outside the United States, it's more difficult to tell venomous snakes from non-venomous ones. However, if you visit the course website I mentioned in the introduction, you can find links to websites that describe venomous snakes in other parts of the world.

Tell someone all you have learned about venomous snakes.

Snake Habitats and Families

Snakes are found everywhere on the planet except Antarctica, Iceland, Ireland, Greenland, and New Zealand. So, if you want to escape snakes altogether, you could move to one of those islands.

Imagine you are a skinny little snake. You need a place to hide and sleep. Where would you go? Well, you might slip into a hole in the ground made by another animal. You might also slip under a rock, log, or bush. You might slip under a house or leaf litter. These are all places a person might find a snake. Snakes are usually found where there are rocks, bushes, and trees. Do you have rocks, bushes, and trees nearby? If so, there are probably snakes nearby as well.

When length and weight are considered together, green anacondas like this one are the largest snakes in creation.

Some snakes are so small they may be mistaken for worms, such as **thread snakes** that grow to be only several inches long. The smallest of them can actually crawl through a pencil if the lead is removed! The largest snakes in the world are **anacondas** and **pythons**. Currently, the longest known snake in the world was a reticulated python found in Indonesia. It was 33 feet long. Imagine that! However, that snake wasn't the heaviest snake ever found. When length and weight are both considered, green anacondas are the largest snakes in the world.

There are several types of snakes, grouped by their physical features and habits. One group, the **blind snakes**, includes the thread snakes mentioned earlier. Blind snakes are not completely blind, but they do have very poor vision. They live almost their entire lives underground. They are extremely thin and covered with smooth scales that allow them to move easily through the soil. They can't open their jaw wide, and they have only a few teeth, which isn't that important since they eat termites and ants. Obviously, these little snakes don't need venom for their lifestyle, so they don't have it.

The pit vipers I already mentioned are a part of a larger grouping of snakes called the **vipers**. Vipers all have one thing in common – long, hollow fangs used to inject venom into their prey. These fangs are hinged so that they fold up against the roof of the mouth and are covered by a thin layer of tissue when not in use. As you might expect, pit vipers are special vipers that have the heat-sensing pits I mentioned earlier. In general, pit vipers are found mostly in the New World, while the vipers that do not have heat-sensing pits (like adders and sand vipers) are found in the Old World.

The next group of snakes is the **elapids** (el' uh pidz). They also have hollow fangs used to inject venom into their prey, but unlike the vipers, they cannot fold their fangs away when they are not being used. The elapids are much more dangerous than the vipers, because their venom (a neurotoxin) is many times more powerful, and they are much more aggressive. Cobras, coral snakes, mambas, and the death adder of Australia are elapids, as are the sea snakes. They are found mostly in the Southern Hemisphere or in tropical regions.

This striped whipsnake is a colubrid. It gets its name because it looks a bit like a whip.

When a snake is found outdoors or in your yard, it is probably a **colubrid** (kol' uh brid). They are sometimes called **typical snakes**, because the majority of snake species are a part of this family. They include garter snakes, grass snakes, king snakes, whipsnakes, and many others. Colubrids are generally venomless, but a few species, like the boomslang and African twig snake, do have venom. In these venomous species, the venom usually comes from fangs in the rear of the mouth. This is different from vipers and elapids, whose venom-injecting fangs are in the front of the mouth. Many colubrids kill by constricting their prey, squeezing them until they can no longer breathe.

Another group of snakes contains boas, pythons, and anacondas. These snakes are not venomous, but are quite good at catching prey, which they bite and then constrict. Once the prey has died of suffocation, the snake loosens its grip and searches for the head. It's always easier for a snake to swallow a creature head first so the legs don't get tangled up. Though these snakes grow to be enormous, they can move easily through water and ambush most of their prey in the shallows when they come to drink. This is how most animals and people are caught by anacondas. Many people keep boas and pythons as pets, and although many are strong enough to suffocate a person by constriction, few people have been killed by their pet constrictor.

Explain what you learned about snakes before moving on to the next section.

Lizards

Scurrying up walls, over fences, and diving out of sight into the brush, lizards are squamates with speed – although some prefer to take it slow. They aren't as hated as snakes, perhaps because we prefer creatures with legs, or maybe it's because most can blink their eyes, which appears friendlier than the unblinking snake. Their reputation is further enhanced with the fact that many believe that lizards are mostly not venomous. It's long been told that only a couple of lizards have venom: the **Gila** (he' luh) **monster** and the **Mexican beaded lizard** – both New World squamates. However, this belief has recently been found false. Many other lizards produce venom as well, such as the bearded dragon, Komodo dragon, and the monitor lizard. How was this venom overlooked? Well, many lizards have mouths teeming with bacteria, and scientists thought that bacteria caused the bad reactions people have to these lizards' bites. However, we now know that it is actually the lizards' venom causing these problems, but the venom is not potent enough to be deadly to people.

This striped whiptail lizard (*Cnemidophorus velox*) has the legs, eyelids, and ear holes common to most lizards.

Most lizards have four legs and five digits (outfitted with claws) on each foot. Unlike snakes, most lizards have ears. You can see their ear holes on the sides of their head. They usually have eyelids that can blink. Many of them also have a tail that can break off if grabbed by a bird, raccoon, or quick-fingered child. This defense culminates with the tail squirming and flipping around for several minutes after it is broken. A wiggling tail distracts the predator so that the lizard can escape. The tail automatically grows back. You can tell when a lizard has grown a new tail because it's a different color from the rest of the lizard.

Not all lizards share the features above. There are some lizards with no ears, and there are some that can't blink. Some lizard species, such as glass lizards and legless lizards, have no functional legs. That's right. There are lizards with no legs. "So," you wonder, "why aren't they just called snakes?" Well, they have eyelids, ears, and a tail that can break off. That makes them lizards.

Lizards have a wide variety of tongues. A few, like Komodo dragons, have a forked tongue that flicks in and out. Chameleons, on the other hand, have a sticky tip to their extremely long tongue that unfurls to nab insects on nearby leaves. In the same way, they have a wide variety of scales. A lizard's scales may be rough, as is the case with the bearded dragon, or smooth, like the scales of an anole. They can also produce horns, ridges, or spikes. Most lizards have rather sharp teeth, but they rarely bite.

A chameleon has a long tongue with a sticky end that can shoot out quickly enough to catch an insect unawares.

Lizards also move around in a lot of different ways. The ones with legs can walk, but many are often great climbers. In a while, you will learn about the gecko, which uses advanced technology to be able to climb on smooth surfaces. Though most lizards stay on all fours when walking, the basilisk lizard can run short distances on two legs. In fact, it can even run across water, which has earned it the nickname "Jesus lizard." If you go to the course website I told you about in the introduction, you will find a link to a video of a basilisk lizard running on water.

Like all squamates, lizards molt. You won't find lizard skins lying around the jungle, however. Their skin molts in patches, coming off a little at a time. Also, many lizards actually eat their molted skin, which contains a lot of protein. While there are many different types of lizards (just as there are many different types of snakes), I will concentrate on the ones that show the diversity of the order.

The Iguania

You are probably familiar with **iguanas**, since they are popular pets. However, you may not know that scientists group them with **anoles**, **chameleons**, and **agamas** because they share similar traits. While anoles can be found in South America, southern North America, and the West Indies, iguanas are found in the tropical Americas, the Antilles, the Galapagos Islands, and Fiji. Chameleons live in Africa, Madagascar, southern Spain, and parts of Asia, while agamas are found in Africa, Asia, and Australia.

This Mediterranean chameleon is normally a very light green, but it turned dark due to being frightened by a dog.

Many lizards in the Iguania grouping can change colors, like the chameleon. Despite what you may have heard, chameleons do not purposely change colors to blend into their surroundings. Instead, each species has a range of colors and patterns that it can display, and many of them are designed to allow the chameleon to blend into its surroundings. However, it is not the surroundings that determine whether or not a chameleon changes color. Usually, things like the amount of light, the time of day, the desire to mate, or specific moods will cause a chameleon to change colors. A chameleon actually has four layers of skin that help it accomplish its color changes. The outer layer (epidermis) is for protection, the next layer down contains yellow and red colors, the next layer down contains darker colors like brown and blue, and the last layer appears white. A chameleon can change the amount of color in each layer, which causes these colors to blend differently, producing various colors and patterns. In addition to this nice color-changing ability, many chameleons have one or more horns growing out of their head.

Iguanas and agamas are rather similar. In fact, agamas are often called the "iguanas of the Old World." One of the more interesting lizards in the agama grouping is the **frill-necked lizard**. Found in New Guinea and Australia, this lizard has a ruff of skin that usually lies back against its neck. When frightened, however, the lizard flares out this ruff of skin to make what looks like an umbrella around its neck. If this isn't enough to scare away the perceived danger, the lizard will also hiss and lunge as if to bite.

This frill-necked lizard (*Chlamydosaurus kingii*) obviously feels threatened.

This anole is showing his dewlap.

Anoles (uh noh' leez) also belong to the Iguania group. These common New World lizards are mostly arboreal, and some of them can be vocal, crying out with squeals when stressed. Most males have a brightly colored flap of skin under the throat called a **dewlap** (doo' lap). It is used to attract a mate, and it can also be used to make the lizard look more formidable than it normally is. Dewlaps appear in other animals throughout creation. For example, go back and look at the picture of the zebu on page 154. Notice the flap of skin under his throat. That's a dewlap as well!

Geckos

Though you may think of lizards as quiet little creatures, this isn't always so. Geckos talk, making chirping sounds that they use to interact with other geckos. They talk a lot, but generally it's at night. In fact, their name comes from a Malay word that is an attempt to imitate the sound they make. Geckos are found in warm climates throughout the world, and in some countries, are known as "chit-chat lizards."

Most geckos have no eyelids and therefore cannot blink. However, they have legs and ear holes, so they are not snakes. While not all species of gecko are able to climb, that is the behavior for which they

This leopard gecko is not a typical gecko, as it has eyelids. It also doesn't climb as well as most geckos.

are best known. Climbing geckos seem to be able to climb on any surface, no matter how smooth or slick. In the next section, you will learn how they can do this.

Geckos are one of the few lizards that have made their home with people. In warm climates, they are a common sight inside homes, businesses, and schools – high up on the walls where they crawl around looking for insects. Leopard geckos are also a good pet for children, as they don't climb well, are slow, and are friendly. One kind of gecko, called the flying gecko, has webbed feet and flaps of skin it can spread out to glide from one high place to another.

Creation Confirmation

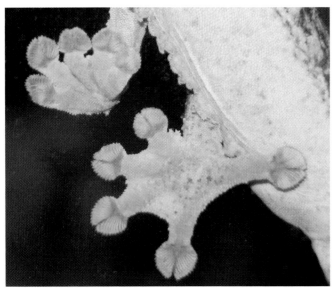

If you magnified the ridges on the pads of this gecko's feet, you would see millions of tiny hairs, called setae.

Some lizards are great climbers. They use their long claws to grip cracks and crevices in a surface. However, climbing geckos use molecular force, which allows them to climb up incredibly smooth surfaces, like glass! You see, a gecko's toes are covered by millions of hair-like projections called **setae** (seh' tee). These setae can lie across any surface and get so close that they can actually stick to the *molecules* that make up the surface! This design is so amazing that to this day, human science cannot come close to imitating it. Indeed, scientists have tried, but the artificial structures they produce when trying to copy the gecko's toes lose their ability to stick to surfaces after only a few uses.

This never happens with a gecko. The very fact that scientists cannot come close to making what the gecko uses by instinct tells you what an awesome Designer made the gecko!

Skinks

Skinks are squamates with long, flat bodies; a long tail; and a small, pointy head. They look snake-like, and while most have tiny legs, some actually have no legs at all. However, they have eyelids and ear holes, so they are not snakes. They can be found all over the world, except in Antarctica. About half of the species lay eggs, while the other half allow the eggs to develop and hatch within the mother. They are generally carnivorous, eating insects, spiders, worms, snails, and other lizards.

Notice how snake-like the body of this skink is.

The Large Lizards

This Nile monitor lizard is 6 feet long.

While we generally think of lizards as small, creeping animals, there are some very large lizards as well. Consider, for example, the **monitor lizards**, which can be found in Africa, Asia, Papua New Guinea, and Australia. They have long necks and a narrow head with a pointed snout. They also have a forked tongue (much like that of a snake), which they use to taste the air. They are carnivorous and cannot chew. Thus, they tend to swallow their prey whole. If the prey is too large (they cannot open their mouths as wide as snakes can), they try to tear the dead animal into smaller pieces and swallow each piece whole.

Many monitor lizards have an interesting way of "caring" for their eggs. They dig into termite mounds, destroying them. There, they lay their eggs. When the termites repair the mound, the eggs are protected in a warm environment, and they have instant access to food when they hatch!

The **Komodo dragon** is an Indonesian monitor that can grow longer than 9 feet, making it the largest lizard in creation. While these bulky giants prefer to eat carrion that is long dead, they are good hunters that hide and ambush their prey when it walks past. When forced to hunt, they will eat almost any large animal, including buffalos, wild pigs, deer, and even each other. As I mentioned before, it was once thought that Komodo

The tongue helps identify this Komodo dragon as a monitor lizard.

dragons were not venomous. However, we now know that they do have venom in their saliva. Though not potent enough to kill a human, it does help them bring down their prey.

Though many lizards have now been found to have venom, few are dangerous to humans. However, there are two lizards with venom fatal to humans, and they both are in the New World: the Mexican beaded lizard, which lives in the Mexican desert, and the Gila monster, found in the deserts and scrubs of the southwestern United States. While the former uses its venom to kill its prey, the Gila monster rarely uses its venom while hunting, indicating that it is used more for self-defense.

Worm Lizards

This is a lizard, not a worm or snake!

Remember how I told you that God's creation doesn't always fit well into people's attempts to classify it? The **worm lizards** are an example of that. These squamates are neither worms nor snakes. They are lizards designed for an underground existence. They spend most of their time underground and are usually legless, though some have small claws near their heads for digging. They use their head to ram into the ground, forming tunnels as they go. Their nostrils face backward so dirt doesn't get inside, and their mouths are on their underside, tightly closed. They have segments, making them look like an earthworm. In fact, the European worm lizard is the color of an earthworm, to further confuse the matter.

So, why are they not earthworms? Well, worms are invertebrates, which means they have no backbones. These squamates have a backbone. They also have the internal anatomy similar to lizards and snakes. Their underground life makes them difficult to study, and their small size makes them difficult to dissect. As a result, not much is known about them.

Tuataras

Although this lesson is mostly about the squamates, I cannot talk about reptiles without mentioning the wonderful **tuatara** (too' uh tar' uh). Even though it looks like a lizard, it is really very different from the animals in order Squamata. Tuatara fossils have been found alongside dinosaur fossils, so some people mistakenly claim that tuataras are dinosaurs. They are not. You'll learn about dinosaurs later on in this course, and you'll understand why tuataras are not dinosaurs. The only place on earth that these interesting reptiles have survived is

You will only see living tuataras in zoos or in New Zealand.

New Zealand and some of the surrounding islands. The name "tuatara" means "spine-bearer" and comes from the language of the Maori people, who are native to New Zealand.

So why aren't tuataras lizards? Well, tuataras have no ear holes, as lizards do. And they also love cool weather, which is not typical among lizards. They do their best when it is about 50 degrees, while most lizards do their best at temperatures of around 80 degrees.

You probably didn't know this, but some reptiles have three eyes. Yes, three! The third eye, often called the **pineal** (pih' nee uhl) **eye**, is on top of the head between the two normal eyes. The tuatara's pineal eye is particularly useful. In young tuataras, you can actually see it – a translucent scale on top of the head. As the tuatara ages, however, it becomes covered with normal skin. That's okay, though, since it is not used for seeing, but for telling light from dark. This is an important feature for this nocturnal reptile.

Tuataras grow for 20 years, but very slowly. They are one of the slowest-growing reptiles of all. They only molt once a year and can live to be over 100 years old. So, although they take a long time to grow and mature, they live a long time as well. They grow to be about 2 feet long when they are fully grown. Fossils of tuataras show that they were once about 4 feet long. So, they have shrunk over the years, as have most animals. They range in color from green to orange, but are usually brownish.

Tuataras hide from danger.

Tuataras tend to run and hide from danger. They find refuge in burrows, even if the burrow belongs to another animal! In fact, they commonly share burrows with seabirds in New Zealand. Since the birds are mostly diurnal and the tuatara is mostly nocturnal, this can seem like a good arrangement. However, it's not as good as you might think, because tuataras do eat bird eggs and young birds, along with insects. The tuatara's favorite meal consists of beetles.

Tuatara eggs take a long time to hatch, usually 13 to 16 months. An egg sitting under the ground this long is likely to be found by rats, foxes, dogs, wild hogs, burrowing crabs, etc. Once an animal finds the nest of eggs, it can return again and again over the course of a year to fill up whenever it is hungry. This is easy for the predator to do, since the parents do not guard the nest. The mother lays the eggs and then leaves.

Why have tuataras survived only in New Zealand? One reason is that they had fewer predators there than in other parts of the world. Once the exploring Europeans arrived, however, rats and dogs jumped off the ships. Also, the Europeans brought foxes for fox hunts and pigs for food. This introduced all sorts of new predators that have decimated tuatara populations. As a result, tuataras are in danger of becoming extinct. Today, tuataras are being introduced to islands that have no rats. This will help their survival.

Living Fossils

Tuataras were once thought of as lizards that were specific to the New Zealand area, until one day a scientist studying its skeleton found it was nearly identical to fossils that had been found alongside dinosaur fossils over much of the world. Until this time, scientists thought those fossils represented a group of reptiles that died out along with the dinosaurs. These reptiles were a part of order Rhynchocephalia, and it was assumed that all members of that order were extinct. Now we know that at least one member, the tuatara, is alive and well and living in New Zealand. As a result, tuataras are often called "living fossils," because they are living versions of something once thought to only exist in the fossil record.

Creation Confirmation

The wonderful tuatara gives us even more evidence for the reality of the global flood as described in the Bible. You see, there are many scientists who believe that the earth is billions of years old. In fact, they think the rocks that contain fossils are millions and millions of years old.

The rocks that contain fossils usually form in layers, and many scientists believe it takes tens of millions of years for each major rock layer to form. As a result, they think that each rock layer you find represents a specific time in earth's past, with the rocks underneath being millions of years older than the rocks above. Since dinosaurs are found in rock layers that are underneath many other rock layers, they think dinosaurs lived long ago – up to 250 million years ago! Since they don't find any dinosaur fossils in rock layers thought to be younger than 65 million years old, they think dinosaurs went extinct about 65 million years ago. If that were true, however, tuataras should be extinct also, since their fossils have not been found in rock layers thought to be younger than 135 million years old!

Fossil-bearing rock forms in layers, and some scientists think the layers represent long periods in earth's past. They also think the lower layers are millions of years older than the upper layers.

Think about it. If the scientists who believe that the earth is billions of years old are right, there should be tuatara fossils found in rock layers that are supposed to be younger than 135 million years old. After all, how in the world could tuataras fail to form fossils for 135 million years if they were living, eating, reproducing, and dying for all that time? They formed fossils just fine before then! The very fact that you cannot find tuatara fossils in layers of rock with other currently living New Zealand animals tells you that these scientists are wrong in their interpretation of the rocks and what they mean.

Of course, you and I know better. We know that science confirms what the Bible says – that the earth was covered by a worldwide flood, which caused the death of many creatures. It's also what formed most of the fossil-bearing rock layers we find today. The fact that we find tuatara fossils only in rock layers that are underneath other rock layers is not because they went extinct 135 million years ago! It's because of the nature of how the Flood took over the earth.

Creation scientists understand that the layers of rock we find in the ground do not represent long periods of time in earth's past. Instead, they represent different stages of the Flood, different regions of the earth, and certain local catastrophes that happened since the Flood. When creation scientists see that tuatara fossils are found with dinosaur fossils, they know this doesn't mean tuataras and dinosaurs lived millions of years ago. It means tuataras lived in the same general areas as did dinosaurs and were caught and fossilized by the Flood in the same areas where dinosaurs were also caught and fossilized.

What Do You Remember?

What do all reptiles have in common? What kinds of animals are in order Squamata? Why don't snakes blink? How are their eyes protected? How do snakes consume their prey? What tooth does a reptile lose after its first molt? Why don't you find molted lizard skins, even though you can find molted snake skins? What is unique about gecko feet? What is the difference between a tuatara and a lizard? If a legless lizard looks like a worm, why isn't it considered a worm? How do tuataras give us evidence for the Flood as described in the Bible?

Map It!

Because snakes and lizards are found all over the world, choose a few from your lesson that only inhabit certain regions and place them on your map. Here are some ideas:

Indonesia – Komodo dragons
North America – Gila monsters, Mexican beaded lizards, anoles, geckos
Africa and Madagascar – Chameleons

Australia – Frilled-neck lizards, death adders
South America – Boas, iguanas
Middle East - Leopard geckos
Southeast Asia - King cobras

Track It!

Snakes and lizards usually don't leave tracks, but in really wet mud or sand, you can sometimes find them. Snakes usually leave a line. If the snake is sidewinding, it actually leaves several lines, each separated from the other. Lizards will leave feet marks with a line between them. That line results from their tail dragging on the ground. See the drawings on the next page for examples of squamate tracks.

Lizard tracks tend to look like the drawing on the left. Depending on the species, the front and back feet may be of different sizes or roughly the same size. The main feature, however, is a tail mark running between the feet. The picture on the right is of snake "tracks" in the sand. This snake was sidewinding, moving diagonally from the upper left-hand corner of the picture to the lower right-hand corner.

Notebook Activities

A Venn diagram is a wonderful tool that helps you compare and contrast different things. The drawing on the right is an example of what a Venn diagram looks like. Use a sheet of paper to make your own Venn diagram where you compare lizards and snakes.

In this space, write things about lizards that aren't true about snakes.

In this space, write things that are true about both.

In this space, write things about snakes that aren't true about lizards.

Make a page for your notebook titled "Special Snake Abilities." On that sheet, describe how snakes "taste the air" with their tongues and can swallow things much bigger than they are. Draw illustrations or cut out pictures to help make your points. Choose two of the lizards discussed in the book and make a page in your notebook that describes those lizards and the interesting things you have learned about them. Finally, write a speech that describes how the tuatara shows that the biblical account of the Flood is more scientifically reliable than the idea that rocks are millions of years old.

Project

Do you know which venomous snakes are found in your state? Your project today will be to research the poisonous snakes in your area. Learn where they are found and how to identify them. When you are done with your research, create a poster with pictures of the different poisonous snakes in your area along with maps of where they can be found.

Optional Project

The best way to learn about squamates is to raise one. Leopard geckos, for example, make great pets. They are fairly easy to care for and don't take up too much space. Go to a pet store or check out the links on the course website to learn where to get a pet gecko (or other squamate) and how to care for it.

Lesson 11
The Rest of the Reptiles…and Amphibians

Let's complete our study of reptiles with a dip into the watery world of orders **Testudines** and **Crocodilia**. Then we'll finish the lesson with a slippery swim amid hopping and creeping creatures that live a dual life.

Order Testudines

Do you remember the sea turtles you studied in Zoology 2? Well, now we are going to study turtles that live mostly on land. I'm sure you remember the identifying feature of a turtle – the shell on its back. In Zoology 2, we discussed how the shell is made of bone covered with scales, or scutes. Do you remember what the parts of the shell are called? The top is the **carapace**, and the bottom is the

plastron. Did you know that the shape of a turtle's carapace tells us about its life? Land species usually have a domed shell that's difficult for predators to crush or break with a bite. Aquatic species, like pond turtles, generally have a lower, streamlined carapace that sails smoothly through the water.

You may think that all turtles can pull their head and feet inside their shell and close it up. However, that's not the case. Sea turtles cannot pull their head and limbs into their shells, but most other turtles can. In fact, scientists use how they pull their head inside the shell to split turtles into two groups. One group (**side-necked turtles**) bends it to the side and flattens it against a shoulder when tucking it under the shell. The other group (**hidden-neck turtles**) pulls the neck straight back into the shell with no bending. Even though sea turtles can't pull their head into their shells, they are put in the second group. Even though most other turtles can pull their heads into their shells, some (like the musk turtle) can't do it completely, and many don't have the ability to close up their shells once their head and legs are inside.

The box turtle (above) can fit completely in its shell, but the common musk turtle's (below) head, feet, and tail do not completely fit inside.

Turtle, Tortoise, or Terrapin?

Though we call some **tortoises**, some turtles, and some **terrapins**, they're all turtles. Many people wonder what the differences are among turtles, tortoises, and terrapins. Generally, a turtle spends most of its life in water, whether freshwater or the sea. A tortoise, on the other hand, lives mostly on dry land. In general, turtles have webbed feet for swimming, while tortoises do not have webbed feet. A terrapin is in between the two. It spends a lot of time both on dry land and in water.

Finding Food

A turtle has a beak instead of teeth.

Like snakes, turtles and tortoises do not have ears. However, they can feel vibrations and even changes in water pressure. This helps them find food. They also have a good sense of smell, which is one of the main ways they look for things to eat. Most turtles are omnivores, although there are several that eat only vegetation. All turtles are missing one thing that helps an animal chew – teeth! Instead, they have a horny beak that actually works quite well at tearing both vegetation and flesh. Since most turtles cannot chew, they must swallow their food one whole piece at a time.

Snapping Turtles

There are two species of snapping turtles: the **common snapping turtle** and the **alligator snapping turtle**. Common snappers typically have shells that are a foot or so long, and their tail is usually about the same length. They can reach weights of 20 to 30 pounds. Is that heavier than you? The alligator snapping turtle, on the other hand, can reach weights of greater than 200 pounds! Both live in freshwater, and while common snappers are found from Canada to Ecuador, the alligator snapping turtle is mostly found in the southern United States.

The common snapping turtle (above) shows you the jagged ridges on its tail. The alligator snapping turtle (below) has jagged ridges on its carapace.

Snappers are easy to identify because their tails have jagged ridges. They also have a really large head, an unusually long neck that can reach back and snap at something behind them, and webbed feet with long claws. The alligator snapping turtle has a horny shell. This makes it look something like a dinosaur, so some call it the "dinosaur of the turtles," even though it has nothing to do with dinosaurs.

The alligator snapper's method for catching prey is remarkable. Under the water, it keeps its mouth open and wiggles its tongue, which is a bright pink. Like a lure, this attracts fish that swim right into its mouth. Guess what happens next. You got it! Snap! The fish becomes food. Not only will it eat fish, frogs, and other aquatic animals that happen by, it'll eat any small duckling or dead animal that floats past as well.

Snappers cannot pull their head into their shell, so the only defense they have is to stay in the water most of the time and be super-aggressive. Indeed, they are fierce creatures; if you see one, leave it alone. Don't chase it, because it will turn around and defend itself by striking forward with amazing speed and force, snapping its jaw down on whatever it can reach. Its powerful jaws can tear flesh quite easily.

If you go swimming in a pond or lake, you may have heard that you need to watch out for snapping turtles. However, you really don't have to worry. Snappers don't go after people in the water. They're really too smart for that. They aren't interested in huge prey. Instead, they make an escape to deeper water when they see or hear something big coming. But if you corner a snapper on land or in a shallow area, that's another story.

Soft-Shelled Turtles

Even though it is only partly extended, you can see how long this soft-shelled turtle's neck is.

Soft-shelled turtles are similar to snapping turtles because they are unable to pull their head fully inside their shell. Like a snapping turtle, a soft-shelled turtle is usually aggressive, and its bite is powerful enough to remove a finger.

Guess why these small creatures are called "soft-shelled turtles"? Their shells are soft, thin, and flat. Rather than being covered with scutes, they are covered with thick skin, making their shell pliable and leathery-looking.

They easily hide by burrowing just beneath the mud at the bottom of a pond or lake. When an unsuspecting creature happens past – snap! Dinner. They have an unusually long neck, and their head is equipped with a long, snorkel-like nose. So, if they are in a shallow pond, they can stretch up and take a breath without leaving their hiding place.

The **pig-nosed turtle** is an interesting soft-shelled turtle. I'm sure you've already guessed the most important feature on this turtle – a pig-like nose. However, this freshwater turtle also looks like a sea turtle. Why is that? Well, instead of webbed feet, it has flippers. Like the sea turtle, it only comes to land to lay its eggs. You can find this turtle swimming in ponds, lakes, and streams in northern Australia and southern New Guinea. It is an omnivore.

Notice both the nose that gives this freshwater turtle its name and the fact that it looks a lot like a sea turtle.

Mud Turtles and Musk Turtles

This scorpion mud turtle is usually found in the water, but it is sunning itself on a log in this picture.

When you hear the word "musk" in nature, think "stink." **Musk turtles** release an offensive odor when bothered. **Mud turtles** do the same. Thus, they are grouped in the same family. Found only in North and South America, these turtles live in waterways that have shallow, muddy bottoms and a lot of grass or vegetation. They can even be found in ditches! While most members of this family are strictly carnivores, some mud turtles do eat vegetation from time to time. The majority of these turtles are moderately sized with carapaces 3 to 7 inches long, but some species have carapaces that are more than a foot long.

Family Emydidea

If you've ever seen a turtle sunning on a log in the spring, it was probably part of family **Emydidea** (em' uh did' ee), which contains **box turtles**, **pond turtles**, **sliders**, **painted turtles**, and **terrapins**. Members of this family are found on all continents except Antarctica and Australia. They live in every water habitat, even **estuaries** (es' choo uh reez). Do you know what an estuary is? It is an area where a river meets an ocean. As a result, an estuary's waters are salty, but not quite as salty as the ocean.

This painted turtle (*Chrysemys picta*) is one of the many members of family Emydidea.

There are almost 100 species of turtles in this family, so it's not surprising that the feeding habits are remarkably different from species to species. Some are strict carnivores, others are strict herbivores, and still others are omnivores. Most of the turtles kept as pets are found in this family. In fact, some species (like the red-ear slider) have expanded their range because people who owned them as pets ended up releasing them where they were previously never found.

Side-Necked Turtles

What do you get if you cross a snake with a turtle? A turtle with a really long neck. Of course, that's just a joke. There are some turtles with really long necks, but they aren't a cross between a snake and a turtle. However, they are sometimes called "snake-necked turtles." Some species have a neck that is longer than the rest of the body! I'm sure you figured out that these are the turtles that don't tuck their head in straight back, but instead turn it to the side to hide it under their shell. These turtles can be found in Australia, South America, New Guinea, Africa, and Madagascar.

Many of the side-necked turtles of Australia and South America have an unusual method for catching prey. When a fish happens past, the turtle opens its mouth wide, thrusting its head in the general direction of the prey. When it opens its mouth, its throat quickly opens up as well. If you opened your mouth and throat in water, what would happen? It would fill with

Can you see why this turtle is called a "snake-necked turtle"?

water. Well, this inrushing water causes a sucking action that both pulls the turtle's head forward and pulls the prey toward the head! In other words, because water is rushing into the turtle's mouth and throat, the prey is sucked in to its mouth as well. That's an amazing way to get a meal!

Now please understand that not all side-necked turtles hunt in that way. In fact, not all side-necked turtles are carnivorous. One species, *Elseya* (el see' ya) *dentata* (den' tah tah), is thought to be a strict herbivore. Generally, side-necked turtles are split into two groups based on their similarities: the **Austro-American side-necked turtles** and the **Afro-American side-necked turtles**. As you can see from the two names, the side-necked turtles in Australia have many things in common with certain South American side-necked turtles, so they are put together in one family. African side-necked turtles have things in common with other South American species, so they are put together in another group.

Tortoises

As I mentioned earlier, tortoises have different feet and shells from other turtles. While turtles have webbed feet – sometimes even flippered feet – tortoises have stumpy feet for trotting along on the land. Turtles generally have flattened shells, streamlined for swimming, while tortoises usually have high-domed shells for protection on land. How does the domed shell protect the tortoise? Well, which of the two hamburgers drawn on the left would be easier to eat? Obviously, the flatter one would be easier to bite, making it easier to eat. Land tortoises have land predators, but their domed shells make it hard for them to be eaten. Not only does the shell act like armor, but it is big enough that many predators don't want to open wide enough to try to eat it. When tortoises live in warm climates, they often grow quite large. The largest tortoise in the world lives on the tropical Galapagos Islands and can grow to be more than 4 feet long. It's so large that a child can ride on its back!

The Galapagos tortoises are quite fascinating and show us how easily a tortoise shell can change shape through natural selection. You see, the Galapagos Islands are a series of islands, some quite different from the others. As a result, the Galapagos tortoises on one island can be different from those on another island. On the lush, green

This Galapagos tortoise lives on an island where most of the food is above ground, so its shell slopes to allow its neck to reach up.

islands, for example, their shells curve downward so that they don't get in the way while the tortoise is walking through bushes and eating fruit. On islands where the food is high up on branches, however, their shells slope so that they can stretch their head up and eat the high-rise food without their neck hitting the shell.

What do you remember about turtles and tortoises?

Order Crocodilia

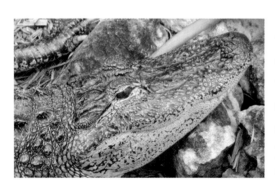

Notice how the only teeth showing on the alligator (top) are a few from the upper jaw. The crocodile (bottom) has many teeth showing, including ones from the lower jaw.

Whoever said "smile and the whole world will smile with you," wasn't talking about the members of order **Crocodilia** (crok uh dil' ee uh). Often called **crocodilians**, these large reptiles have quite an evil grin! They include **alligators**, **caimans** (kay' muhnz), **gavials** (gay' vee uhlz) and, of course, **crocodiles**. It is best that I start by telling you how to distinguish between the four members of order Crocodilia. The most important distinction between alligators and crocodiles is their teeth. When an alligator or a caiman closes its mouth, you cannot see many of its teeth. If you see any, they are the ones from the upper jaw and are pointing down. However, even with its mouth closed, you can see a crocodile's (or a gavial's) teeth. The ones to look for are the teeth from the lower jaw that are pointing up. If you see such teeth when the mouth is closed, you know you are looking at a crocodile or a gavial. Also, an alligator or caiman has a U-shaped snout, while a crocodile or gavial usually has a V-shaped snout.

But what about alligators and caimans? How can you tell them apart? That's very hard. In fact, you really have to look at a skeleton. Alligators have a bone that separates the two nostrils in the nose, while caimans do not have such a bone. In addition, caimans have a lot more bony plates protecting their underside than do alligators. It is very easy to tell a gavial from a crocodile, however. A gavial has a very long snout with a bump on the end (see the picture on page 201).

There are a few other differences among these interesting crocodilians. For example, crocodiles and gavials have special glands that help them to get rid of excess salt in the body. Alligators and caimans are unable to rid their bodies of excessive salt. Based on this information, can you guess what kind of water crocodiles and gavials can often be found in? Indeed, crocodiles and gavials frequent places like estuaries, where the water is salty. A few even live in the ocean, like the Australian saltwater crocodiles (called "salties" by Australians). Because alligators and caimans can't get rid of excess salt, they prefer to live in freshwater, but they can visit salty water for short periods of time.

Located on the skin around the upper and lower jaws of both crocodiles and alligators are special, pimple-like bumps. These little pimples are actually sensory organs. Scientists believe they can detect changes in water pressure and possibly help the reptiles detect prey under the water. These pimples are called dermal pressure receptors, or DPRs. Look at the upper picture on the right. Do you see the little bumps on each scale? Those are the DPRs. Crocodiles have DPRs over almost their entire body, while alligators and caimans have them only on the skin around their jaws. This is how you can tell alligator or caiman skin from crocodile skin. Crocodile skin will have a small spot or dimple on most of the scales, while alligator skin will not.

These are close-up pictures of the skin on the neck of a crocodile (top) and alligator (bottom).

Share with someone all that you have learned about the differences between crocodiles and alligators.

Crocodilian Conventions

If you were ectothermic, where would you prefer to live? I know I would choose a warm location, probably somewhere close to the equator. It just so happens that warm locations are where most crocodilians live. Two species of crocodilians (the **American alligator** and the **Chinese alligator**), however, can live in colder climates. They survive the cold times by hibernating in burrows they dig themselves.

Not only do crocodilians like to be where it's warm, they also must be where it is wet. Search as long as you like, but you just won't find a crocodilian in the desert. If a drought comes to their watery world, these creatures are designed with a special ability to dig holes that retain what little water might be around. These holes, often called **gator holes**, stay wet and muddy long after other places have dried up. This wet area lures other animals also in search of water. So, it's not just a mud hole, it's a trap!

Notice how this alligator's eyes and nose stick out of the water, while most of the rest of its body is submerged.

Crocodilians spend most of their lives in the water and are designed to swim fast. Tucking their legs up next to their body, they swish their powerful, paddle-shaped tail in an "S" pattern, which propels them through the water. When they are resting in the water, with their nostrils and eyes peeking out above the water, their legs tread the water doggie-paddle style. If they decide it's time to take a stroll on the bottom of the river, they jut out their feet, spread their toes, and sink. They then walk along the river bottom, holding their breath.

God designed crocodilians with special underwater swimming gear. For example, a crocodilian can open its mouth underwater to capture prey without worrying about the water going down its throat. That's because it has a special valve in the back of its mouth to keep its throat watertight while underwater. Its eyes are even supplied with special goggles – a set of transparent lenses that slide over the eyes, keeping them protected under water. Once a crocodilian has gone underwater, how long might it stay down there? Depending on the species, it could stay for as long as two hours if it's not using much energy. However, it will probably come back up after fifteen minutes or so.

Crocodilian Chow

Crocodilians are apex predators. Typically, the only predator a crocodilian has to worry about is another crocodilian! They aren't too picky about what they eat, but they are excellent hunters. Crocodilians can eat many times their own weight each day. Yet, their bodies store enough fat and they can conserve energy so well that they can survive without food for several months! I sure wouldn't want to meet up with a crocodilian that hadn't eaten for several months, would you?

If you did meet up with a hungry crocodilian, do you think you could outrun it? Perhaps, but these creatures are surprisingly fast on the ground. They can run faster than 10 miles per hour over short distances. Most people can sprint faster than that, but most crocodilians can reach their top speed surprisingly quickly, so you will be able to outrun the crocodilian only if you react quickly enough.

Most crocodilians don't chase their prey, however. They lie in wait, partially submerged under the water – looking just like a log floating in the water – until their prey comes close to them. When the prey is close enough, the crocodilian grabs the hapless creature before it knows what happened. If the prey happens to be an animal that breathes air, the crocodilian will drag the poor creature underwater to drown it.

Some crocodilians actually use their tail to sweep schools of fish into shallow water; then open their mouth wide and sweep the fish in. When there are large schools of fish present, Nile crocodiles will sometimes hunt in groups, forming a circle around the fish so they have nowhere to escape.

While crocodilians will eat just about anything, fish is often on the menu.

With their powerful jaws and spiky teeth, you would think crocodilians could chew up their food. However, they cannot. They must either swallow their food whole, or they must whip the carcass back and forth until a piece small enough to swallow comes off. Many crocodiles will actually trap their dead prey under the water by piling rocks on top of its body. Leaving the dead animal underwater allows the carcass to rot and become softer, making it easier to rip pieces off. This amazing example of tool use shows us just how intelligent crocodilians are.

Crocodiles instinctively swallow stones. These stones, called **gastroliths** (gas' truh liths), are stored in the stomach and grind up the food once it has been swallowed. They also add weight to the crocodilian to keep it submerged under the surface of the water.

Crocodilian Young

Like all reptiles, crocodilians hatch from leathery eggs. Most build nests for their eggs. Some simply dig holes; others construct layers of sticks and brush to protect their eggs. After constructing the nest, a crocodilian mother digs a hole and lays many eggs. Some crocodilians fill the hole with dead plant matter. The warmth generated as the dead plant matter decomposes helps keep the eggs warm as they mature. If it's extremely warm, all the eggs will produce male crocodilians. If it's a little on the cool side, the eggs will produce female crocodilians. Medium temperatures will produce a mixture of males and females.

This young crocodilian just recently hatched.

Though most reptiles aren't great parents (remember the tuatara), most crocodilian mothers protect their young before and after they hatch. The mother will often sit right near her eggs, forsaking food for two or three months, waiting for the young to hatch. When the baby crocs are ready to hatch, they squeal and holler inside their eggs so loudly that even you and I could hear them. Like many animals born from eggs, the hatchlings are specially designed with an egg tooth on the end of the snout. They use this egg tooth to crack open their shell. In some species, as soon as the mother hears their yelps, she digs up the eggs and helps the new hatchlings break out of their shells. Remarkably, some mother crocodilians do this by actually putting the eggs in their mouth and gently cracking them!

If the babies aren't already in their mother's mouth after they hatch, they often crawl in there. No, mom isn't looking for a quick meal. She is carrying her babies to the safety of a shallow pool. After bringing them to a safe place, crocodilians will watch over their young carefully for while. The American alligator keeps track of her young the longest – for more than two years. She wins the prize as the best mom in the reptile world! Yet, even with all these precautions, only one in a hundred newborn crocodilians will survive to have their own offspring. The others become meals for sea birds, turtles, snakes, raccoons, large fish, and even other alligators.

Crocodilians are the biggest reptiles alive today, some reaching more than 28 feet long. Yet that's nothing compared to one fossilized crocodile that stretched about 40 feet! Not many animals could escape once that mouth clamped down on it, for the mouth alone was 6 feet long (longer than most adults are tall) and contained 132 razor-sharp teeth.

Explain all you have learned so far about crocodilians.

Crocodiles

Now that you have learned a bit about crocodilians in general, let's talk about some specific types. We will start with the most common crocodilians – crocodiles. Different species of crocodiles can be found in many parts of the world: South America, North America, Central America, Africa, Australia, and Asia. The American crocodile is one of only two crocodilians that reside in the United States. It can be found in the southern parts of the United States (Florida, mostly), throughout Central America, and in the northern parts of South America.

Because they are so aggressive, crocodiles can be a real problem for people who live near them. Two of the more aggressive crocodiles in the world are the Nile crocodile of Africa and the saltwater crocodile of Southeast Asia and Australia. Nile crocodiles occasionally grow to be more than 20 feet long. They prefer fish, but will eat any creature that comes into the water – even a zebra or a small hippo.

Despite its name, the saltwater crocodile doesn't always live in salt water. In fact, most "salties," as they are called, spend the wet season in freshwater swamps and rivers. They tend to move to saltier

Saltwater crocodiles like this one are known as "salties."

waters during the dry season, when many of the freshwater sources dry up. Generally considered to be the most aggressive of all crocodilians, salties will eat about anything that comes into their path, including sharks! Obviously, then, they are not afraid of people.

Gavials

It is easy to recognize a gavial because of the very long snout and the bulb on the nose.

These interesting crocodilians are instantly recognized by their long, narrow snout. Gavials are really much different from other crocodilians because they don't come out of the water much. In fact, their legs are so weak, and their feet so webbed, they just aren't very fast or powerful on land. They only leave the water to lay eggs or bask in the sun on the water's edge. Like a seal or turtle, a gavial must push its body along as it struggles to get around on land. Gavials are also called "gharials," because the bulb on the nose is called a "ghara."

Because of their aquatic lifestyle and their narrow snout, gavials specialize in eating fish. They catch them by swishing their head to the side, snagging the fish, then flipping it to go down their throat in one piece. They don't prey on animals that must be ripped into pieces to eat. So, if you happen to be swimming in a lake in India and see a gavial, there is no need to fear. It will not be a danger to you.

Caimans

There are several species of caimans, and they are found in Central and South America. They are almost exactly like alligators. As I told you before, you must examine the skeleton or the scales on the underside of the animal to tell a caiman from an alligator. While caimans are all nocturnal, the size varies dramatically with species. The largest, the black caiman, can grow to be 12 feet long, while the smallest, Cuvier's dwarf caiman, rarely reaches 5 feet in length. Not surprisingly, then, while all caimans

As you can see, this caiman is very similar to an alligator.

are carnivorous, the specific animals they eat vary quite a bit from species to species. With the exception of the black caiman, these crocodilians are too small to post a threat to people.

Alligators

This Chinese alligator is floating in the Yangtze River.

When the Spanish settlers came to South America, they saw a huge, lizard-like creature and called it "The Lizard" – "el lagarto" in Spanish. "El lagarto" eventually became "alligator." There are only two kinds of alligators in the world: the large one that lives from the southern United States down through the northern parts of South America, and a smaller one that lives in China. The American alligator, sometimes called the "Mississippi alligator" or simply "gator," is the only other crocodilian, besides the American crocodile, that lives in the United States. It's more abundant than the American crocodile, and the greatest number can be found in Florida and Louisiana. In Florida, alligators can be found in almost every single body of water; they love swamps, marshes, lakes, and drainage canals. The Chinese alligator is very rare and can only be found in the Yangtze River Basin in China.

Gator Farms

While the Chinese alligator is currently on the brink of extinction, alligators in the New World are thriving. However, that wasn't always the case. As recently as the 1960s, the American alligator was almost extinct. Why? Because alligator meat tastes good and alligator skin looks nice on boots, wallets, briefcases, and purses. Also, alligators aren't really a welcome sight in someone's backyard pool (where they sometimes turn up). As a result, they were hunted by the millions. In less than a hundred years, they went from overpopulated to near extinction. In 1967 they were put on the endangered species list, and killing them was forbidden. This helped a little, but not a lot. After all, the fact that it was illegal to hunt them made them even more valuable, so people took the risk and hunted them anyway. Then, an interesting plan was set in action – alligator farms!

Alligator farmers go out into the wild and collect alligator eggs. They incubate them and raise the young for two years. This ensures the survival of nearly every hatchling. Do you remember how many newborn alligators usually survive? Only about one in a hundred! With gator farming, survival is increased dramatically. After two years, 20 percent of the gators are sent back into the wild to breed, while the rest are killed for their meat and hides. This increases the population of alligators in the wild, and at the same time it makes alligator skin and meat less expensive. When the skin and meat are less expensive, poachers don't want to kill them because they don't bring enough money. This has helped to save the alligator population. There are said to be more than a million wild alligators roaming around Florida. So, they are no longer endangered, but Florida residents must be careful or they'll find themselves in danger.

What have you learned about the different kinds of crocodilians?

Amphibians

Although you learned a lot about amphibians in Zoology 2, this lesson will explore the amphibians you'll find living much of their lives on land. The word amphibian actually means "dual life," which suits these animals well, since they begin life like a fish in the water and later develop legs and lungs to live on land. Basically, the life cycle of most amphibians follows several stages. I'll explain it by using a frog as an example. Please note, however, that not all amphibians (not even all frogs) develop in exactly this way. For example, some frogs don't have a tadpole stage. They go straight from egg to frog. However, the *typical* frog lifecycle is as follows:

1. **Spawning:** This is when the frog lays its eggs. Frogs lay a lot of eggs, because most of the eggs (or the hatchlings) will get eaten. Many frogs lay their eggs in water, but others lay them on land.

2. **Egg Stage:** The egg contains a tiny baby frog and the food it needs to be able to grow. At first, the baby is so small that you cannot see it without the aid of a microscope. As it feeds on

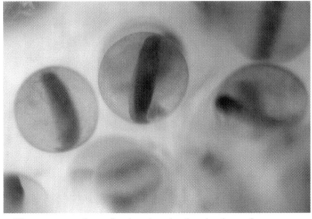

You can see the tadpoles developing in these frog eggs.

the yolk of the egg, however, it begins to grow and develop. Within one to three weeks (usually), the egg will hatch, and a little tadpole wiggles out.

3. **Tadpole Stage:** After hatching, the tadpole feeds on the remaining yolk that is still attached. Only when that food supply is exhausted will it begin to eat with its mouth. At that point, it feeds on microscopic organisms in the water. During this stage, the young frog is breathing with gills, like a fish. Unlike a fish, however, the gills can be on the *outside* of the tadpole's body!

In the tadpole stage, the gills can be on the outside of the body. This is most often the case in salamanders.

4. **Metamorph:** After about a month of development, tiny hind legs start to sprout. The head becomes more frog-like, and the body grows more round. In addition, the gills begin to be replaced by lungs so that the frog can breathe outside of water. In short, it is beginning to look more like a frog. It also begins to eat more like a frog – insects and other protein sources are on the menu. Before long the front legs pop out, leading to the next stage.

You can see the tiny hind legs emerging in this tadpole.

5. **Froglet Stage:** By a few months (in most species), the only difference between the young frog and an adult is the presence of a tail. Over time, the tail will disappear, indicating the frog is now an adult.

This froglet still has a tail.

6. **Adult Stage:** Usually around four months of age, the frog has completed the cycle and is now an adult. It's time for the frog to start the process again by finding a mate and laying more eggs.

This lifecycle is one thing that separates amphibians from reptiles. They begin life in the water, and end life as a terrestrial, or land-dwelling, creature. Most don't like to be too far from water or dampness. Because they can breathe through their skin, it must remain moist; if their skin gets too dry, they are unable to breathe.

Like all animals, amphibians have glands in their skin that produce certain chemicals. In amphibians, these chemicals protect the animal in a variety of ways. Some kill bacteria found in water. Others are poisonous to animals that might want to eat the frog. If the frog is quite colorful, it's more

This poison dart frog's bright colors warn predators to stay away.

likely to have poison. Do you remember how bright colors might protect an animal from being eaten? As you learned in Zoology 1 and 2, the bright colors serve as a warning sign to predators. Predators remember eating brightly colored prey and getting sick. This makes them avoid eating the same prey again. The bright colors shout, "Remember when you tried to eat something my color before? Don't even try it!"

The beautiful poison dart frogs of Central and South America are used by natives to poison the tips of their darts. They catch the frogs using leaves to protect their hands from the poisonous chemicals. They then rub a frog with the tip of a dart they shoot out of a blowgun. One frog can coat many darts. The frog is then released, and the hunters can disable or kill their target when they blow these darts at the animals they are hunting. Some species of poison dart frogs are more toxic than others. A few kinds have poison strong enough to kill a large animal or person.

Frogs and Toads

Frogs can be found on every continent in the world except one. Can you guess which one? Antarctica, of course. The warmer the climate, the more frogs you will find. Frogs can be found living in the water or on the land, in holes or under rocks. Tree frogs even live in trees. They have sticky pads on their toes to help them cling to the tree trunks and branches. Other frogs are burrowers, hibernating in holes they dig to make it through the cold winter months.

You may remember the difference between frogs and toads from Zoology 2. Frogs have smooth, wet skin; toads often have bumpy, thicker skin that retains moisture but doesn't feel very moist. Frogs must live in or very near water, while toads can travel across dry land for quite some time before they dry out. Frogs usually have webbed hind feet, while toads usually do not. But this is not always the case. Tree frogs and poison dart frogs don't have webbed feet. In fact, adult tree frogs can't even swim! They keep wet by soaking in small pools and living in places like rainforests.

Many amphibians lay wet, jelly-like eggs that hatch in the water. It doesn't take much water. Poison dart frogs lay their eggs in puddles of water that form on leaves, and they watch over their developing young carefully. They'll even move them to another puddle if the first puddle isn't working out. If you are walking through a forest or jungle, check every little puddle for tadpoles – even a puddle in the fork of a tree may have developing frogs.

Australia's gastric brooding frogs actually *swallowed* their eggs. The eggs contained a chemical that "turned off" the frog's digestion, so the eggs would hatch and the tadpoles would actually develop *in the mother's stomach*! The mother would then vomit the tadpoles out when they were ready to live outside. Unfortunately, as far as we know, these unique frogs became extinct in the 1980s. A frog called Darwin's frog has a similar way of protecting its young. The eggs are laid in moist soil, and the male guards them. When they hatch, the male swallows them and keeps them in his **vocal sac**, where they develop. One day, the father opens his mouth and little froglets jump out!

This male painted reed frog is using its vocal sac.

What is a vocal sac? Well, most male frogs have a thin membrane of skin that they can "blow up" to make what looks like a little balloon under the neck. This "balloon" actually amplifies the sounds the frog makes so that his calls carry over long distances. Why do males do this? Mostly, they do it to find a mate!

Some frogs, like the African foam-nest tree frog, actually mate in tree branches that hang over streams and rivers. The female secretes a sticky foam substance, and the male whips the foam into a nest with his legs. Then, the female lays eggs in the foam mixture. The nest hangs over the water, and the outer shell of foam dries in the sun, preserving the moisture and protecting the developing embryos inside. After a few days (or when it rains), the outer shell breaks, and the tadpoles fall into the water below to continue their development.

What have you learned so far about amphibians?

Frog Food

Though you may have seen cartoons of frogs eating flies, they eat a lot more than flies. They'll consume almost any small critter, including earthworms, minnows, and spiders. Large frogs will even eat birds and mice! Most frogs and toads usually catch their food using their long, sticky tongue. When inside the mouth, the tongue is folded. To catch prey, the frog or toad will open its mouth, quickly flipping the tongue to extend it out. If the animal aimed right, the prey will stick to the tongue and be brought back to the mouth, where it is swallowed whole. Please note that not all frogs and toads have long, sticky tongues. Ground frogs that eat ants and other crawling insects, for example, don't have long tongues. They just bite at their prey.

Frog Defense

Frogs have many enemies, though they aren't very frightening. Because of their enemies, they have a lot of defenses. Their first defense is escape. God has given frogs very large eyes positioned high on their head, giving them panoramic vision. In other words, they can see almost the entire area around them, helping them keep a watch out for predators.

In addition, frogs have an amazing ability to escape danger. Their powerful legs are specially designed to spring them several feet away in one leap. The longest recorded jump was done in 1986 buy a frog named "Rosie the Ribiter." This feisty frog jumped 21 feet, 5¾ inches in one leap! Think about that! Go outside with a yardstick or tape measure and measure that distance out. Now, stand at one end and jump as far as you can. Continue to jump until you have traveled the entire distance. How many jumps did it take you? Obviously, your legs aren't designed as well as a frog's when it comes to jumping!

This frog's mottled green color gives it good camouflage while it swims in water that is covered with leaves.

As I already told you, some frogs have toxic or poisonous chemicals that will harm any animal that tries to eat them. Bright colors typically warn potential predators that they should stay away. However, colors aren't just used to warn predators. Sometimes, they are used as camouflage to help the frog blend into its environment. This makes it much easier to hide from predators.

A few species of frog (like the four-eyed frog) have spots on their hind end. These spots look like large eyes. When threatened, the frogs lift their hind end, which startles predators into thinking they are being attacked. Typically the predators run away, or at least they pause long enough for the frog to make its escape. Sometimes, a frog will puff itself up to look bigger, harder to swallow, or more menacing.

Deformed Frogs

Throughout North America, scientists have been finding deformed frogs – frogs that have too many legs, too few legs, only one eye, etc. The number of such findings has grown substantially over the years, but there is no clear-cut answer as to what is causing it. Scientists know that such deformities can be caused by naturally occurring parasites, but they can also be caused by pollution. However, pollution levels in general have been decreasing all over North America, so if pollution were the only cause, you would not expect an increase in the number of deformed frogs found. Research is being done to determine exactly what is causing the increase in the numbers of deformed frogs. The course website I told you about in the introduction to the book has links that discuss this interesting scientific mystery in much more detail.

Frog Foe

One frog foe that has caused entire populations to become extinct is a fungus, called the chytrid (kye' trid). This fungus eats away the top layer of an amphibian's skin. Sadly, this fungus has affected frogs and other amphibians all over the New World and in Australia. Not much is known about the fungus, but it has caused the extinction of many species of frogs.

Did you know that it is against the law to transport wild animals from one country to another without a license? Sometimes you can't even take a creature or plant from one state to the other. One of the many reasons for such restrictions is the fear of spreading fungi like the chytrid. You see, when we transport a living organism, it might be carrying something that could infect other living organisms. If you release the animal, or touch another animal after touching the infected one, you could spread the disease to more creatures. If it were something as serious as a chytrid infection, you could be the cause of an extinction of an entire species. This is one way that fungi, viruses, and bacteria are spread from one region to another.

Salamanders and Newts

Though they look like slimy lizards, **salamanders** are amphibians. They differ from frogs, however, because they have tails and long, slender bodies. They are generally small; few of them grow to be bigger than several inches long. They also walk along the ground like a lizard, swinging their tail back and forth. Their legs are so short that their belly sometimes drags along the ground when they walk, but they swim with the best of them. Salamanders have smooth, slimy skin, like frogs. **Newts** are specific salamanders that have rougher skin that is not as slimy. Thus, a newt's skin is more like that of a toad.

Like frogs and toads, salamanders and newts must keep their skin moist. Some salamanders do this by staying in the water almost all the time. We call these **aquatic salamanders**, and some of them are so adapted

Note that the salamander (above) has smooth, slimy skin, while the newt (below) has rough skin.

to the water that their legs are very small or non-existent.   Other salamanders and newts are **semi-aquatic**. They spend some of their time as adults in water and some on land. Many salamanders and newts, however, are **terrestrial**. That means they spend most of their adult life on land, some returning to the water only to mate. These amphibians keep their skin moist by living in wet areas and under rocks and logs where the surroundings stay moist.

Though salamanders and newts don't have ears, they can "hear," much like a turtle. They feel vibrations that travel through the ground. This tells them when predators are nearby so they can run (or swim) away. That's why they are so difficult to spot, though they are quite numerous. Salamanders and newts use other senses besides feeling vibrations; they happen to have great senses of sight and smell.

What did you learn about salamanders and newts?

What Do You Remember?

What are the differences among turtles, terrapins, and tortoises? Can snapping turtles pull their head into their shell? How do they protect themselves? How does the alligator snapping turtle catch prey? What is interesting about the snake-necked turtles of South America and Australia? Explain the differences among the different kinds of crocodilians. How do crocodilians care for their young? Explain the stages in an amphibian's life. What is the main difference between a salamander and a newt?

Map It!

Galapagos Islands – Galapagos tortoises
United States – American alligators and crocodiles (southern), many varieties of turtles, salamanders, newts, frogs, and toads
Central and South America – Caimans, alligators, crocodiles, many frogs (including tree frogs and poison arrow frogs), newts, toads, and salamanders.

Eastern China – Chinese alligator, many varieties of frogs, toads, newts, salamanders, and turtles
India – Gavial, many varieties of frogs, toads, newts, salamanders, and turtles
Africa – Nile crocodile, many varieties of frogs, toads, newts, salamanders, and turtles

Track It!

If you live in an area with a warm climate, you might see alligator or crocodile tracks near lakes, rivers, or marshes. The front feet are smaller than the hind feet, and the tail generally leaves a trail in between. As you look in the mud around waterways, you might also find frog or toad tracks. These usually have a splotch in the middle where the animal's belly left its mark.

tail mark

belly mark

alligator or crocodile

frog or toad

Notebook Activities

You finished your study of reptiles and learned a lot about amphibians. Now, it's time to compare and contrast the two. Make a Venn diagram (like you did in the previous lesson) for reptiles and amphibians. If you can't remember all the differences and similarities, think about what you learned about each animal. If it's really hard, go back and review the previous lesson, as well as Lesson 4 in Zoology 2.

Make three sections for your notebook. In the first one, write down the things you have learned about turtles. In the second one, write down what you learned about crocodilians. In the third one, write down what you have learned about amphibians. Include pictures in each section. Finally, for the amphibian section, write a "diary" as if you were a baby amphibian. Start your diary while you are in the egg, and end it when you find your mate. In the diary, discuss what happens to you as you develop into an adult.

Project

Keeping turtles as pets is a great way to learn about these interesting reptiles. While you can probably find a turtle outside, it is best not to keep it as a pet. Many turtles look harmless, but their strong beaks can pack a nasty bite. In addition, wild turtles can carry diseases that could possibly infect you or your other pets. Thus, it is best for you to get a turtle from a pet store.

Since there are so many different kinds of turtles, you first need to choose the turtle you want to keep. Most people start small, with something like a red-ear slider. These turtles can be found in most pet stores and don't take up too much room. They can be kept in a watertight plastic container that has both water for the turtles to swim in and dry places that the turtles can crawl up on. One of the dry spots should be under a warm lamp, but the lamp should not be so hot that it heats up the turtle's entire area. In other words, the turtle should be able to warm itself under the lamp when it gets cold, but it should also be able to cool off by going to another part of its habitat. The pet store will sell you food pellets for your turtle to eat. Be sure to spend some time learning about the needs of your turtle before you just jump in and start. The course website I told you

Red-ear slider turtles are probably the most popular of all pet turtles.

about in the introduction to this book has links to websites that discuss the things you will need to do in order to properly care for your turtle. You can also learn about your turtle's needs by talking to someone at your local pet store.

Lesson 12
Dinosaurs

Long ago, the world was crawling with enormous animals the likes of which we have never seen. The picture on the right shows what one of these animals, *Triceratops* (try sehr' uh tahps), might have looked like. Not only were strange animals like *Triceratops* roaming around at that time, but also giant forms of the animals we know today, like giant wombats, sloths, crocodiles, and kangaroos, were also plentiful on this planet. What happened to these animals? We know they once existed, because we find their fossils. We also know that many of the plants they tromped on are plants that exist today. However, these huge animals don't exist today. Did something happen to their food supply? Were they hunted to extinction? Was the environment different when these creatures walked the earth?

This model shows you what a dinosaur called *Triceratops* might have looked like.

Whatever the reason, the giant versions of the animals we know today are gone, as are specific types of animals like *Triceratops*. In this lesson, we'll focus on the extinct creatures known as **dinosaurs** (dye' nuh sawrz). Though they came into existence on the sixth day of Creation, they were given the name "dinosaur" (which comes from Latin words meaning "terrible lizard") fairly recently – in 1841.

What's in a Name?

Since the term "dinosaur" is relatively new, you won't find it in writings that are more than about 170 years old. However, if we can find ancient writings with accounts of animals that fit the description of what we now call dinosaurs, we can find out what they were once called. Also, if there are ancient drawings of such animals, we might get a better idea of what they looked like. As you learned in Zoology 1, fossils can't tell us everything we want to know, so drawings could be helpful.

Well, there are historical descriptions of animals that seem to be what we would call dinosaurs today. One of the oldest descriptions comes from the Bible. Archaeology and historical science have shown that the Bible is the most accurate historical work of ancient times, so the accounts in it can be trusted to give us solid information about what the world was like back when it was written. Possibly the oldest book in the Bible is the Book of Job, and in Job 40:15-24, we read the words of God as He is speaking to Job.

"(14) Behold now, Behemoth, which I made as well as you. (15) He eats grass like an ox. (16) Behold now, his strength in his loins and his power in the muscles of his belly. (17) He bends his tail like a cedar; the sinews of his thighs are knit together. (18) His bones are tubes of bronze; his limbs are like bars of iron. (19) He is the first of the ways of God; let his maker bring near his sword. (20) Surely the mountains bring him food, and all the beasts of the field play there. (21) Under the lotus plants he lies down, in the covert of the reeds and the marsh. (22) The lotus plants cover him with shade; the willows of the brook surround him. (23) If a river rages, he is not alarmed; he is confident, though the Jordan rushes to his mouth. (24) Can anyone capture him when he is on watch, with barbs can anyone pierce his nose?"

Look at those verses again. Job is told to consider an animal named **Behemoth** (bee' uh muth). Could this be a dinosaur? Some say it could be an elephant or a hippopotamus, because the passage describes a large herbivore that likes to be in water. However, look at verse 17, which describes Behemoth's tail. Now look below at the tails of an elephant and a hippopotamus. Look also at the tail of the dinosaur called *Apatosaurus* (uh' pat uh sawr' us), which is a member of a group of herbivorous dinosaurs, called **sauropods** (saw' ruh podz), thought to have spent a lot of time in water.

The hippo (left) and elephant (middle) have small tails. Fossils indicate that sauropods (right) had long, muscular tails.

Which tail fits the description given in Job? A cedar is a massive tree. Which tail do you think bends "like a cedar"? Clearly sauropods had tails like the one God says Behemoth had. It seems likely, then, that this dinosaur was once called Behemoth by the people in Job's land.

Suppose the description of Behemoth as found in the Book of Job really is talking about a sauropod dinosaur. What does that tell us? Well, God speaks to Job as if he should know what Behemoth was. Since the study of fossils did not exist back in the times of the Old Testament, the only way Job would have known what Behemoth was is if he had seen Behemoth, seen a drawing of Behemoth, or at least spoken to someone who had seen Behemoth or a drawing of it. That means Behemoth must have been seen by people. Is that possible? Some evidence suggests that it is.

The Natural Bridges National Monument in Utah, for example, contains ancient artwork that has been etched on rocks. The drawings are called **petroglyphs** (peh' truh glifs), and scientists tell us they were made prior to the year 500 A.D. That's more than 1,500 years ago! One of these petroglyphs is a very good representation of a sauropod dinosaur. Look at the photograph and drawing below:

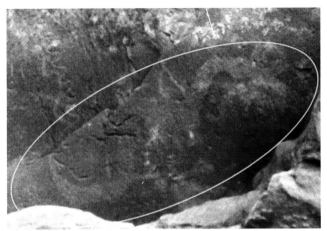 

The photo (left) shows a petroglyph (circled to help you see it) of what appears to be a sauropod dinosaur. The drawing (right) is based on the petroglyph, giving you a better view of the details.

Now how do you suppose people from more than 1,500 years ago were able to draw such a good representation of a dinosaur? Scientists didn't know sauropod dinosaurs existed until the 1840s (about 170 years ago). Nevertheless, someone drew a pretty good picture of one more than 1,500 years ago! Most likely, the person drawing the dinosaur had seen one, had seen a drawing of one, or at least had spoken to someone who described it to him.

Creation Confirmation

If Behemoth really was a dinosaur, and if the petroglyph I just told you about is of a dinosaur, what does that mean? It means that dinosaurs lived on earth at the same time as people did. I know this goes against what a lot of people want you to believe, but there is evidence to support that idea. The petroglyph mentioned above is not the only ancient drawing of dinosaurs. The tomb of Bishop Bell, which was built in England over 500 years ago, contains brass artwork that accurately represents sauropod dinosaurs. In addition, Arizona's Havasupai Canyon contains an ancient drawing of a creature that has the unmistakable proportions, stance, and tail of a theropod (thuh' ruh pod), which is another type of dinosaur. It is unlike any other kind of creature known to man. If dinosaurs lived "millions of years ago" like some scientists believe, how did ancient people who had no access to fossils of these animals produce such accurate artwork depicting them? It is more reasonable to conclude from such pictures that people and dinosaurs were created together and shared this planet until the dinosaurs went extinct.

Fossils also give us evidence that dinosaurs haven't been extinct for very long. Scientists studying a *Tyrannosaurus rex* fossil in Montana, for example, found flexible tissue including blood vessels and blood cells! Tissue does not remain flexible for long, even in the best of situations, and cells tend to disintegrate fairly quickly after an animal dies. If the animal lived many millions of years ago (as some would have us believe), the blood cells would have disintegrated long before now, and the flexible tissue would have long ago fossilized. Thus, this fossil shows every indication of being only a few thousand years old (at most). This fits with the idea that dinosaurs and people lived at the same time.

Tell someone about the evidence that dinosaurs lived at the same time as people.

Bone Basics

Regardless of how long ago dinosaurs lived, most of what we know about them comes from fossils, and most of what fossilizes is bone. Thus, most of what we know about dinosaurs comes from their skeletons. Unfortunately, just seeing an animal's skeleton doesn't tell us everything we need to know about it. **Paleontologists** (pay' lee on tol' uh jists), the scientists who study fossils, must make guesses about what an animal looked like and how it lived. They do this by looking at animals today with similar skeletons. Then, they make drawings of the animal with flesh on its skeleton, usually guessing at its skin coloring and other features. This is why many paleontologists also study art, because it can help them "fill in the gaps" that are left when they have only bones to study. Unless they find a fossil imprint of the dinosaur's skin (which is very rare), they have to guess about what kind of skin it had.

Paleontologists also make guesses about behavior. For example, a giraffe's teeth are different from a zebra's teeth, because giraffes eat the soft leaves at the tops of the tall trees, while zebras eat tough, dry grass on the ground. If a dinosaur had teeth like a giraffe, we think it may have browsed for food in trees and bushes. If it had teeth like a zebra, we guess that it might have grazed on tough grass on the ground. If a fossil dinosaur has sharp teeth, we guess that it was a meat-eater. However, as I have already mentioned earlier in this book – that's not always a good indicator. Some herbivores have teeth that are sharp and resemble those of carnivores!

This is the skull of a dinosaur known as *Iguanodon*. The skull is large because the animal was probably about 30 feet long. Since its teeth are very similar to (but bigger than) those of an iguana, we assume it was an herbivore like an iguana. Since *Iguanodons* are extinct, however, there is no way to be sure.

So paleontologists have to make a lot of guesses. They compare the bones of extinct animals to those of animals that are currently alive. When they find a lot of similarities, they assume that the extinct animal looked and behaved similarly to the animal that is still alive. Nevertheless, it is important to understand that we cannot be sure about such conclusions.

What's Your Stance?

If paleontologists have only the bones to look at, how do they know if a fossil comes from a mammal or reptile? Well, remember what you learned in Lesson 2. Mammals have a lower jaw made of only one bone, while the lower jaw of a reptile is made up of several bones. In addition, while the joint that connects the lower jawbone to the rest of the skull allows only simple up-and-down motion in a reptile, it allows for side-to-side motion in a mammal. This allows mammals to chew their food, while reptiles generally swallow their food whole.

Once a fossil is identified as coming from a reptile, what causes paleontologists to call it a dinosaur fossil? It's all in the way it walked. Lizards have a sprawling stance, where their legs are positioned out to the sides of the body. They walk by swinging themselves from side to side. Dinosaurs had a joint at the top of the leg that fit into a hole in the hip bone. This allowed the legs to be positioned more directly under the body. As a result, they did not have to throw their bodies from side to side to move. This enabled them to run more efficiently. Imagine trying to run while tossing your hips from side to side. You would tire *a lot* more easily. That's why lizards stop running every few minutes and crocodiles can only sustain short bursts of speed. Dinosaurs, however, could probably run quite well.

The gecko (left) is a lizard. Notice its sprawling stance, with its feet far out on its sides. Compare that to the stegosaurus skeleton (right), in which the legs are more directly under the body. That makes stegosaurus a dinosaur.

Since their legs help determine that they are dinosaurs, it's not surprising that paleontologists further classify dinosaurs based on their hips, which is where their legs attached. Some are "lizard-hipped" dinosaurs, and others are "bird-hipped" dinosaurs. We call them **Saurischia** (saw ris' kee uh) and **Ornithischia** (or' nuh this' kee uh). The names are easy to remember when you realize that in Greek, "sauros" means "lizard" and "ischion" means "hip joint," while "ornitheos" means "of a bird." The Saurischia, then, are the lizard-hipped dinosaurs. Their legs were attached to a pelvic bone shaped and positioned like that of a lizard. The Ornithischia were the bird-hipped dinosaurs, and their legs were attached to a pelvic bone shaped and positioned like that of a bird.

Saurischian Hip Structure

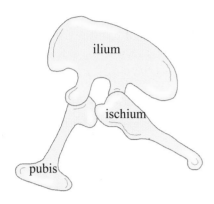

Dinosaurs with hip structures like that drawn on the far left are members of the Saurischia. Like lizards, these dinosaurs' hips were arranged in a triangle, with the pubis and ischium pointed in different directions. *Tyrannosaurus rex*, whose hip is shown in the picture, was a saurischian.

Ornithischian Hip Structure

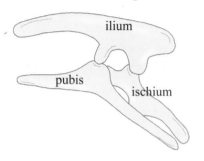

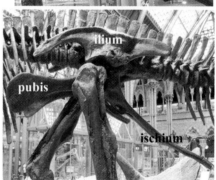

The Ornithischia had hip structures as drawn on the far left, where the pubis and ischium point in the same direction. *Edmontosaurus*, whose hip is shown in the picture, was an ornithischian.

All dinosaurs fit into one of these two groups. For example, the animal called Behemoth in the Book of Job is mostly likely a sauropod dinosaur, which is a saurischian. As you can see from the skeleton on the previous page, stegosaurus was an ornithischian.

Name Game

The names of individual dinosaurs usually come from some physical feature. Usually (but not always) "saur" or "saurus" is included at the end of the name, because it means "lizard" in Greek. So for example, *Heterodontosaurus* means "different-toothed lizard." It is the name of a dinosaur with teeth unlike other reptile teeth. Look at the dinosaurs below and see if you can match the drawing to the following names: *Monoclonius* (one horn), *Corythosaurus* (helmet lizard), *Monolophosaurus* (single-crested lizard), and *Dilophosaurus* (double-crested lizard). The correct answers can be found with the "Answers to the Narrative Questions" at the back of the book.

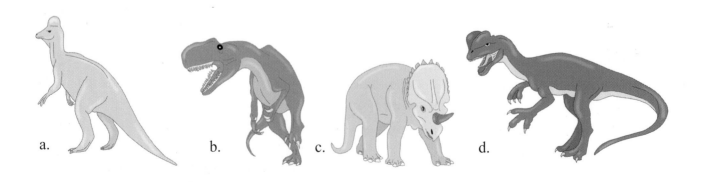

a.   b.   c.   d.

Some dinosaurs are named after the place where their fossils were found or the person who found the fossils. *Albertosaurus*, for example, was named after Alberta, Canada, where the fossils are mostly found. On the other hand, sometimes dinosaurs are given names to honor people. For example, *Fabrosaurus* was named in honor of Jean-Henri Fabre, a famous French scientist best known for his discoveries about insects. One dinosaur is even named "deceptive lizard," or *Apatosaurus*. It was given that name because some of its bones made it look like it was another dinosaur. Thus, the discoverer thought the bones were trying to deceive him.

Actually, while *Apatosaurus* bones can't really try to deceive anyone, a paleontologist did try to deceive the world with them. Have you ever heard of a *Brontosaurus*? Well, for years, everyone knew what a *Brontosaurus* was, because its fossils had been found and placed in museums. Pictures were drawn and toys were made based on the famous *Brontosaurus*. Then, one day, it was discovered that there was no such thing as a *Brontosaurus*. You see, the truth is that the dinosaur's skeleton was found without a head. So, to make it look like a complete dinosaur, the scientist who found the skeleton secretly put a head from a different dinosaur whose fossils were found far away. Eventually, however, other paleontologists figured out the deception, and we now know that there was no such thing as a *Brontosaurus*. If you become a paleontologist, please don't try to deceive people like that!

Tell someone all remember about dinosaurs so far.

Sauropods

Now that you have learned some general things about dinosaurs, it is time to get a little more specific. Let's start by discussing the types of dinosaurs found in the Saurischia. These "lizard-hipped" dinosaurs are separated into two groups – the **sauropods** and **theropods**. Sauropod ("lizard-footed") dinosaurs were colossal herbivores that walked on all fours. Theropod ("beast-footed") dinosaurs were carnivores that walked on two legs. Let's start with the sauropods.

Most sauropods looked quite similar, except some were the size of a huge ship, while others were the size of a small horse. You'll notice that their fossilized skeletons fill entire rooms in museums, with their long neck and tail reaching from one end of the room to the other. Interestingly, they usually had a small head with nostrils placed right on top of their head, close to their eyes. What other animals do you know that have

The people looking at this *Brachiosaurus* skeleton give you a good idea how huge the sauropod was.

nostrils on top of their head, and why are they located there? Alligators, hippos, and frogs have this same arrangement. These are animals that often spend a lot of time submerged under the water with just their nostrils on the surface, giving them the ability to breathe while under water. It is thought that this was the case with sauropods as well. Can you imagine relaxing at the lake, and all of a sudden an enormous sauropod rises up out of the water next to you? That would be frightening!

Though other dinosaur fossils have been confined to certain areas or continents, sauropod fossils have been found on every continent, even Antarctica! This explains why ancient art from both the New World and the Old World depicts sauropod dinosaurs.

Based on its neck, *Brachiosaurus* probably ate from the tops of trees.

No one knows for certain what sauropods ate. In 2005, fossilized dung (called coprolite – kop' ruh lyte) thought to be from a group of sauropods was found. It had fossilized remains of grasses, so at least some sauropods probably ate grasses. This is interesting because before 2005, many paleontologists were certain that dinosaurs *could not have eaten grasses*, since they thought sauropods lived millions of years before grasses existed. Of course creationist paleontologists never made such an error, because they understand that dinosaurs lived only a few thousand years ago, along with many different types of grasses.

Looking at the teeth structures of different sauropods and understanding the teeth of today's animals, scientists think that different sauropods had quite different diets. Those with peg-like teeth, such as *Diplodocus* (dih plod' uh kus), probably ate aquatic vegetation (like water lilies). Those with large, spatula-shaped teeth like *Camarasaurus* (ka' muh ruh' sawr us), however, probably ate tougher vegetation, like tree leaves. Studying sauropod necks also indicates that different sauropods ate different veggies. For example, fossils indicate that *Brachiosaurus* (bray' kee uh sawr' us) probably held its neck straight up (like a giraffe), so it probably ate the leaves at the tops of trees. *Diplodocus*, however, probably held its neck out horizontally, which makes us think that it sought after plants near the surface of the water.

Whatever they ate, we do know that they probably didn't chew their food. How do we know this? Well, their jaws have the kind of hinge that indicates they couldn't chew their food. Also, paleontologists have found gastroliths inside some fossilized sauropods, and you already learned that some animals swallow such stones to help them digest their food. Animals that swallow stones today do not chew their food, so we assume that the presence of gastroliths in sauropods indicates they didn't chew their food.

Try This!

Place some leaves inside one plastic bag with several stones. Then place some leaves of the same kind inside another plastic bag without stones. Seal up both bags. Now, squeeze and move around the leaves inside each bag, trying to crush and mash them. How much more quickly did it happen when you had stones in your bag? Now you know how gastroliths work!

Common Sauropods

There are many different types of sauropod fossils that have been found. I want to briefly tell you about a few of the more common sauropods.

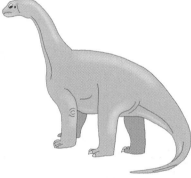

Brachiosaurus, which means "arm lizard," is a genus that contains at least two species that grew to lengths of more than 80 feet. Their fossils have been found in Europe, Africa, South America, and North America. The front legs were longer than the back legs, which is where they get their name. They had a skull with a very large nose opening close to the top of the head.

Diplodocus, which means "double beams" due to the appearance of certain bones under its tail, is a genus that contains several species. Found in the same areas as *Brachiosaurus*, these dinosaurs' front legs were shorter than their back legs, giving them a more horizontal posture. The tail was longer than the neck, and some paleontologists think it was used for defense. They grew to about 90 feet in length.

Camarasaurus, which means "chambered lizard" due to holes in its vertebrae, is a genus of smaller sauropods that grew to "only" about 60 feet long. They had a bigger head but shorter neck and tail than *Brachiosaurus* and *Diplodocus*. Their fossils have been found in North America and Europe. Some fossils from Asia are also thought to belong to members of this genus.

Cetiosaurus, which means "whale lizard," was actually the first sauropod discovered. The scientist who analyzed the fossils initially thought they were from some large sea-living reptile (like a crocodile). That's how this genus got its name. The species grew up to 60 feet long and are mostly found in Europe and Africa. Like *Diplodocus*, these dinosaurs probably had a more horizontal posture, because their front legs were smaller than their rear legs.

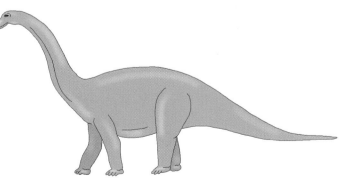

Theropods

Now let's talk about the other saurischians – the theropods. These beast-footed dinosaurs were probably the largest carnivorous dinosaurs that ever made the earth tremble. It appears they were not nearly as common as sauropods, since fossils of these creatures are extremely rare, and when they are found, it is usually only one bone or a few pieces of bones. Though scientists believe there were many species of smaller, lizard-sized theropods, few fossils of small theropods have been found.

This drawing of what the theropod *Allosaurus* might have looked like shows you its bipedal stance and the fact that its claws and toes were of different sizes.

Theropods were bipedal and generally had five fingers and five toes, but they were of much different size. There were usually three large fingers or toes and two smaller ones. In some species, there were only three fingers. Their toes all had claws, but usually only the three long fingers had claws. Most theropods had sharp, serrated teeth, believed to be used for tearing flesh.

Because there are some similarities between theropod feet and bird feet, many scientists think that dinosaurs and birds are somehow related to each other. Some go so far as to draw feathers on them, even though no feather imprints have been found on theropod fossils. Unfortunately, this point of view affects the way in which these animals are sometimes grouped. Some paleontologists even say that birds should be in the same order as these dinosaurs. You may even read in books that say birds are dinosaurs or dinosaurs were birds! We know that's not the case, and if you become a paleontologist one day, you'll be able to help people understand that theropods are not related to birds in any way.

All the bird issues aside, it's hard to classify theropods and separate them into groups, because new specimens are always being found. Scientists once believed that theropods were all carnivores, but they now believe that some of them, such as *Segnosaurus* (seg' noh sawr' us) were actually strict herbivores.

Common Theropods

While there are many types of theropods, I want to discuss only a few of the common ones. Where better to start than with the most famous, ***Tyrannosaurus***? This genus, whose name means "tyrant lizard," contains the well-known species *Tyrannosaurus rex*. Found mostly in North America, these were some of the biggest meat-eaters to stomp around God's creation. Strangely enough, for a creature thought to be a rough and scary animal, it had extremely short arms – like those of a kangaroo. Nobody is sure what the arms were used for, but the bones indicate there were strong muscles attached to them. Also, they are often found broken and injured, so they must have had some use.

A *Tyrannosaurus rex* skeleton in a museum

Tyrannosaurus rex (also known as T-rex) was huge, as you can see from the picture on the right. It had a body that could be more than 40 feet long, a head that was up to 6 feet long, and some of its 60 sharp teeth were up to 7 inches long! Get out a ruler and measure out 7 inches. Can you imagine seeing an animal with teeth that size? It was once believed that the *Tyrannosaurus rex* was the largest of all theropods, until new fossils were found.

Spinosaurus probably ate a lot of fish.

Currently, most paleontologists believe that a member of genus ***Spinosaurus*** (spy' noh sawr' us) is the largest of the theropod dinosaurs, with species thought to have been almost 60 feet long! This genus contains those species of theropods with large spines on their back. The spines could reach lengths of more than 6 feet, but no one is sure exactly what purpose they served. Based on the structure of its jaws and teeth, paleontologists believe that fish made up a large part of its diet. Fossils of this genus have been found in northern Africa.

Ceratosaurs (ser' uh tuh sawrz'), which means "horned lizards," are a large group of theropods that ranged from 20 feet to almost 30 feet in length. Their fossils are found in North and South America, Africa, Antarctica, Australia, and India. They get their name from a small horn on their snout. As shown on the right, some are found with one or two crests. These crests are tall, thin, plate-like bones on the top of the head. Paleontologists believe they were social animals, because their fossils are often found in groups. Members of one genus, *Coelophysis*, were found in a

This drawing represents what *Ceratosaurus*, an important ceratosaur, probably looked like.

mass burial that contained hundreds of them all jumbled together. So, even though movies portray all theropods as hungry, solitary stalkers, some appear to have been social creatures.

This drawing represents how *Velociraptor* most likely appeared.

Dromaeosaurs (droh' mee uh sawrz'), which means "swift-running lizards," were a group of medium-sized theropods (2 to 20 feet long) whose fossils have been found in Asia, North America, and possibly Australia. They had stiff tails, claws on the feet and hands, and one retractable, sickle-shaped claw on each foot, which was probably used for tearing flesh. The movie *Jurassic Park* made one type of dromaeosaur, the *Velociraptor*, famous. These are the theropods most likely to have feathers drawn on them, because their bones have many features in common with bird bones. This has led to a lot of confusion in paleontology. Some scientists think that dromaeosaurs like *Velociraptor* had feathers, although there have never been feather fossils found with *Velociraptor* fossils. Many paleontologists even classify animals that are obviously birds, like *Microraptor*, with the dromaeosaurs. It is a rather sad development in paleontology, which one famous expert on fossil birds, Dr. Alan Feduccia, says indicates a serious meltdown in the field.

Oviraptors, which means "egg thieves," were a group of smaller (3 to 9 feet long) theropods whose fossils are found in Asia (actually just Mongolia). They were given their name because the first oviraptor fossil was found on top of a nest of eggs, and scientists believed the eggs belonged to a different dinosaur. Based on later discoveries, however, scientists now believe that the eggs actually belonged to the oviraptor. So the first-discovered oviraptor had actually been found protecting, not stealing, eggs. Recently, many oviraptor skeletons have been found on top of nests, showing that this

Some oviraptors, such as the *Citipati* (chit' ih puh tih) drawn above, had crests on top of their head.

protection must have been a common behavior. Apparently, these dinosaurs were devoted parents, protecting their young with their lives as they were buried under massive sludge that poured in and froze them in time. Oviraptors had no teeth. They did have two small, tooth-like prongs in the roof of their mouth. It is hard to tell exactly what these dinosaurs ate. Most paleontologists think they had an omnivorous diet that included plants, seeds, and some eggs.

Ornithischia

The bird-hipped dinosaurs make up all the rest of the dinosaurs you have seen in books and toys. Despite their name, the paleontologists who think theropods are related to birds do not think these dinosaurs are related to birds. This group of dinosaurs is quite diverse. Some were quadrupedal, some bipedal; some were plated, others weren't. Some had skull structures that indicate they had cheek pouches for storing food; others don't. The one thing that unites them all, however, is the hip structure I already told you about. Let's have fun exploring some examples of these bird-hipped dinosaurs!

The **thyreophora** (thy ree' uh for uh) were the knights of the dinosaur world, with armor protecting their slow and steady frame. One of the most famous of these dinosaurs is *Stegosaurus*. The name of this genus means "covered lizard," because the well-known plates on its back were once believed to lie flat, like a cover. What were the plates for? Well, like *Spinosaurus'* spines, paleontologists aren't sure, but many think they may have helped regulate the dinosaur's body temperature. Averaging about 30 feet in length,

Paleontologists once thought that *Stegosaurus'* plates laid flat on its back, but they most likely stood up, as shown here.

Stegosaurus fossils have been found in western North America and perhaps Europe. Their greatest weapon was probably the 2-foot long spikes at the end of the tail. There were four or eight of them, depending on the species. The front legs of *Stegosaurus* were a bit shorter than the rear legs, which means it walked a lot like an elephant would today. Their brain was probably the size of a walnut. For such a large creature, that's a small brain!

Ankylosaurus was heavily armored.

Another famous genus of thyreophora is *Ankylosaurus* (ang kee' loh sawr' us). Its name means "fused lizard," because the plates on its back seem fused together. Although no complete skeleton has been found, the partial fossils indicate it might have grown as long as 30 feet. Dinosaurs like *Ankylosaurus* have been found in North America, Europe, and Asia. They are often called "tanks" because of their heavy armor. They also had a club at the end of the tail that was most likely used for defense.

The **marginocephalia** (mar jin' oh sih fal' ee uh) were the dinosaurs with margins (or shelves) on their heads. The model pictured on the first page of this lesson is of the most famous member of this group, *Triceratops*. The "tri" refers to the fact that it has three horns in addition to its head shelf. Some of the marginocephalia had no horns, and some had several. Most of them had a beak at the end of their nose, like that of a snapping turtle. Their fossils are found in North America, Europe, and Asia.

The *Pentaceratops* drawn here were marginocephalia that had ornate margins and five horns.

Creation Confirmation

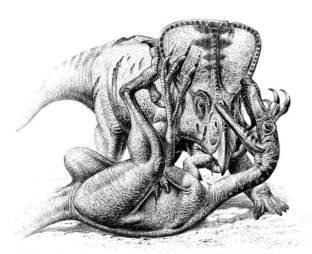

This drawing is an attempt to depict the fight that the famous Mongolian fossil seems to have preserved.

In 1971, a fossil was discovered in the Gobi Desert in Mongolia. It is considered remarkable because it appears to record a fight between a *Velociraptor* and a hornless marginocephalian known as *Protoceratops*. While we can never know whether or not the two dinosaurs really were fighting, the *Velociraptor's* hands look like they are grabbing *Protoceratops'* margin, while one of its arms is in *Protoceratops'* mouth! That sounds like a fight, doesn't it? How could these two creatures be fossilized in the middle of a fight? Well, they must have been buried quickly by a lot of sediment so their fight would be "frozen in time." This, of course, is exactly what we would expect if the fossils were formed in the Flood mentioned in the Bible. The huge number of rapidly formed fossils like this one, found around the world, gives solid support to the creationists' views on how fossils were formed.

The **ornithopoda** (or nuh' thuh puh duh), or bird-footed dinosaurs, were mostly bipedal with three toes. All of them were herbivores. The group of dinosaurs we call **hadrosaurs** (had' ruh sawrz) were the most common of all the ornithopods. The name means "bulky lizard," but a better name would be "billed lizard." You see, these dinosaurs had an elongated face that ended in a broad, flattened snout. In some species, the snout was so flat it resembles the bill of a duck! As a result, these dinosaurs are often called "duck-billed dinosaurs." Their remains have been found in North America, South America, Europe, and Asia.

While not all hadrosaur "bills" were as pronounced as this one, they are often called "duck-billed dinosaurs."

The "bill" of a hadrosaur had no teeth, but the dinosaur could have more than a *thousand* teeth in the back of its mouth. These teeth, called **cheek teeth**, helped it to grind rough vegetation so that it would be easier to digest. Scientists believe that hadrosaurs ran on two feet, but they could get down on all fours when grazing. Some had elaborate crests on top of the head; others didn't. In general, their sizes ranged from about 10 feet to about 40 feet long.

Paleontologists think there were at least five species that belonged to the ***Iguanodon*** genus of the ornithopods. As I told you before, the name means "iguana teeth," because these dinosaurs had teeth that strongly resemble those of an iguana. Remains of these dinosaurs have been found in Europe, Africa, North America, and Asia. The first iguanodon was found in England and named well before the word "dinosaur" had been used. The man who discovered it thought it was some large, extinct reptile. However, he wasn't aware that it was really different from a lizard. Later, miners found a group of 31 iguanodons together. They

It was first thought that *Iguanodon* was quadrupedal. Now most paleontologists think it was bipedal but often got down on all fours to graze, like the hadrosaurs.

had obviously been suddenly buried together. In addition to evidence for the Flood, this suggests they were social creatures. They had a spiked thumb on each hand, which is believed to have been used for defense or to strip leaves off tree branches.

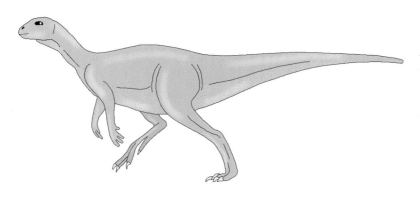

Paleontologists think *Hypsilophodon* could run very quickly.

Another set of interesting ornithopods can be found in the genus ***Hypsilophodon*** (hip sih loh' fuh don), which means "high-crested tooth." This "smaller" dinosaur was about 6 to 7 feet in length, and its remains are found in Europe. It had smaller front arms that ended in five-fingered hands, and its longer, rear legs ended in four-toed feet. It had a horned beak, cheek pouches (where it stored food like a chipmunk), and a mouth full of cheek teeth. Close to twenty *Hypsilophodon* fossils found together on an island in Great Britain make us believe it was another social dinosaur that needed to be around large groups of dinosaurs like itself.

Although I have not come close to covering every type of dinosaur that paleontologists think once existed, I have given you a good overview of the major ones. Take a moment to skim through the different dinosaurs I presented, and note how many similarities they all have. Even though the appearances of these dinosaurs varied quite a bit, there are only a couple of basic body plans (bird-hipped and lizard-hipped), and within each of those groups, there are really only a few basic distinctions. So what can we conclude from this? Do you remember when I told you that the Bible talks about creatures reproducing after their own *kind*? Well, the many similarities among dinosaurs tell us that while there were many *species* of dinosaur, there were probably only a few *kinds* of dinosaurs. This fact will be important in the next section.

What Happened to Them?

Even though dinosaurs were once plentiful on earth, they are now extinct. What happened to them? It is impossible to know for sure, but the Bible tells us that Noah took two of every *kind* of animal on the ark, and seven of each kind of "clean animal." Did that include the dinosaurs? Of course, because the Bible says two of *every* kind. Could Noah really have fit dinosaurs on the ark?

www.LostWorldMuseum.com

As I mentioned previously, there were not that many *kinds* of dinosaurs. Thus, Noah would not have needed to take many. Two of each basic body plan would probably have been enough. In addition, Noah wouldn't have needed to make room for two fully grown sauropods, for example! He probably took younger ones, which were much smaller. In the end, then, there were dinosaurs on the ark.

If dinosaurs got on (and got off) the ark, why aren't they alive today? Well, for starters, the Flood-induced ice age I told you about previously might have limited their food supply. If food is scarce or the weather isn't warm, reptiles don't thrive, and many times they die. Thus, many dinosaurs might have died as a result of the climate changes caused by the Flood. Some must have survived, however, because we see dinosaurs depicted in ancient artifacts. What happened to those survivors? Well, when people don't like a creature (or want to use a part of it), they often hunt the creature to extinction. Mastodons, Tasmanian tigers, dodo birds, and passenger pigeons are examples. The dinosaurs that survived the ice age were probably hunted to extinction, either for protection or for food. In fact, the term "dragon slayer" might have come from people trying to describe those who hunted dinosaurs.

What Do You Remember?

What evidence do we have that dinosaurs lived during the same time as people? What's the difference between dinosaurs and other reptiles? What are the two main groups of dinosaurs? What are some special features of sauropods? Which animal does Behemoth best describe and why? What are some special features of theropods? In which group of dinosaurs is *Stegosaurus* placed? In which group are the duck-billed dinosaurs placed? What are some possible reasons for the extinction of dinosaurs?

Map It!

North America: *Tyrannosaurus rex, Brachiosaurus, Diplodocus, Camarasaurus*, dromaeosaurs, *Stegosaurus, Ankylosaurus*, ceratosaurs, marginocephalia, hadrosaurs, *Iguanodon*
South America: *Brachiosaurus, Diplodocus*, ceratosaurs, hadrosaurs
Africa: *Brachiosaurus, Diplodocus, Spinosaurus, Cetiosaurus,* ceratosaurs, *Iguanodon*
Europe: *Brachiosaurus, Diplodocus, Camarasaurus, Cetiosaurus, Stegosaurus, Ankylosaurus*, marginocephalia, hadrosaurs, *Iguanodon, Hypsilophodon*
Asia: *Camarasaurus*, dromaeosaurs, Oviraptors, *Ankylosaurus*, marginocephalia, hadrosaurs, *Iguanodon*
Australia: Sauropods, ceratosaurs, dromaeosaurs
Antarctica: Sauropods, ceratosaurs

Track It!

Dinosaur tracks are remarkably abundant. When those heavy reptiles were tromping around trying to escape the Flood, they left many tracks in their wake. Like the hadrosaur footprint shown on the right, the most common dinosaur tracks have three lobes and look a bit like a leaf. Keep your eyes peeled when you're in dinosaur territory!

Notebook Activities

Now I want you to add a dinosaur section to your notebook. Start by writing about the two basic kinds of dinosaurs. Include drawings or pictures like those on page 216 so that someone who reads your notebook will know how to tell the two groups apart. Next, include information about the basic kinds of dinosaurs: sauropods, theropods, thyreophora, marginocephalia, and ornithopoda. Include an illustration for each kind.

Experiment

At the beginning of this lesson, you learned about the main difference between lizards and dinosaurs – their stance. I want you do to an experiment in which you will get some experience with how this difference affects both the weight of the reptile as well as how the reptile walks. To do this, you will build two models – one that represents a lizard and another that represents a dinosaur. After that, you will try to walk like a lizard and then like a quadrupedal dinosaur.

You will need:

♦ Scientific Speculation Sheet
♦ Two cardboard cylinders, like those used in toilet paper rolls
♦ A few metal coat hangers your parents will allow you to destroy
♦ Pliers
♦ Wire cutters or very strong scissors
♦ A timer, like a stopwatch
♦ Someone to help you

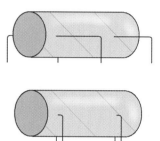

1. Use the wire cutters to cut the coat hangers so you have eight straight pieces of wire 6 inches long.
2. Bend the wires (use the pliers if you need to) and attach them to the cylinders by sticking one end of the wire right through the cardboard. The wires are the legs for your "reptiles." One of the cylinders should have legs bent far from the cylinder, as shown in the top drawing on the right. The other should have legs bent close to the cylinder, as shown in the bottom drawing.
3. Push down on each cylinder from the top. Which resists your push better?
4. The cylinders you made each represent a type of reptile. On your Scientific Speculation Sheet, make a hypothesis about which type of reptile could run faster.
5. Give your helper the timer and go to a hallway in your home.
6. Get on all fours, holding your legs and arms "splayed" out, like the top cylinder drawn above.
7. Have your helper time how long it takes you to crawl down to the other end of the hallway if you keep your arms and legs splayed out the entire time.
8. Go back to where you started and repeat steps 6 and 7, but this time, have your arms and legs more directly under your body, like the bottom cylinder drawn above.
9. Now that you have completed the experiment, finish filling out your Scientific Speculation Sheet.

In this experiment, the cylinder with the wires bent far from the body represented a lizard, while the other cylinder represented a dinosaur. From what you found in step 3, can you see why dinosaurs could be so much heavier than lizards?

The main purpose of this experiment was to give you some first-hand experience with what the different stances of lizards and dinosaurs mean for the animal itself. In steps 6–7, you were crawling like a lizard, while in step 8, you were crawling like a quadrupedal dinosaur. Which was faster? Was your hypothesis correct?

Lesson 13
Arthropods of the Land

We are now going to explore the exciting but creepy world of some of the **arthropods** (ar' thruh podz), such as spiders, harvestmen, scorpions, mites, centipedes, and millipedes. You may remember from Zoology 1 and 2 that arthropods are identified by their tough exoskeleton and segmented body, and that the word "arthropod" means "jointed foot." Like most creatures, they do not have a backbone. Do you remember what scientists call creatures without a backbone? That's right – **invertebrates**. Let's crawl into our study of arthropods by examining the **arachnids** (uh rak' nidz).

Arachnids

Do you know what arachnophobia (uh rak' nuh foh' bee uh) is? Doctors use the word to describe an excessive fear of spiders. Can you believe that the fear of spiders is so intense for some people that doctors have a medical name for it? Where do doctors get that word? Well, **spiders** are members of class **Arachnida** (uh rak' nih duh), so they are called arachnids. The Greek word "phobos" means "fear," so arachnophobia is the fear of arachnids! But of course, arachnids include more than just spiders. **Scorpions**, **harvestmen**, **ticks**, and **mites** are also arachnids. If you want to know whether or not the creature you are looking at is an insect or an arachnid, just count its legs. Do you remember how many legs an insect has? Six. Well, unlike insects, arachnids have eight legs.

Like all arachnids, this golden silk spider has eight legs.

abdomen   cephalothorax
pedipalps   chelicerae

In addition to their eight legs, arachnids have two **pedipalps** (ped' uh palps) that are so long in some species they look like an extra pair of legs. They are sensitive appendages that give arachnids a good sense of touch and can be used for handling food as well as for defense. Arachnids also have mouthparts called **chelicerae** (kuh lis' ih ree) that end in tiny "swords" called **fangs**. The body of an arachnid is made up of two parts: the **abdomen** (ab'duh muhn) and the **cephalothorax** (sef uh loh thor' aks). The legs and pedipalps are attached to the cephalothorax, while the abdomen contains several organs, including the lungs (or in some cases, gills).

Spiders

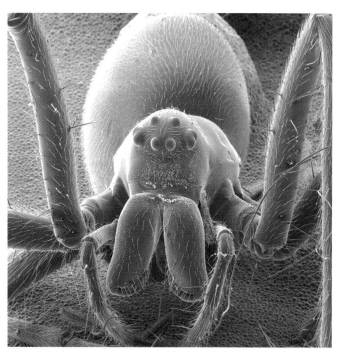

The eight bumps on this magnified spider's head are its simple eyes, and the "hairs" on its legs, pedipalps, and chelicerae are its setae.

Wherever you live, you are usually near a spider, or two, or ten, or a thousand. Along with their dreadful eight legs, most spiders were created with the same number of sinister-looking eyes. The majority of spiders do not have good eyesight, however. Their eyes mostly serve to detect light from darkness as well as movement. So, if you spot a spider staring at you with its eight beady eyes, fear not; it probably can't see you well. But, it can sense you with its legs. Indeed, the legs are better at "seeing" than are the eyes.

A spider's legs are equipped with thousands of "hairs" called **setae**. These setae serve many purposes, mostly related to sensing the outside world. Some can smell, others can sense vibrations and motions, and a few can even taste. The setae are so sensitive that some spiders can sense an insect without touching it! You might see a spider like a tarantula pounce on its prey without even looking at it, because the spider's hairy legs could sense the prey's location. Remove a spider's legs, and you've removed its ears and nose, some of its eyes, and its legs, of course, which it needs for walking and climbing.

At the bottom of each leg is a **tarsus**, otherwise known as a foot. If the spider is a web-making spider, its tarsus will also have a tiny claw. The claws help the spider hang onto the thin threads of its web. If the spider doesn't make webs, it often doesn't have claws, but each tarsus has a tuft of setae called a **scopula** (skop' yuh luh). Many web-making spiders have both a claw and a scopula on each tarsus. What do the scopulae do for the spider? Well, do you remember how geckos climb on smooth surfaces? Their setae get so close to the surface that they stick to the individual molecules of the surface. The setae of a spider's scopula do the same thing!

claw on the tarsus

You can see the claw this web-making spider has on its tarsus. It uses the claw to grip its web.

Remember the fangs we discussed earlier? Well, to make the spider even more uncivilized, its fangs inject venom when it bites. Perhaps if spiders were herbivores, instead of carnivores, this wouldn't bother us as much. But a spider likes to eat meat. In fact, it actually *drinks* meat! You see, because a spider has a tiny mouth, it is unable to ingest solid food. It must first liquefy its food before eating it. Here is how it works: the spider injects a venom mixture into the body of its prey. The venom kills the prey and actually *liquefies* its body. The spider then sucks up the liquid as its meal.

Spider Friends and Foes

Although it may seem like a good idea to kill every spider you see, spiders actually do a lot of good. Because of their voracious appetite, they eat many of the insects and creatures we consider to be nuisances. In fact, spiders eat more insects each day than birds do! Of course, we tend to dislike spiders because they bite us if we are not careful. These bites usually aren't serious, however, because a spider's venom is usually not powerful enough to harm people in any severe way. It is, however, often powerful enough to cause an annoying itch for several days! Of the more than 30,000 species of spiders known to exist, only about a dozen have powerful enough poison to be a threat to people. In the United States, there are only two: the **brown recluse** and the **black widow**.

The brown recluse lives in the midwestern, midsouthern, and southeastern United States. Measuring from the end of one leg to the end of the corresponding leg on the other side, the brown recluse is about an inch wide. Yellow to brown in color, it has a violin pattern on its cephalothorax. The wide part of the violin pattern is the head of the spider, while the neck of the violin points to the abdomen. A brown recluse will only bite people when touched. It is generally active at night, and it likes to reside in buildings where it

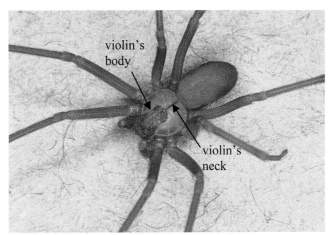

The violin pattern is easy to see on this brown recluse.

can hide in warm, dry places during the day. Don't worry, though. When you come close to a brown recluse, it usually scurries off as quickly as it can, and you never even know it was there.

The brown recluse's venom is highly poisonous, more powerful than that of a pit viper. The good news, however, is that the brown recluse doesn't have *as much* venom as a pit viper. As a result, its venom can't do quite as much damage to you. Thus, brown recluse bites are rarely fatal. Nevertheless, this spider's bite can produce a deep, painful wound that takes a long time to heal.

Unless you live in the northern parts of the world or in remote parts of Africa, you probably live in black widow territory, because they can be found in most of the warm areas of the world. Many know that these spiders are black and shiny with a red, hourglass-shaped mark on the underside of the abdomen. However, most people don't realize that this description is only true for the *female*. Male black widows are all or partly brown, depending on the species, and they do not have the hourglass-shaped mark. The picture on the next page illustrates the differences between males and females.

Like the brown recluse, black widow spiders are nocturnal. They build their tangled webs of coarse silk in dark places where humans rarely frequent. Like the brown recluse, the female black widow's venom is more toxic than that of many snakes, but it injects so little when it bites that people rarely die from it. The bites can be very painful, however, and they can cause nausea, severe perspiration, chest pains, cramping, difficulty in breathing, and slurred or labored speech.

What have you learned so far about spiders?

Spider Silk and Spiderlings

The female black widow is on the bottom left, and the male is on the top right. The female is protecting the egg sac she spun.

Spiders have the special ability to produce silken threads, which many weave into webs. These silken threads actually have many uses – helping the spider protect its young, catching food, creating a home, and even helping the spider move around. Have you ever wondered where all that silken thread comes from? The silk is made inside tiny, silk-producing organs, called "spinnerets." These organs are most often found at the very back of the abdomen. Spiders usually have four, six, or eight spinnerets, depending on the species. Silk glands attached to each spinneret contain the liquid silk. The liquid silk hardens into thread when forced through a spinneret.

A spider has several silk glands, all filled with different kinds of silk. Why does a spider need different kinds of silk? Well, each kind of silk serves a different purpose. The different types of silk common to most web-making spiders are **dragline silk**, **capture silk**, and **egg-case silk**.

Dragline silk is the strongest silk a spider makes. Most spiders, even if they don't build webs, lay down dragline silk as they forage. These strands are like safety lines the spider uses to make a quick escape if danger approaches. Capture silk is used to catch prey in a spider web, and it is also used by those spiders that actually shoot out strands of silk to catch prey. The egg-case silk is a special waterproof silk the spider wraps around its eggs, making an egg case. If you go on a spider web hunt, you might notice little round balls of silk. Inside these silk balls are the developing young – there can be as many as several hundred spider eggs inside one little egg case! Most baby spiders, called **spiderlings**, stay inside the egg case after they hatch until they molt for the first time. Remember from Zoology 1 and 2 that arthropods must molt to grow, so spiderlings do a *lot* of molting!

What do the spiderlings do once they leave the egg case? They actually want to get away from their mother, father, brothers, and sisters. Why? If they all stayed close to one another, they would have to compete for food, and there are too many of them! As a result, they need to get far away from each other. Believe it or not, many spiderlings get away from their families by going ballooning. That's right! A young spiderling will often climb up and up, as high as it can go. When it has reached the tip-top of whatever it has found to climb, it's ready to "fly." From its spinnerets, the spiderling lets out strands of silk that wave like a kite in the wind. As the silk lines get longer, the wind finally whisks the spider away. It glides through the air, traveling far and wide, into new territory. The distance it travels depends on the wind; it could fly across the lawn, or it might fly all the way to the next city!

Creation Confirmation

Spider silk is a technological marvel that points unmistakably to its incredible Creator. Dragline silk, for example, is one of the strongest substances known. If you had two tubes of the same size – one made of steel and one made of dragline silk, which would you think would be stronger? Believe it or not, the *dragline silk* would be. A tube of dragline silk about the thickness of a garden hose would be able to support the weight of *two* Boeing 747 airplanes, complete with passengers and luggage! And not only would it be stronger than steel, it would be flexible! Dragline silk can stretch up to 40% of its original length and then spring right back to normal.

To understand how marvelous spider silk is, all you have to do is compare it to what modern technology can produce. The strongest fiber that human science and technology can produce is Kevlar®. Do you know what we make from Kevlar? Bullet-proof vests. A vest made of Kevlar can actually stop a bullet before it reaches the person wearing the vest. Sounds amazing, doesn't it? However, spider silk is *stronger and more elastic* than Kevlar. In fact, an article in a respected science journal compared the structure of spider silk to human-made fibers (called "synthetic fibers"). It says that spider silk "makes synthetic fibers seem crude." [Fox, D., "The Spinners," *New Scientist* **162**:38–41, 1999]

Wondrous Webs

Though not all spiders build webs, the web-building spiders are industrious little creatures that spin these works of art in order to catch prey. They produce different kinds of webs, depending on their species. Let's take a look at the webs you may see on your nature hikes or in your backyard. **Orb webs** are composed of round elements, because the word "orb" means "ball." The web itself is not necessarily round,

This is an orb web.

but is composed of strands that form circles, more or less. Spiders that weave orb webs typically stay on or near their web, waiting to sense vibrations on one of the strands. This tells the spider that an animal is struggling in the sticky fibers of the web. If it feels violent vibrations from a creature too large to eat, the spider typically hides until the creature quits struggling. Then, the spider cuts the threads and lets the creature fall. If it senses small vibrations, the spider knows it's a small creature and pounces. It may eat the captured animal right away, or it may wrap the prey in silk and save it for later.

Try This!

Step 1:

Step 2:

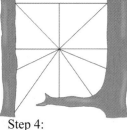

Step 3:

Step 4:

Step 5:

Do you think you could build your own orb web? Get a ball of yarn and some tape and find a place to build your web. You can make it really large (between two trees) or small (between two chairs).

An orb weaver follows a general strategy when building its web. First, it looks for a place where there are two "posts" (like tree branches) and something in between them (like a small twig as shown in the drawings on the left). Next, it holds onto one of the posts and releases some dragline silk. The silk is blown by the wind and, with some luck, it eventually hits and sticks to the post on the other side. The spider then carefully crawls on that line, adding more and more silk until it's sturdy and strong, as shown in the drawing labeled "Step 1."

Next, the spider creates a Y-shape, anchoring the web to an object below, as shown in the drawing labeled "Step 2." Look at the illustration to see where the Y is attached. After that, it makes rays, called **radial lines**, which stretch across the entire web, spreading it out in several directions, attaching to all sides, as shown in the drawing labeled "Step 3."

Once the radial lines are done, it creates strands in large circles. The circles are constructed so the spider can walk across the entire web using the radial lines and these circles. Why? Well, so far, the spider has used non-sticky silk. A spider would get caught in its own capture silk, which is sticky. So it creates a lot of its web (the part shown in the drawing labeled "Step 4") out of non-sticky silk. It then adds more circular structures so that the web eventually looks like the drawing labeled "Step 5," but the *extra* circles added between the two steps are made of the sticky, capture silk. When the spider's prey hits the web, it will get caught in the capture silk. However, since the spider knows its own web, it walks on only the non-sticky strands, so it never gets stuck. Isn't that clever? So how did your web turn out? If it didn't turn out too well, don't worry. You aren't designed to make webs – spiders are!

Orb webs are not the only kinds of webs you will see in nature. Some spiders spin **funnel webs** that are like little webbed sinkholes in the ground. As the name implies, the web is usually funnel-shaped, and it is designed so that something will fall in if it walks past. A spider that spins such a web usually waits at the bottom, hoping an unsuspecting creature, like a lizard or insect, will stumble into the trap. Then, when the prey falls in, the spider quickly bites its prey using its sharp, venomous fangs. Many of the spiders that spin such webs have very strong venom, and some scientists consider them to be the deadliest types of spiders.

A funnel web is a deadly trap for insects that crawl on the ground.

A tangle web has no discernible shape.

Tangle webs, also called **cobwebs**, look like random masses of threads that sprawl out here and there. While orb webs are flat, and funnel webs have a definite funnel shape, cobwebs are just bulky, tangled masses of spider silk. The black widow spider, which you learned about previously, spins a tangle web. These webs typically contain a lot more silk than orb webs or funnel webs, and the spider usually spins them over a period of several days.

Sheet webs are flat web sheets that lay across vegetation or outdoor structures. They can be found over fences, or they can be spread over grass or other plants. Typically, a spider that builds a sheet web strings several criss-crossing strands of silk above the sheet and hangs upside down on the underside of the sheet. When a flying insect hits one of the criss-crossing strands, it is knocked down onto the sheet. The spider then rushes to where the insect landed and pulls the prey through the web.

A sheet web looks like an acrobat's safety net, but it is not safe for the spider's prey!

Try This!

While the four types of webs I have shown you in this book are not the *only* kinds of webs you will find in nature, they are the most common. Go on a nature hike or a walk around your yard and try to identify the different kinds of webs you find.

Describe some of the different webs that spiders build. For what purposes might a spider use its silk?

Hunting Spiders

Some spiders don't use their webs to catch food; instead, they hunt or ambush their prey. Even though most spiders don't have great eyesight, hunters and ambushers often do, because they cannot just wait for their prey to come to them. They must find their prey. Let's take a peek at some of these hunters and ambushers.

Notice the two large eyes on this wolf spider.

Wolf spiders are fast-moving hunters that track down their prey, like a wolf. There eyes are arranged in three rows: two medium-sized eyes in the top row, two large eyes in the middle row, and four small eyes in the bottom row. Although their venom is deadly to their prey, it is not deadly to people. It will cause burning, itching, and pain, but that's about it. One interesting thing about these spiders is how carefully they watch over their young. The mothers actually carry the egg sac around with them, attached to their spinnerets, everywhere they go. They are even able to hunt while carrying their egg sac! When the young are born, they climb upon mother's abdomen and stay there until after the first molt. I first learned about this when I stepped on a wolf spider in my basement, and hundreds of tiny spiders scurried in every direction. Yes, these spiders enjoy damp basements. They also can be found outside under rocks and pieces of wood. Most wolf spiders are gray, black, or brown. They are often striped and somewhat hairy.

Instead of hunting their prey, **crab spiders** wait in ambush to pounce on it. They typically sit inside a flower, camouflaged, hoping for a pollinator to visit. When a bee, gnat, or other insect comes searching for nectar, the crab spider quickly snatches the prey with its long front legs. With their quick maneuvering and powerful venom, crab spiders are able to catch insects much larger than themselves. They look a little like a crab with their long front legs and flat bodies. Many are brightly colored, matching the flowers in which they hide.

Notice how well this crab spider blends in with the flower upon which it is sitting.

Tarantulas are probably the best known type of ambushing spider. They creep about the dry, warm areas of the world, including the southern United States, South America, Africa, Asia, and Australia. They are notoriously hairy and can be tan, red, black, or a mixture of these colors. Because the venom in most species is harmless to humans, they are often kept as pets.

Tarantulas are quite slothful and spend most of their day in hiding – usually in holes in the ground. But as the evening approaches, the tarantula creeps out of its shelter, seeking something to devour. It typically hides, waiting to ambush something good to eat (a lizard or other small animal) as it passes. Tarantulas can strike with amazing speed – zipping over and biting their prey with their large fangs. When it comes to protecting themselves, most tarantulas have barbed hairs on their abdomen that contain an irritating chemical. When threatened, tarantulas spew these barbed hairs into the potential predator. Though most

Although they look scary, most tarantulas are harmless to people and are often kept as pets.

tarantulas only grow to be about 3 inches from tarsus to tarsus, some grow much larger; for example, the goliath tarantula has a leg span of up to 12 inches!

Fishing spiders can be found at the edge of the water.

Fishing spiders are very similar to wolf spiders but tend to be thinner. These interesting spiders usually live very near a river or lake. They sit at the edge of the water, or on a leaf floating in the water, and put one or two of their legs in the water. The legs sense the motion of insects that have fallen into the water, and they can actually *run on the surface of the water* to get the struggling insect. If a small fish happens to be swimming by while a fishing spider has its legs in the water, the spider can also catch the fish for its meal.

Jumping spiders, as you would expect from their name, hide while hunting and then ambush their prey by jumping on the creature. Their legs are so well designed for jumping that they can jump 20 to 30 times the length of their own body. Think about that! How far would you go if you could jump 20 times your own height? Interestingly enough, before a jumping spider jumps, it generally attaches a line of dragline silk to its hiding place. That way, if it doesn't land where it intended, it can climb back up the line and try again! Jumping spiders are so common in creation that they represent about one-eighth of all spider species.

This jumping spider successfully ambushed a fly.

You have completed your study of spiders. Explain to someone all that you have learned.

Mid-Lesson Notebook Activity

For your notebook today, I would like for you to go on a spider hunt. Carefully look for spiders in your house or yard – a web is a great indicator that a spider lurks nearby. Sit down and draw pictures of the spiders or webs you find for your notebook. If you see an egg sac, write down its size and where you found it.

Mid-Lesson Project
Create a Web Frame

Spiders are always looking for places to build their webs. I want you to create a special web frame and put it in an alluring location in hope that a spider will come and use it to build its web.

You will need:

♦ A long, sturdy wooden dowel or broom handle
♦ A foam board about 1½ feet long and 1½ feet wide
♦ A marker
♦ An adult with sharp knife (like an X-ACTO® knife) or sharp blade
♦ Duct tape or glue

hollow hexagon shape made of foam

dowel or broom handle

1. Use the marker to draw a large hexagon (six-sided shape – see the drawing on the right) on your foam board. Make it as large as you can.
2. Draw a smaller hexagon inside the first so there is about 1 or 2 inches between the inner hexagon and the outer one.
3. Have an adult use the knife to cut out both hexagons so that you have a hollow hexagon shape like that shown in the drawing.
4. Insert the wooden dowel into the bottom of the hexagon shape. Use glue or duct tape to make sure the hexagon is securely fastened to the dowel.
5. When the weather is warm outside, choose a spot for your frame near one of your home's windows or an outside light. The light will attract insects, which will, in turn, attract spiders that want to eat them. Insert the web frame into the ground several inches deep so it doesn't blow over.
6. Keep the lights near the web frame on at night to attract insects. Within a few weeks, your web frame may become the most desired property in town – for spiders, that is. If no spider moves in to build a web, move the frame to a new location.

Harvestmen

You've probably seen spider-like harvestmen running about outdoors. They are sometimes called **daddy longlegs**. Though this eight-legged arachnid may look like a spider, it's not a spider at all. Instead of having two parts to its body, like a spider, it has only one. Also, instead of having eight beady eyes, it only has two. In addition, a daddy longlegs can eat chunks of food. It need not drink its meals. Finally, daddy longlegs produce no silk, so even though they are a part of class Arachnida, they are not spiders.

Notice that the body of this harvestman is not separated into two segments like the body of a spider.

When I was a child, I was told that the daddy longlegs had the most powerful venom in the world, but its fangs were too small to break your skin. What I was told, however, was wrong on both counts. Daddy longlegs have no venom at all, and they also do not have fangs. Sometimes people will tell you things that are not true; often the person telling you something untrue is just repeating what he heard from someone else. If you ever wonder whether or not something you hear is true, ask your parents. If they don't know the answer, they will find out the truth for you.

Harvestmen have a couple ways to protect themselves from predators. If something picks one up by a leg, the harvestman can detach its leg, which even keeps moving for a few moments. This confuses predators long enough for the harvestman to escape. In addition, most harvestmen can use another defense – chemical warfare! They are able to spray nasty-smelling fumes from their body. Birds and other predators don't like that at all!

Though harvestmen may look scary, they're pretty good to have around. You see, they consume all kinds of small garden pests like aphids, flies, mites, etc. They also consume decaying plant and animal remains, animal waste, and some kinds of fungi. So, these omnivores are a garden friend, not a foe.

Scorpions

For some, the sight of a scorpion is more frightening than that of a spider. This might be because of misconceptions people have about these fearsome-looking creatures. A scorpion has lobster-like pedipalps used to capture and tear up prey. At the other end of the animal, we see the menacing **metasoma** (tail) topped with a sharp **telson**. The telson ends in a nasty, venomous stinger used on predators and prey. Rest assured, a scorpion isn't an aggressive creature; when in danger, it prefers escape to stinging. Though it favors flight instead of fight, when a scorpion must sting a human, it will. Interestingly enough, however, scorpions have two types of venom – one that simply causes pain, and the other that causes real harm. Unless it feels *really* threatened, a scorpion will use the less harmful poison, saving the potent stuff for when it really needs to use it. Of the many, many scorpion species, only twenty or so can do serious harm to people, even with their potent venom. Only one of those species lives in North America: the **bark scorpion** that can be found in the southwestern United States.

Though the potent venom is usually reserved for a predator on the hunt for a tasty scorpion snack, it's also sometimes used to disable prey so that the scorpion can eat in peace. Dinner consists of anything the same size or smaller than the scorpion, but the venom is specifically designed to be most effective against other arthropods. With all their weapons, however, scorpions are still not at the top of the food chain. Many creatures, like Elf Owls, enjoy a scorpion snack. Grasshopper mice are immune to the scorpion's venom, as are pallid bats, desert shrews, and some snakes and lizards. Centipedes and tarantulas also hunt scorpions, as do meerkats, who consider scorpions a true delicacy.

Although scorpions are common in desert environments such as those found in Arizona and Texas, these creatures of the night can be found in a variety of habitats, from the highest mountain to the densest rainforest. Most scorpions can be found crawling out of their self-made burrows on the forest floor. They generally grow only a few inches long. However, a few species can grow to be 8 inches in length.

False and Whip Scorpions

This whip scorpion has pedipalps, but there is no telson on the end of its whiplike tail.

Even though their name includes the word "scorpions," **whip scorpions** aren't really scorpions at all. Instead of having a metasoma ending in a telson, they have a thin "whip" for a tail. These animals have no venom. Instead, they have glands that emit foul-smelling chemicals. In some species, the smell is a lot like that of concentrated vinegar, which has led some people to call them "vinegaroons." Even the largest of these small arachnids grows to be just over 3 inches long. They feed on insects, worms, and slugs. They are considered necessary animals for the control of the roach and cricket populations.

False scorpions are also called **pseudoscorpions** (soo' doh skor' pee uhns), because "pseudo" means "false." These tiny creatures don't even reach an inch in length, and they can spin silk like spiders! They sometimes build a webbed nest under papers and books in your home, which has led some to call them "book scorpions." Although they have pedipalps, they don't have any kind of metasoma – not even a thin whip like the whip scorpions. These tiny arachnids are beneficial to people, because they eat the larvae of moths that can destroy your clothes. They also eat ants, mice, and other tiny pests.

What are some facts you have learned about scorpions and scorpion-like creatures?

Acarina

More numerous than all the other arachnids put together are the tiny parasites called the **acarina** (ak uh ree' nuh), otherwise known as **mites** and **ticks**. It's been said that 1 square yard of forest has more than a million different kinds of mites creeping about under and above the dirt. Mites are so plentiful that an entire colony might be living inside the follicle of your eyelash right this very minute. Let's hope not!

Most species of acarina are parasites. They live off plants or animals or their waste. They can be microscopic, like follicle mites, or as big as a raisin, like some ticks. Even as small as these creatures are, they can really cause serious problems for those plants or animals they infest – spreading disease, decay, and even death.

This peacock mite has been magnified to about 300 times its normal size so you can see it clearly.

Because they are arachnids, they are similar to the animals you have studied so far. For example, most of them have eight legs. The head and abdomen are fused together, much like you see in harvestmen. They generally have piercing, fanged mouthparts, and they often excrete toxic digestive juices into their hosts. Let's look at a few types of acarina that may be residing in or near your home.

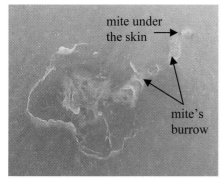

mite under the skin →

← mite's burrow

This picture shows you skin infected by a scabies mite. The skin damage that is not from the mite or burrow is from the person scratching the area.

The word **scabies** (skay' beez) comes from the Latin word for "scratch." That's because the scabies mite causes people to scratch. It burrows under the skin of people and animals, creating an itchy patch. Female scabies mites will lay eggs under the skin, and when the larvae hatch, they cause a severe rash. People tend to scratch themselves so much when they are infected with scabies that they open themselves up to other infections as well.

If you've ever spent a day out in nature and come home with several red spots that itched for days and days, you probably had **chiggers**, which are the larvae of **harvest mites**. Adult harvest mites eat insects and insect eggs, but their own eggs hatch into larvae that need to eat skin cells to survive. If you are unlucky enough to brush your skin against plants or soil that contain these larvae, they will jump onto your skin and feast on it. They don't burrow under your skin or drink your blood. They just punch a hole in your skin and inject digestive juices that make your skin a drinkable slurry. These juices cause severe irritation, forming red, itchy welts on your skin.

Have you ever heard the term "mangy dog?" It refers to a dog that has patches of skin showing through its coat. Those patches are caused by **mange**, a disease that a dog gets when it is attacked by **mange mites**. The mites bore into the dog's hair follicles and grow colonies that make the dog itch, lose its hair, and eventually stink.

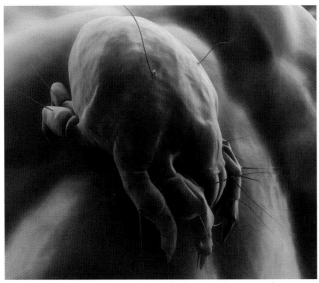

This dust mite has been magnified more than 250 times so you can see it clearly.

Do you realize that your skin is shedding every single day? Dead skin cells are constantly falling off your body and being replaced with new ones. So, where does all that shed skin go? Well, it ends up in the carpet, on the floor, in your bedding, etc. But thankfully, it doesn't just stay there forming huge mounds of skin. Tiny creatures come to the rescue, feasting on this dead skin. But, we really don't offer the **dust mites** much thanks for this cleaning job. That's because of the harm they do us. These little mites aren't meaning to harm anyone, but their droppings and the chemicals they produce while eating your skin can cause terrible allergies.

Some homes are literally crawling with dust mites, and some have relatively few. The difference is, of course, on how often you sweep, vacuum, wash the bedding, and get rid of dust. Houses that have high humidity levels also have more dust mites. So, go wash your sheets! Who wants to sleep in dead skin…or with the animals that eat it?

There are several different types of acarina that we call ticks. In all stages of a tick's life, it feeds on blood, blood, and more blood. There are two kinds of ticks: **hard ticks** and **soft ticks**, and their behaviors are quite different. When a hard tick finds an animal or person to feed on (called the **host**), it feeds for a long time (several days or even weeks). It generally leaves its host when it needs to molt so it can grow. Once it has molted, it goes and looks for a new host. Soft ticks, on the other hand, feed on their hosts for shorter periods of time (several minutes to a few days). They are commonly found in nests and burrows, where there is easy access to hosts. Soft ticks look different from hard ticks as well. The easiest way to tell them apart is to look at their backs from above. If you can see the mouthparts, you are looking at a hard tick. If the mouthparts are all or mostly hidden on the underside of the body, you are looking at a soft tick.

How do ticks get onto their hosts? Well, they are patient creatures. Many of them climb up to the very tips of grass and shrubbery, waiting, waiting, and waiting for a warm-blooded creature to pass by. When someone or something brushes past, they latch on and crawl upward, looking for a well-concealed spot to grab on and feast.

This hard tick is waiting for a host upon which to feed.

Ticks can be dangerous to people because they can transmit several kinds of diseases: Lyme disease, Rocky Mountain spotted fever, American fever, Colorado tick fever, Q fever, encephalitis, and tick paralysis are examples of tick-borne diseases. However, most ticks are not infected with these diseases, and a tick usually has to be attached to you for several hours to make you ill. If you check yourself well after a hike in the woods, you'll be just fine.

If you do find a tick on you, pull it off carefully. The best way to do it is to grasp the tick with tweezers as close to the skin as possible and pull steadily. If you pull steadily enough, the tick will let go rather than break apart. Once you have the tick out of your skin, wash the site with alcohol. You can then put the tick in a jar that has some alcohol in it. This will kill the tick but preserve it if your doctor wants to identify or test the tick.

Although we have concentrated on acarina that feed on warm-blooded animals, there are many that feed on plant matter as well. Some are beneficial, consuming dead plant matter to clean the forest, but several are known to harm plants. Spider mites, gall mites, and other mites can cause harm to plants grown by gardeners and farmers. In fact, the peacock mite pictured on page 241 can cause damage to certain fruit crops in the tropics.

Explain all you remember about arachnids before we move on to other arthropods.

Centipedes and Millipedes

Centipede means "hundred feet," and **millipede** means "thousand feet," but don't be fooled. Depending on the species, centipedes have between thirty and a few hundred feet, while millipedes don't have anywhere near a thousand feet! Both centipedes and millipedes are long-bodied creatures with two parts to their body – a head and a long, segmented trunk. The head is equipped with two antennae for sensing the environment. Though they eat different kinds of food, both creatures have chewing teeth in their jaws. Preferring areas with high humidity, such as forests and basements, these two creatures are not difficult to find. Though there are a few similarities, the centipede and millipede are really very different.

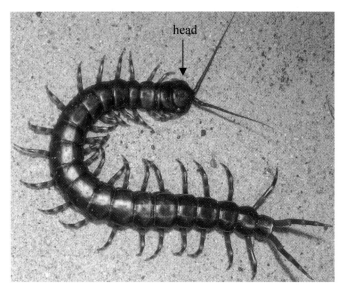

Although they are fierce predators in the arthropod world, most centipedes can't harm people.

Centipedes are more aggressive than millipedes. These carnivores are a part of class **Chilopoda** (kye lah' puh duh) and sport venomous fangs that kill prey. Their nasty bite can also be used on an animal that wants to be a predator. However, only one kind of centipede can bite hard enough to really hurt a person; that would be the giant centipede found in exotic places like the Amazon rainforest. It can grow up to a foot long and catch bats in mid-air to feed on them! Strangely, though, giant centipedes are sold as exotic pets. The centipedes that you might find in your yard or home grow to be only an inch or two long.

Centipedes have longer legs than millipedes, which carry them about speedily. This is important, since they are predators. Their long body is divided into segments. Only one pair of legs is attached to each segment of the centipede, compared to the two pairs attached to the millipede's segments. The body of a centipede is much flatter than that of the millipede.

You can usually find centipedes under decomposing leaves and other places where they hunt their prey. Although outdoors is ideal, one species of centipede makes its home in a most unwelcome spot – your house! The **house centipede** has thirty very long legs, making it look hairy and…scary. Yet, it is not fearsome, and it is no more harmful than a bee. In fact, though it isn't the most attractive visitor you'll ever have, it will eat the spiders, roaches, bedbugs, and silverfish inhabiting your home.

Millipedes are members of class **Diplopoda** (duh plah' puh duh), and you can tell them apart from centipedes in several ways. First, a millipede's body is more rounded than that of the centipede. Also, when you look closely, you'll see more than one pair of legs attached to each segment. In fact, this is why their class is called Diplopoda, which means "double foot." They have two feet on each side of each segment. Another thing that distinguishes a millipede is that it curls up for protection.

When threatened, a millipede will curl itself into a spiral.

While the centipede has speed and a nasty bite for defense, the slow-moving millipede just curls up, hoping its tough exoskeleton will protect it from harm. Also, if you can see what they eat, most millipedes are not carnivores. They prefer to feed on decaying plant matter.

In addition to curling up into a spiral, some millipedes have a chemical defense. When these millipedes are frightened, they produce chemicals that can smell terrible and irritate the skin. The smell is enough to ward off most predators, but if the animal is determined to eat the millipede, it could suffer a skin rash that will make it think twice about eating another one!

These smelly little creatures don't often make their way into people's homes because they prefer eating decomposing plant matter. I don't know about you, but we don't have a lot of decomposing plant matter in our house. However, even if you find one, they

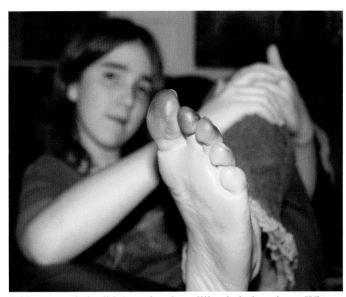

This young lady didn't notice the millipede in her shoe. When she stuck her foot inside, the millipede released its chemicals, which caused the rash you see here.

were not created with fangs and therefore don't bite. Many do stink, however, because of their chemical defense. Millipedes are usually good for gardens and can help clean up the dead plant matter in the yard. Because of this, they are easy to find under moist leaf piles. Since they are very slow, they're quite easy to catch. Some people even keep millipedes as pets. Of course, you always want to wash your hands after handling them.

If you watch a millipede walk, you'll notice their legs move in the most fascinating wavelike motion. They range in size from an inch to about 9 inches long. With simple eyes that can only detect light and dark, they are dependent on sensory hairs and their short antennae to find food and escape danger.

Explain some of the differences between centipedes and millipedes.

Isopods

A woodlouse is not a bug. It is a crustacean.

Is it a roly-poly or a pillbug? Perhaps it's a sow bug. Some call it an armadillo bug, potato bug, or a cheese log. Where I grew up, we called it a doodlebug. All these names represent a little creature that's more accurately called a **woodlouse**. The woodlouse is an example of an **isopod**, and it isn't a bug at all. It is actually a crustacean, like a crab, lobster, or shrimp. You may remember from Zoology 1 what features an animal must have to be a bug, and perhaps you remember the characteristics of crustaceans from Zoology 2.

The woodlouse is the only crustacean completely at home on land. However, their bodies do dry out easily, so they must stay in moist environments. In fact, even though they live on land, they

actually breathe through gill-like structures. Thus, they must have moisture in order to get the oxygen they need. To avoid too much evaporation, they are nocturnal, coming out at night to feed on decomposing plant and animal matter, including animal feces.

There are many isopods that live in the water as well. Interestingly enough, they look a lot like their terrestrial counterparts, but are often bigger. In addition, some isopods are parasites that attach to their host on the skin, fins, or gills. They then feed on the tissue to which they are attached.

This squirrelfish has an isopod parasite attached to it. Notice how similar the isopod is to a woodlouse.

Try This!

Isopods can be caught easily. They don't bite, stink, or carry diseases. So, if you have some in your yard, it would be fun to study one up close as you read the next section about their anatomy. If you think you can find one in your yard right now, go get it. Look for them under damp leaves, pieces of wood, or rocks. They might be gray, tan, or white, so keep your eyes peeled. If you catch one, keep it handy as you read the next section.

Isopod Anatomy

antenna

eye

cephalothorax

pereon

pleon

pleotelson

Like all arthropods, isopods have jointed legs. The head is at the front, housing the tiny compound eyes and the antennae. The next section of the body is the **pereon** (puh ree' ahn), and it acts as the isopod's thorax. It is composed of seven large plates. Turn your isopod over and count its legs (the longer limbs on the underside). Did you count seven pairs? You should have, because isopods have a pair of legs on each segment of the pereon. Behind the pereon is the **pleon** (plee' ahn),

which ends in the **pleotelson**. The pleon also has limbs attached to it, but the isopod doesn't use them for walking. Those limbs are where you find the gills. The fact that an isopod's body is composed of individual plates enables it to roll into a ball. Can you guess why it would do this? To defend itself. A few species can't roll into a ball, but they have longer legs that they use to speed away.

Though many people see woodlice as pests, they are usually very helpful to the environment, because they recycle dead animal and plant matter, adding nutrients to the soil. However, having too many isopods is not a good thing…they may run out of dead animal matter and begin eating your plants.

What Do You Remember?

How can you identify an arthropod? How can you tell the difference between an insect and an arachnid? What are the two most dangerous spiders in the United States? How do spiders consume their prey? Name some of the things spiders do with their silk. From where does the silk come? What are some of the different kinds of webs that spiders build? What are some ways spiders capture their prey? What are harvestmen? How do they defend themselves? Why are harvestmen good for your garden? What animals eat scorpions? What are the acarina? Name some specific kinds of acarina. Why are ticks dangerous? Name some differences between centipedes and millipedes. Where do woodlice live? How do they defend themselves?

Notebook Activities

If the weather is somewhat warm outside, the invertebrates are waiting for you to find them. Why don't you try to see if you can find some in action? Go outside and spread apart the grass, turn over some rocks, and study the creatures as they scurry out of sight. What arthropods do you see? Write about what you saw in your notebook, drawing pictures if you can.

Choose some of the arthropods from this lesson that you found interesting and make pages for them in your notebook. You might want to do a little independent research to learn more about them. The course website I told you about in the introduction is a great place to start!

Experiment
Woodlouse Population Study

We often hear scientists give estimates of how many insects live in a particular area. How do scientists know how many insects might be in an area unless they have counted them all? Well, scientists use a simple procedure called **mark and recapture**. Along with a math equation, this method gives you a good estimate of the population in a given area. You are going to use this same method to estimate the population of woodlice in your yard.

You will need:

♦ A flashlight
♦ A shoebox
♦ Oil-based paint (yellow is best, but any bright color will do)

♦ A paint brush (one with a small tip, like what an artist would use)
♦ A yardstick or measuring tape
♦ Chalk

1. Begin by looking around your yard and finding some places where woodlice might be hiding.
2. Once you have found a likely area, measure out a square yard of space in that area. This means you need to measure out a square that is 1 yard long on each side, and mark the area with chalk.
3. At night, go outside with your shoebox and gather all the woodlice you find in that square yard. Be certain to count the minutes you spend doing this. You will want to repeat the experiment exactly the next night – reenacting the length of time and time of night.
4. Take your woodlice inside and count them. Record the number you caught.
5. Dab a small amount of paint on the back of each one you captured.
6. The same night, release them back where you caught them.
7. The next night, go to the same area at the same time and spend the same amount of time trying to capture all the woodlice in that same square again.
8. Once again, take the woodlice inside.
9. Count the number of woodlice you captured.
10. Count the number of captured woodlice that have paint on them.
11. Write down these numbers and then do the calculations described below.

The key to understanding the **mark and recapture** method is to realize that woodlice are good at hiding and escaping. So even though you caught all the woodlice that you could *find*, it wasn't all the woodlice *in the area*. As a result, you need some way of estimating what percentage of the population you were unable to capture. You do that by marking the ones you captured and trying to capture them again the next night. If, on the second night, you could only recapture ½ of the ones you caught the first night, this tells you that, most likely, you will always miss ½ of the woodlice in the area. Algebra (see, it is useful) tells us that under those assumptions, the true population is:

True population = (# caught the first night) x (# caught the second night) ÷ (# recaptured)

You can check the course website I told you about in the introduction to learn why this equation works. Here is how you use it: Suppose you caught 25 on the first night and 31 on the second night. Suppose also that 13 of the ones caught on the second night had paint on them, indicating they were recaptured. The true population would be:

True population = (25) x (31) ÷ (13) = 59.6, which is essentially 60

So, the population of woodlice in that square yard would be 60. To get the total population of woodlice in the entire yard, measure how many yards long and wide the yard is. Then, multiply the number of woodlice in the one square yard you studied by the length of your yard, and multiply the answer by the width of your yard. Now you have a good estimate for how many woodlice are in your entire yard. Is it more than you expected?

Lesson 14
Gastropods and Worms

Have you ever seen a glistening trail of dried ooze streaked across a section of your garden? If not, you probably didn't notice it was there. After all, the oozing, slippery creatures that make those trails are everywhere. Slugs, snails, and worms may seem like a slimy way to end your study of zoology, but I think you'll find them quite fascinating.

Just by glancing at the pictures on this page, you probably guessed that these creatures aren't arthropods. What are they missing? They are missing jointed legs and a hard exoskeleton. Slugs, snails, and worms are legless, soft-bodied, invertebrate creepers that God created on the sixth day. Though they lead secretive lives, they affect us in many ways – some bad, some good. Some destroy our gardens (or even our bodies), living as predators or parasites on or in plants and animals. Others are so helpful that their presence ensures we have a healthy garden.

Slugs and Snails

Slugs and snails belong in phylum **Mollusca** (mah lus' kuh), class **Gastropoda** (gas truh' puh duh). The class name comes from two Greek words that mean "belly" and "foot." When you think about how these animals move, it makes sense, because they use their belly as a foot! You probably already know that the difference between a slug and a snail is that a snail carries an obvious shell on its back, while a slug doesn't. If you think of a

Both are in class Gastropoda, but a slug (left) has no noticeable shell on its back, while a snail (right) does.

snail's shell as its home, you can think of slugs as the "homeless" members of class Gastropoda. In actuality, many slugs have a kind of shell, but it is not very noticeable. It is more like a small plate found under the skin.

Slugs and snails are oval-shaped, slimy mollusks like the ones you studied in Zoology 2. You can think of them as a foot with organs and a head attached. The muscular foot produces a lot of mucus to help the snail or slug slide around the world. The head has tentacles, two of which are topped with eyes! Although you might find it hard to believe, some people really enjoy eating cooked snails. Of course, restaurants don't call them snails on the menu; they call them **escargot** (es kar goh'). Have you ever eaten escargot? It may sound fancy, but don't be fooled. It's nothing more than cooked snails!

The holes in this leaf indicate a snail has been munching on it.

If you grow vegetables, you definitely aren't pleased at the sight of a slug, snail, or even the shiny paths they leave behind. After all, these spineless creatures are midnight thieves, creeping quietly into your garden during the dark of night, stealing from you as much as they can – which can be quite a lot for such a tiny creature. As daylight dawns, you can't find them. They're gone; but like a thief, you know they were there – the leaves on your plants have holes, and your fruit, seedlings, and buds have been bitten. The thieves came in and ruined your beautiful garden. But, like a good detective, you can find their footprints; just look for the streaks of dried, shiny slime. Interestingly enough, studies show that an easy way to discourage these little thieves is to water your garden in the morning rather than at night. Gastropods need plenty of water to survive, and since they are nocturnal, they tend to be attracted to places that are wet at night.

Special Slime

Though their preferred time of feeding is during the middle of the night, a cloudy, sunless day will also do for a hungry gastropod. They must stay out of the sun or something dreadful will happen to them. Can you guess what? Slick, soggy creatures dry out quickly in the sun. Staying moist is their only means of survival. They depend on the slimy mucus they secrete from their skin – it keeps them from drying out, and it allows them to slide along at top speed…for a snail, that is. This mucus protects them so well that they can *crawl over a razor blade without injury*. Now, that's some well-designed mucus! Only God could design a liquid that works like a shield.

It is easy to understand how slugs and snails move. They have strong muscles in the foot, and those muscles expand and contract in a rippling pattern that pushes the gastropod forward. The mucus secreted from the foot helps to smooth the path and anchor the foot to the surface over which the gastropod is traveling. Interestingly enough, even the gastropods that live in water must crawl along surfaces this way. They cannot swim. Most gastropods travel at speeds that range from slow (2½ feet per minute) to very slow (6 inches per minute).

The snail's mucus not only helps it crawl around; it is also a great defense. If a frog or toad decides a gastropod would make a nice snack, the gastropod produces an enormous volume of mucus. The predator finds its mouth so full of slime that it must spit the creature out or choke to death on the frothing foam. Yuck!

The trails that the slugs and snails leave behind are very important, and other slugs and snails often follow them. Why? To conserve energy. You see, it takes a lot of energy for a gastropod to make the mucus it uses to move around. If a gastropod can find another's slime trail, it doesn't need to produce nearly as much mucus. These little animals are clever, aren't they? You can also usually tell whether a slime trail was left by a snail or a slug. Snails generally leave slime trails that are broken into small blotches, while slugs tend to leave an unbroken trail of slime.

Can you name three ways a gastropod's mucus is helpful to the gastropod?
Can you name one way it is helpful to other gastropods?

Try This!

The best way to see how a gastropod moves is to watch it for yourself. Go outside and capture a snail or slug. When you find one, put it on the bottom of a glass baking pan or bowl. Now look at the snail's foot from underneath the glass surface so you can see how it moves. If you can't find a snail outside, try going to a place that sells fish. Many of the aquariums that hold the fish will also have snails. See if you can find one crawling along the side of the aquarium so you can see its foot in action.

Gastropod Anatomy

Although they may not be the most beautiful of all of God's creatures, gastropods are equipped with the tools they need to survive. Take a look at the illustration and picture below to learn a bit about how God built gastropods.

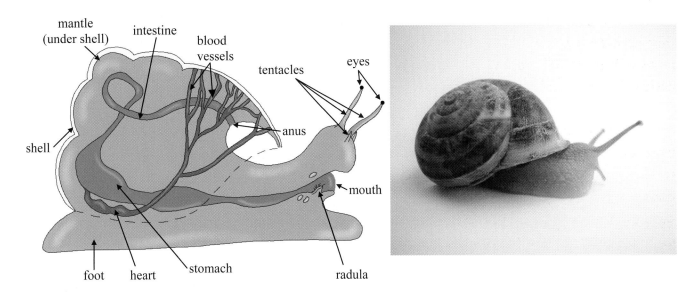

In some ways, you can think of a gastropod as a stomach built on top of a foot. It eats by scraping food into its mouth with its **radula** (ra' dyoo luh), which is a rasping tongue that looks like a ribbon covered in teeth. Each species has different food preferences. In addition to eating your tomato plants, some of them also eat algae, animal feces, carrion, centipedes, insects, and worms. Some are even cannibals, eating others of their same kind.

A snail's shell often hides its pneumostome, but the breathing valve is easy to see on a slug when it is open.

The shell of a snail is produced by the **mantle**, which is the soft tissue directly under the shell. While a slug's mantle does not produce a noticeable shell, it often produces a hard plate. In both snails and slugs, there is a valve called a **pneumostome** (new' muh stohm) in the mantle. The gastropod breathes by opening its pneumostome and sucking in air.

As you can see from the drawing on the previous page, these creatures were created with two pairs of tentacles on their head. The two tentacles on the top are called the **optic tentacles**. On the tip of the optic tentacles are eyes that allow the gastropod to detect shapes and light. In front of the optic tentacles are the **sensory tentacles**, which are used for feeling and tasting. Have you ever touched the tentacles of a snail or slug? If so, what happened? You might have seen the tentacle disappear, because a gastropod can retract its tentacles back into the body if it thinks they are in danger. How's that for eye protection?

Like many aquatic gastropods, slugs and snails are hermaphroditic. You may remember that term from Zoology 2. It means they are both male and female at the same time! When two snails mate, they *both* end up producing eggs, which are typically buried under a couple inches of soil. The eggs are very small and come in many shapes and colors. The tiny eggs usually hatch in a few weeks, unless winter is around the corner. Eggs laid in the fall will overwinter and hatch in the spring.

Snail Stowaways

Snails and slugs can carry parasites that are harmful to people and animals. One of the more interesting parasites is particular to the amber snail. Because it lives near the water, it is exposed to the water-dwelling larvae of a particular kind of worm. If the larvae infect the snail, they begin growing inside the snail's body. As they grow, they extend into the poor snail's tentacles. The once normal-looking tentacles suddenly become large, swollen and green. Because they are swelled up, the snail cannot retract them, and the larvae control them.

This is a healthy amber snail.

Unfortunately, the larvae are on a mission to get eaten by a bird, their final host. They wiggle the swollen, green tentacles, making them look like tasty insects. This entices a bird to come down and eat them! You might think that spells the end for the larvae, but it does not! The larvae survive being eaten and end up maturing into adult worms. Then, they lay eggs that will come out in the bird's feces and hopefully land in water, where the larvae will grow and start the process all over again.

In this case, the worm uses the snail as an **intermediate host** and the bird as the **final host**. There are also other parasites that infect snails as intermediate hosts, with the primary host being a person instead of a bird. For example, some snails eat rat feces, which can have certain worms in them. If a person eats a raw or undercooked snail that has eaten worm-infected food, the person can be infected with the worms as well. Although you might never think of eating a snail, remember what escargot is!

Before you begin your journey into the world of worms,
tell someone everything you have learned about slugs and snails.

Worms

To the untrained eye, worms may seem similar to slugs, but they are completely different creatures. There are three basic types of worms: **flatworms**, **roundworms**, and **segmented worms**, called annelids. You studied aquatic flatworms and segmented worms in Zoology 2, but in this book, I will dwell on those that live on land or inside land-dwelling creatures. In addition, I will discuss roundworms, which you didn't study in Zoology 2.

Flatworms

Flatworms are…well…flat. There are thousands of different species of these thin invertebrates roaming around the world, and unfortunately, some of them live as parasites in people and animals. In fact, the worm that invades the amber snail is a kind of flatworm. Though most flatworms live in aquatic habitats, many live in damp soil or inside bodies.

Some of the most nightmarish parasites in the world are flatworms. For example, one type of flatworm, called the tapeworm, begins its torturous lifecycle by infecting a small animal like a flea. When the flea (or an egg) is eaten by another animal, that animal becomes infected. If a person eats an infected animal, the person can become infected. Once inside its final host, the tapeworm inserts itself into the intestine, attaching itself to the intestinal wall using suckers and hooks. It doesn't need its mouth to eat, as

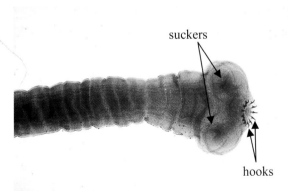

suckers

hooks

This magnified image of the front of a tapeworm shows you the hooks and suckers it uses to attach itself to its host.

its skin simply absorbs the nutrients from the already digested food in the person's intestines. As the tapeworm grows, the person gets less and less of the nutrition from the food he or she eats, which leaves the person often feeling hungry. So the person keeps eating more and more but never really gains any weight. This may sound like a great weight-loss plan, but it is incredibly unhealthy. Besides, who wants a large worm growing in their intestines?

In people, tapeworms can live for many years and grow up to 30 feet long, winding their way through a person's intestines! As the tapeworm continues to absorb nutrients and grow, it begins to add segments to its body. Each segment is like a separate worm, with its own reproductive system. Each segment produces its own eggs.

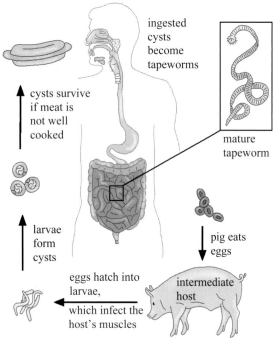

ingested cysts become tapeworms

cysts survive if meat is not well cooked

mature tapeworm

larvae form cysts

pig eats eggs

eggs hatch into larvae, which infect the host's muscles

intermediate host

Although not common in industrialized nations, people can be infected by tapeworms in this way.

Tapeworms that infect humans usually come from undercooked pork, beef, or fish. Here's how: A pig might eat some vegetation that has tapeworm eggs on it. Those eggs most likely came from the feces of an infected animal. The eggs hatch and form larvae, which infect the pig's muscles, which is what people cook and eat as pork. When the pig is killed for food, the larvae form **cysts**, which are like temporary shells that make them very hard to destroy. If the meat is not cooked thoroughly, those cysts survive and end up maturing into one or more tapeworms in the intestines of the person who eats the meat. In industrialized countries, tapeworms are not a big problem for people, because there are so many regulations on the sanitation of meat-based products. Also, tapeworms are easy to treat with medication if a person does happen to get infected.

Even in industrialized countries, however, tapeworms are common in dogs and cats. They typically get tapeworms from fleas. Fleas eat the feces of an infected animal, and they then live on the skin of a dog or cat. In the course of grooming, the animal might accidentally eat a flea or its eggs, giving the tapeworm a new host. Once inside the intestines of the dog or cat, it hooks itself onto the intestinal wall, soon growing to be several inches long. As it grows, some of its segments break off, and you can see them as white, wiggly bits visible in the animal's feces. These aren't complete tapeworms; they are just segments of a tapeworm still in the animal. However, since a segment is like an individual, it can produce lots of eggs in the hope that something else will be infected.

A dog or cat with tapeworms should be immediately treated. It is best for the animal's health, but it is also possible for you to be infected by your pet's tapeworm. Fleas eat the eggs of a tapeworm, and since fleas are the intermediate host, they cannot infect a mammal unless the mammal eats a flea.

Now you might say, "I don't eat fleas." Well, maybe not on *purpose*, but it is possible to swallow an infected flea by accident, because they are so small. If you do, you could end up with a tapeworm.

Land Planarians

Land **planarians** (pluh nair' ee uhnz) are the most common flatworm you will find in a garden. This type of flatworm has a shovel-shaped head, and often there are stripes down the body. Like all flatworms, they don't breathe. They just absorb the oxygen they need through their skin. In addition, a planarian has only one opening for both eating and eliminating waste. Like slugs and tapeworms, land planarians must stay moist to live, so they stay under rocks and leaves during the heat of the day and produce mucus on their skin to seal in the moisture. They were introduced to the Americas from Asia and are not good for gardens, since they eat earthworms. However, they are also cannibalistic and will eat their own children if they find them. One of the

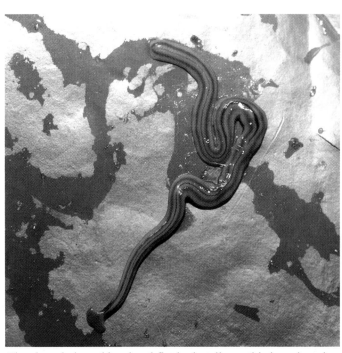

The shovel-shaped head and flat body tell you this is a planarian.

most interesting things about planarians is that they can regenerate body parts that are cut or torn off. In fact, sometimes a planarian will *intentionally* break itself into two pieces so that both pieces can regenerate. In other words, planarians can rip themselves apart in order to reproduce!

About fifty years ago, planarians were used in an experiment that produced amazing results. Planarians usually are attracted to light, because that is where food is often found. However, two scientists trained planarians to avoid light by shocking them every time a light was turned on. After repeating this many times, they took away the electric shock, but the worms still avoided light, as if they expected a shock from it. That's not the amazing part, however. They then cut the flatworms in half, and as expected, both halves grew new parts so there were two new flatworms for each original one. It turned out that *all* the new flatworms still avoided light. Later on, one of the scientists did an even more amazing experiment. He ground the flatworms into small pieces and fed them to other flatworms that had never been trained to do anything. When he started training the well-fed flatworms to avoid light, they learned much more quickly than the first set of flatworms! This showed scientists that perhaps memory can be transferred chemically, at least in some animals. This experiment sure gives new meaning to the phrase, "You are what you eat."

Tell someone what you remember about flatworms.

Roundworms

Roundworms, which scientists usually call **nematodes** (nem' uh tohdz), are the most abundant of all the worms. They are found everywhere. While reading this book, how many times have you heard that a creature lives everywhere except…see if you can say it with me…Antarctica? Well, believe it or not, roundworms even live in Antarctica. In fact, they are one of the few creatures found everywhere, even at the deepest depths of the sea. They are survivors. But unfortunately for us, of the tens of thousands of known species of nematodes, about a quarter of them are parasites.

Although flatworms take in food and excrete waste through the same hole, roundworms have a digestive system more like vertebrates – a hole at each end, one for eating and the other for eliminating waste. And instead of a layer of mucus for protection, roundworms have a **cuticle** (kew' tih kul), a tough-but-flexible outer covering, that protects them. Most roundworms have one long muscle that runs from the front of the body to the back. When the muscle contracts and relaxes, it makes the roundworm thrash from side to side like a whip. If you've ever had the misfortune of seeing a pinworm, you have witnessed this thrashing. Though it does not seem very efficient, it gets the parasite where it wants to go.

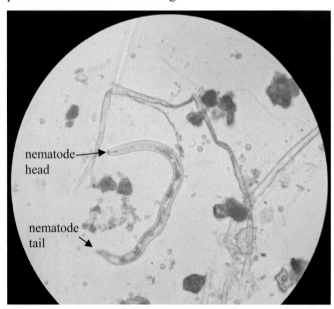

nematode head

nematode tail

The nematode in this picture is a tiny parasite that infects the roots of plants. It is so small you can only see it with the aid of a microscope.

If a nematode is not parasitic, we call it a **free-living roundworm**, because it lives without a host. If it is parasitic, we call it (surprise) a **parasitic roundworm**. Most nematodes are microscopic, but some (especially certain parasitic ones) can grow to be quite large. Let's take a look at some of the common parasitic roundworms that are dangerous to people and animals. Remember, infection with these worms is more common in Third World countries where people don't have access to clean water. If, after learning about all the animals in this book so far, you have decided that the best places to live are the jungles of South America, Southeast Asia, and Africa, you might think differently after reading this section!

Try This!

Before beginning this next section on parasites, draw (or print) eight copies of a diagram that shows the human body with its internal organs visible. There is an example of such a drawing on the next page. You can find a copy of it on the course website I told you about in the introduction to this book. For each worm that you learn about, mark on one of the copies where the worm enters and where it lives inside the body. Write down anything special you learn about each worm, including where it is found and how to avoid getting one.

Ascaris and Whipworms

Ascaris (as' kuh ris) and **whipworms** are two very common parasitic roundworms. In fact, experts estimate that about 25 percent of the world's population is infected with ascaris worms! There are some countries where almost 90 percent of the population is infected. Although ascaris and whipworms look different from each other, people get them in similar ways. The feces of an infected person or animal are full of the worms' eggs. The eggs must first spend some time in the soil in order for the embryos inside to develop properly, but then they must be eaten to hatch. People and animals get these worms by eating food that has not been washed or by drinking unpurified water. They can also get them by eating food without washing their hands of contaminated soil. Once the eggs hit the small intestine, they hatch.

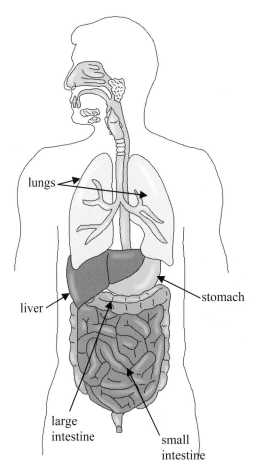

The differences between these two nasty nematodes are their appearance and what happens after the eggs hatch. When ascaris eggs hatch, the larvae get into the bloodstream and travel to the liver and then the lungs. From the lungs, they travel to the throat and are once again swallowed (yuck). This sends them back to the small intestine, where they mature into worms that look much like earthworms but are smaller and white. There they mate and release eggs that get into the host's feces. Whipworms don't travel as extensively as ascaris worms. When their eggs hatch in the small intestine, the larvae move to the large intestine, where they mature into flesh-colored worms that are rarely over 2 inches long. There they mate and release eggs that will end up in the host's feces. When people are infected by these worms, they have problems absorbing the nutrients from their food, and often have belly pain. Ascaris-infected people can actually cough up worms or have worms crawl out of their nose! The consequences of whipworm infections can often be worse, because bad infections can lead to severe diarrhea, other problems with eliminating waste, bleeding, and severe weight loss.

Hookworm

In Georgia, I once met a kitten that had been rescued from the wild. It had a red wound on its throat caused by a **hookworm**. Hookworm larvae burrow beneath a mammal's skin in order to enter the body. Once inside, they get into the bloodstream and are carried to the lungs. Like ascaris worms,

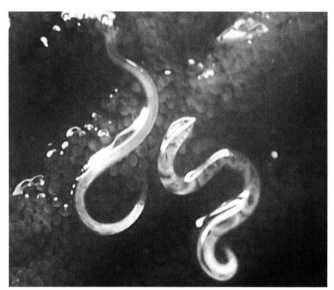

These are adult hookworms attached to the lining of an intestine. The actual length is about 1½ inches.

they then crawl up the throat and are swallowed, ending up in the small intestine. There, they grow into adults, laying eggs that are released in the host's feces. The eggs then actually hatch in the soil, and the larvae wait for an unsuspecting mammal to dig into. Regular bathing can help stop hookworm infections, but the best thing to do is keep any soil that might be contaminated with feces away from your bare skin. For example, wear shoes when walking outside. Serious hookworm infection can result in belly pain, diarrhea, and weight loss. Very serious infections can cause stunted growth and incomplete mental development.

Guinea Worm

In parts of the world where clean drinking water is hard to find, millions and millions of people get the **Guinea** (gihn' ee) **roundworm**. You see, everyone must drink water, and if your only choice is water from a pond or river, you will drink it in order to stay alive. The problem is that ponds and rivers can have small animals called **water fleas** in them. Although not microscopic, they are very small, about one-tenth of an inch long. These water fleas can eat Guinea worm larvae, and those larvae can start to develop in the water fleas.

When a person drinks water that has infected water fleas in it, the water fleas are destroyed by the acid in the person's stomach, but the Guinea worm larvae are not destroyed. They make it to the small intestine and then burrow out into the rest of the body. There, they mature and mate. Once she has mated, the female will actually move to the skin of the host, forming a blister. The blister itches and hurts, often causing the host to put the blister in water. When that happens, the female releases her young, which are then eaten by water fleas, starting the process all over again.

People with Guinea worm infections experience a lot of pain when the female worms reach the skin, but the real problem is the blister the female forms. It is an opening in the skin, and all sorts of other nasty, infectious things can enter the body that way. As a result, people with Guinea worm infections often get other sicknesses as well. To stop Guinea worm infection, infected people must not expose their blisters to water, and everyone must drink water that has been filtered to remove the water fleas.

Filarial Worms

Don't you hate mosquito bites? They itch, don't they? Well, sometimes, a mosquito bite can do more than itch. Mosquitoes can carry many parasites that harm people and animals, including certain types of **filarial** (fil air' ee uhl) **roundworm**. As you learned in Zoology 1, a mosquito has a long, tubular mouthpart called a proboscis (proh bos' kis) with four cutting and piercing tools, which are often called stylets (sty lets'). The mosquito uses these tools to stab into the skin, and then the proboscis is inserted into the wound and is used to suck blood from the victim. It is during this process that a mosquito can infect a person with filarial roundworms.

You see, in order to keep a person's blood flowing freely up its proboscis, a mosquito releases fluids that mix with the blood. If a mosquito is carrying roundworms, they come out with the fluid and make their way into the person's bloodstream. Soon, the worm gets into the person's **lymph nodes** and can live there for up to six years. During that time, they can produce young that go back into the bloodstream. If an uninfected mosquito happens to bite that person, the mosquito eats the young along with the blood. Once the young mature in the mosquito, they will start coming out with the fluid, infecting any people the mosquito bites.

If you haven't studied the human body yet, you might not know what lymph nodes are. Basically, your body has a network of vessels that are separate from your blood vessels. They are called **lymph vessels**, and they carry fluid from your tissues and eventually put it back into your blood.

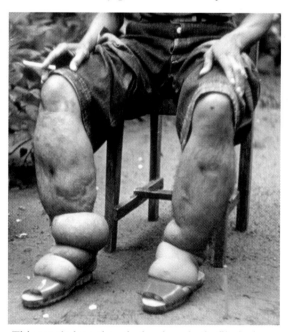

Along the way, however, the fluid is cleaned at little bean-shaped stations called lymph nodes. Since the filarial roundworms live there, they hamper the body's ability to clean and recycle the fluid, which can make it much easier for an infected person to get sick. Also, through a process that scientists still don't completely understand, the roundworms can cause body tissue to swell, making parts of the person's body thick and puffed up. This condition is called **lymphatic** (lim fa' tik) **filariasis** (fil uh ry' uh sis), but it is more commonly known as **elephantiasis** (el' uh fuhn ty' uh sus). Do you have to worry about getting elephantiasis from a mosquito? Well, only if you travel to parts of South America, Africa, and Southeast Asia, because that's where the infected mosquitoes can be found.

This man's legs show he has lymphatic filariasis.

Now don't get the idea that elephantiasis is the only problem caused by filarial roundworms. There are many different species, and they cause many different diseases in both people and animals. For example, another type of filarial roundworm causes **river blindness**. This roundworm is spread much like the roundworm that causes elephantiasis, but rather than mosquitoes, it is carried by certain species of black fly. Once the fly bites a person, the roundworms enter the person's bloodstream and travel to various locations, mostly the skin. If they end up in the **cornea** (kor' nee uh), the transparent cover for the eye, they can cause blindness.

Speaking of blindness, do you know what **spiritual blindness** is? Well, the Bible tells us in 2 Corinthians 4:4 that Satan (the god of this world) also causes blindness, "in whose case the god of this world has blinded the minds of the unbelieving so that they might not see the light of the gospel of the glory of Christ, who is the image of God." In other words, the Bible tells us that people who do not believe the truth about Jesus have been blinded by Satan. Satan is a lot like a worm that blinds people. However, Jesus tells us that He is greater than Satan. So you can pray for people to be set free from this blindness so that when you share the truth about Jesus with them, they will be able to see and understand it.

Tell someone what you remember about the parasites we have studied so far.

Trichinella

The diseases we have studied so far tend to exist mostly in less developed countries, but let's take a look at some roundworms that cause diseases in developed countries such as the United States. We will start with ***Trichinella*** (trik' uh nel' uh), a genus of roundworms that cause **trichinosis** (trik' uh

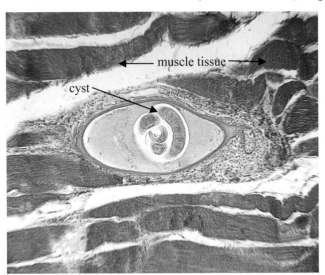
muscle tissue
cyst

This microscopic picture shows you muscle tissue that is infected with *Trichinella* cysts.

noh' sis). We learned a little bit about trichinosis when we studied pigs. *Trichinella* larvae live in carnivores, including pigs. Animals get infected by eating other carnivores, like certain rodents. When mammals (including people) eat meat from an infected animal, they eat the roundworm's cysts along with the meat. The cysts break open in the stomach, and the roundworms move into the intestines, where they mature. The mature roundworms release larvae that then travel through the intestine and go to the host's tissues. Eventually, they form cysts in the host's tissues, waiting for the chance to be eaten by another potential host.

People can become infected with these roundworms when they eat infected meat (like pork) that is not well cooked. It's common in places where pigs eat infected animals like rats. Even though pork is inspected, some *Trichinella* can be missed, but the cysts are destroyed if the meat is cooked thoroughly. However, because some people consume undercooked meat, about a dozen cases of trichinosis are reported each year in the United States. The disease causes fever, muscle soreness, and swelling. If not treated, it can be fatal.

Pinworm

Pinworms are the most common roundworm parasites found in developed countries, and their lives are similar to those of the whipworms you already studied. The easiest way to get this infection is to eat pinworm eggs. The eggs hatch in the small intestine, and once the larvae mature, they go to the large intestine. The females lay eggs, which cause your rear end to itch. When you scratch there, you pick up some of the eggs under your fingernails and can transfer them to anything you touch. If you touch food with pinworm eggs under your fingernails, for example, the person who eats that food can become infected. Washing your hands regularly is the best way to avoid pinworm infections. Nevertheless, because people don't do this, it is estimated that as many as one-third of people in the United States have pinworm infections. Fortunately, the itchiness is the only real problem caused by pinworm infection, and the parasites can be killed with the proper treatment.

Toxocara

Another roundworm parasite found in developed countries comes from the genus *Toxocara* (tahk' suh kar' uh). These parasites infect dogs and cats. People can get them if they accidentally eat something that has dirt that contains an animal's infected feces. Once ingested, these worms move out of the intestines and are carried by the blood to all sorts of tissues. If they end up in the eye, they can cause vision loss or even blindness. If they end up in the heart, they can cause heart problems. If they end up in the lungs, they can cause breathing problems. These worms are very, very common in parks and playgrounds where dogs and cats frequent. To keep from becoming infected, always wash your hands after handling animals and don't put your hands in your mouth or eat until you have washed them. When you go to a park, wash your hands before you begin your picnic.

Explain what you have learned about roundworm parasites in developed countries. How can you avoid getting these parasites?

Annelids

Leaving our study of parasites, let's conclude our safari with the study of the animals in phylum **Annelida** (an uh lee' duh), which are typically called **annelids**. The phylum name comes from the Latin word "anellus," which means "little ring." You are probably already familiar with one of the most common annelids – the earthworm. Look at the earthworm pictured here and see if you can figure out why its phylum name comes from a word that means "little ring."

Earthworms are annelids.

Indeed, these worms have little rings around their body, which form segments. As a result, annelids are called segmented worms. As they grow, most of them add more and more segments to their body. Now don't think that the only annelids in creation are the helpful garden creatures we call earthworms. The blood-sucking leech is also an annelid! There are thousands of other species of annelids as well. Most are aquatic, several are terrestrial and, thankfully, not many are parasitic.

Since earthworms are the most common terrestrial annelid, we'll focus on them. Do you know why I called earthworms "helpful garden creatures"? Well, they do lots of things to make the soil more fertile. First, earthworms dig tunnels under the ground, because they actually *eat dirt*! Even though they eat dirt, they don't necessarily digest it. You see, an earthworm ingests dirt by its mouth, and the dirt travels through its digestive system. Anything the earthworm can digest as food gets digested, and the rest comes out the back end. We call what comes out the back end an **earthworm casting**. These castings are full of nutrients that make plants healthy! So gardeners love earthworms and their castings. In fact, some gardeners even purchase earthworm castings to spread in their garden. It's like buying fertilizer – God's fertilizer.

Castings are not the only thing great about earthworms. The tunnels that these annelids make become special underground systems that allow water and oxygen to reach the roots of plants. This makes the soil much better at supporting plant life. As a result, it is well known among gardeners that if you dig into the ground and find several earthworms, you have healthy soil – good for both plants and earthworms! If a garden has no earthworms, the dirt probably has few nutrients, and plants will most likely not survive well there. The best way to remedy this problem is to add compost to your soil and buy some earthworms to increase the soil's fertility.

Try This!

Go outside with a ruler, bucket, and a large spoon, a spade, or a shovel. Find an area that your parents will allow you to dig up and use the ruler to mark a square on the ground that is 1 foot on each side. Dig out that entire square foot, about 7 inches deep. Place all the dirt in the bucket as you dig.

When you are done, sort through the dirt in the bucket and count how many earthworms are there. If you find a lot of earthworms (ten or more), you have very healthy soil. The more earthworms you have, the better your soil. Save a few of these earthworms in a container of moist (not soggy) dirt. We'll use them soon.

Annelid Anatomy

Like roundworms, annelids have a cuticle that helps protect their skin. The cuticle must stay wet, however, because they breathe through it. As you may have noticed, earthworms dry out pretty fast in the sun. If a hard rain washes an earthworm into the middle of a driveway, it's usually unable to reach the moist dirt before it dries out. Earthworms crawl much better on the ground than they do on hard surfaces. That's because of the way they are designed to move.

The way an earthworm creeps along is quite complex. You see, it is designed with specialized muscles that cause parts of it to shrink down into stubby, fat sections or stretch out into long, thin sections. How does this make the earthworm move? Well, annelids have hairs or bristles on their skin. Some annelids are actually quite furry, like the bristleworm. An earthworm, however, has four pairs of little bristles on the bottoms of each of its segment. If you get a magnifying glass, you can see these bristles, called **setae**.

Get one of the earthworms you just saved and see if you can find its setae. Rub your finger along the underside of the body from back to front and feel the setae on each segment. These bristles are quite important to the earthworm, because they are like anchors. Have you ever tried to grab hold of an earthworm before it tunnels into its burrow? Did you find it difficult to pull it out? That's because when an earthworm doesn't want to leave its burrow, it sticks out its setae like little anchors, holding on to the burrow. You, like a bird, will have to break the worm in half to get it out. That's not necessarily the worst thing in the world for an earthworm, though. Can you guess why? As long as the bird got its rear half, it can regenerate a new one. However, it cannot regenerate its front half.

The earthworm uses its muscles and setae to tunnel through the dirt and to crawl around on the earth. When the worm decides it needs to go somewhere, it makes itself as long as it can, then it anchors its front setae into the soil. After this, it releases its back setae and pulls its tail end forward, making itself short and thick. Once the tail end is set in place, it anchors its rear setae into the soil. The front setae release, and the worm stretches out, propelling the front end forward, bumping against the solid dirt or tunneling into it as it stretches out farther and farther.

This earthworm is all stretched out. To move in the direction of the arrow, it will anchor its front setae into the ground, release its back setae, and scrunch up to become short and stubby. That will move its tail end forward, closer to where its head is.

Once the dirt is moved, it releases the back setae and starts over. In this way, an earthworm moves dirt as it moves along. Put an earthworm on a flat surface and see if you can watch how it crawls along. As you watch, you might notice that the earthworm doesn't have to use its entire body to move. Sometimes, it just stretches and scrunches a part of its body in order to crawl.

tail   clitellum   head

Now that you know how an earthworm crawls, let's get back to looking at its anatomy. Continue to study a real earthworm as you read. If you look at your earthworm (or the picture on the left), you will see that it has a band near one end of its body. That's called the **clitellum** (klye tel' uhm), and it helps you determine which end of the worm is which. The head is the end closer to the clitellum, and the tail is the other end. If your worm doesn't have a clitellum, it is either not a complete worm or it is a young one, as only an adult earthworm will have a clitellum. You will also notice that the earthworm's body has many segments. Some species of earthworms have over 100 segments. How many segments does your earthworm have?

The head of the worm is more properly called the **anterior** end. It is designed with light-sensitive regions, kind of like eyes. But, you probably noticed the worm doesn't have any actual eyes. Even though it's missing real eyes, the earthworm can sense when it is night and day with these light-sensitive regions. When it senses night, it emerges from its tunnel, searching for an above-ground meal. It is sometimes called a "night crawler" because of this nighttime habit. Many people place red cellophane over their flashlights and go out to collect earthworms at night for fishing. The red cellophane keeps the earthworms from sensing the light, because if they sense the light, they retreat back into their hole. Earthworm hunters also have to tip toe very carefully around the yard, because earthworms can sense vibrations from walking feet and will crawl away from them.

The most obvious thing at the anterior end of the earthworm is its mouth. Though many animals don't have lips, earthworms do! They have a flap, called a **prostomium** (proh stoh' mee uhm), that covers the mouth. If you look at the anterior end of your worm closely, you can see its mouth under its prostomium. The earthworm has no teeth however. Food entering the mouth sucked up by the muscular **pharynx** (fair' inks) and stored in the **crop**. Afterward, it goes into the **gizzard**, which contains tiny stones that grind the food. Once the food is ground up, it is sent through the rest of the body, where the nutrients are absorbed into the blood. The

The prostomium is clearly visible as this earthworm sucks things into its mouth.

waste is sent out its tail end (called the **posterior** end) as castings. Like some of the other creatures you have studied, earthworms are hermaphrodites. When two earthworms mate, they *both* end up laying eggs that hatch into small worms!

Try This!

Create a wormery to naturally compost some of your trash and create rich soil for your garden. Believe it or not, it's really easy to create your own wormery. All you need is a five-gallon bucket with a lid, newspaper (just the black and white sections), water, and some worms.

Drill or puncture about ten holes in the top of the lid near the center. You need to keep the holes away from the edges of the lid. Tear the newspaper into strips and fill the bucket with them. Then, add about a cup of water. Add it in small amounts until all the newspaper is moist. It should not be dripping wet, though. If there is excess water in the bottom of the bucket once you are done, pour it out. The newspaper should be compacted now, nearer to the bottom of the bucket.

Place six to twelve earthworms in the bucket. Use the earthworms you found previously, or buy them at a bait shop or large department store. Try to get the worms called red worms or red wrigglers, as these are the best at composting. These worms produce a lot of babies, so you'll have quite a lot of worms in only a few months. Watch as the worms wriggle down to the bottom of the container.

Add a few uneaten fruits or vegetables or their peels to the top of the newspaper every few days or so. You can also add tea bags (with no staples) and coffee grounds. Don't add meat, oils, or grains, because they will rot and stink. If the vegetables begin to rot, wait until the earthworms have had a chance to eat what you have in there before adding more.

Once the worms catch up, you can begin to add more food for the worms. Within a couple months, the worms will break down the plant matter and create rich dirt that you can use in your garden. When you are ready to use the dirt for your garden, you can save several of the worms, start over with more newspaper, and put the dirt and the rest of the worms in your garden.

You can keep this five-gallon bucket in your kitchen. If it is done correctly, it won't stink. If it does stink, you are either over feeding the worms, feeding them the wrong materials, or you don't have enough holes at the top. Just make sure that wherever you store your wormery, the temperature does not get above 80 degrees or below 50 degrees.

What Do You Remember?

What are the meanings of the two Greek words that form the name "Gastropoda"? Why do slugs and snails produce mucus? How do slugs and snails eat? Name the three basic types of worms. How does a tapeworm get inside a dog or a cat? Explain the tapeworm life cycle. Which of the three basic worm types are pinworms? What are some ways you can avoid getting parasites? What kind of worm is an earthworm? Why are earthworms important to people? How do earthworms move from place to place?

Notebook Activities

Put the drawings you made while you studied roundworms into your notebook. Make a gastropod page in your notebook, and draw the basics of gastropod anatomy. Use the drawing on page 251 as a guide. In addition, make a page about how tapeworms infect dogs and cats. Explain the process, and draw a picture that explains it, much like the drawing on page 254 explains how tapeworms infect people. Finally, explain how an earthworm moves. Draw pictures to help illustrate the process. In one of the drawings, point out the clitellum, anterior end, and posterior end of the earthworm.

Experiment
Worm Temperature Preference

Do worms prefer warm or cold temperatures? Does it matter at all? Write your hypothesis on a Scientific Speculation Sheet and conduct the following experiment to find out.

You will need:
♦ Earthworms
♦ An oblong baking tray
♦ Moist paper towels
♦ Heating pad
♦ Ice pack

1. Place a heating pad under one half of the baking tray and an ice pack under the other half.
2. Line the bottom of the baking tray with moist (not soggy) paper towels and place four worms in the center of the tray.
3. Cover the tray completely so no light gets in.
4. After about 30 minutes, lift up the cover to see where the worms are. If they have moved toward one side, that tells you which temperature they preferred. If they haven't moved or there are worms that have moved in both directions, this tells you there was no temperature preference.
5. Was your hypothesis correct? Finish filling out your Scientific Speculation Sheet and place it in your notebook.

Answers to the Narrative Questions

Your child should not be expected to know the answer to every question. These questions are designed to jog the child's memory and help him put the concepts into his own words. *The questions are highlighted in bold and italic type*. The answers are in plain type.

Lesson 1

Explain what animal habituation is*.* Habituation is the process by which animals get used to people. ***What is a safari?*** A safari is a journey across a stretch of land, usually made to observe or hunt wild animals. ***What does it mean to be a predator?*** A predator eats other animals. ***What does it mean to be prey?*** A prey is eaten by other animals. ***Have there always been predators and prey?*** No. There were no predators and prey in the Garden of Eden. ***What is a zoonotic disease?*** Zoonotic diseases are illnesses transmitted between animals and people. ***Name a few careers that involve working with animals****.* Zoology, biology**,** animal trainer, animal control officer veterinarian, veterinarian technician, horse breeder, and farrier are examples of such careers. There are many others.

Lesson 2

What characteristics do mammals have? Mammals have vertebrae, are endothermic, breathe oxygen from the air, nurse their young with mother's milk, and have hair. ***How can you tell the skull of a mammal from the skull of a reptile?*** Mammals have a lower jaw made of only one bone, while the lower jar of a reptile is made up of several bones. Also, in reptiles, the joint that connects the lower jawbone allows it to open and close only. In mammals, that joint allows it to not only open and close, but also move from side to side. ***Which sense does a dog use the most?*** It uses its sense of smell most. ***What are some of the ways dogs communicate?*** Dogs communicate with scent, body postures, and facial expressions. ***What four major kinds of teeth do mammals have?*** The four major kinds of teeth are incisors, canines, premolars, and molars. ***How many of each gene do you have?*** You have two of each gene. ***Where did you get them?*** You get one from your father and one from your mother. ***If a gene is recessive, what does that mean?*** It means the gene will be masked by the dominant gene if it is present. ***How does a pack of dogs usually hunt prey?*** They work to separate one straggler from the rest, and they chase it until it falls. ***What do we call the male leader of a pack?*** We call him the alpha male. ***What do we call the female leader?*** We call her the alpha female. ***Why are wolves so rare today?*** They have been hunted almost to extinction and "squeezed out" by cities. ***What is a digitigrade?*** An animal that walks on its toes is a digitigrade.

Lesson 3

What is a plantigrade? A plantigrade is an animal that doesn't walk on its toes; it uses the entire bottom of the foot. ***Do bears eat mostly meat?*** No. Most bears are predominantly vegetarians. ***What do bears do instead of hibernating?*** They go into a state of dormancy. ***Should you ever feed a bear?*** No. It is dangerous for you and the bear. ***Name one way to tell the difference between a black bear and a brown bear****.* Brown bears have a hump above the shoulders. If a black bear has it, it is small. Black bears are also smaller than brown bears. NOTE: Color is not a way to tell them apart. ***What color is polar bear skin?*** It is black. ***What is different about a panda's wrist compared to a brown bear's wrist?*** A panda's wrist bone is extended so it can be used much like a thumb. ***What kind of otter spends almost all its time in the water?*** A sea otter spends almost all its time in water. ***Which is more likely to have rabies: a skunk or a raccoon?*** A raccoon is much more likely to have rabies.

Lesson 4

"Try This" calculations: The state of Indiana contains 36,420 square miles. Number of male cougars: 36,420 square miles ÷ 200 square miles per cougar = 182 male cougars. Number of male bobcats: 36,420 square miles ÷ 60 square miles per bobcat = 607 male bobcats. The city of Indianapolis, Indiana contains 373 square miles. Number of male cougars: 373 square miles ÷ 200 square miles per cougar = just under 2 male cougars. Number of male bobcats: 373 square miles ÷ 60 square miles per bobcat = just over 6 male bobcats. ***Page 53 pictures:*** left: leopard, middle: cheetah, right: jaguar. ***What special sensory organ do cats have?*** They have their whiskers. ***If a leopard or jaguar is black, what is it often called?*** It is often called a black panther. ***Which cat cannot retract its claws?*** The cheetah cannot retract its claws. ***What is an apex predator?*** An animal is an apex predator if the other animals around it do not consider it to be their typical prey. ***Which cat forms strong family bonds?*** Lions form strong family bonds. ***Which cat is the most dangerous to humans?*** Bengal tigers are the most dangerous to humans. ***Which cat is the fastest runner?*** The cheetah is the fastest cat. ***Name the three wild cats that live in North America****.* Bobcats, cougars, and Canada lynxes live in North America. ***Which***

requires the largest hunting territory? The cougar requires the largest territory. *How is a hyena similar to a dog?* It's face is similar to a dog, and it runs in packs, like a dog. *How is it similar to a cat?* It purrs when it nurses. *How is the spotted hyena different from other hyenas?* Most hyenas are peaceful scavengers, while spotted hyenas are fierce, apex predators. *What does an aardwolf eat?* It eats termites. *What is a mutation?* A mutation changes an animal's genes, either putting something in the genes that wasn't there to begin with or eliminating something that was there. *What kind of homes do creatures from the family Herpestidae create for themselves?* They dig underground tunnels. *Which animal is the mongoose famous for being able to kill?* It is famous for killing snakes. *How do meerkats care for their family members?* They all work together to dig their tunnels, and some "stand watch" to warn the colony of danger.

Lesson 5

What do most female marsupials have that other female animals do not? They have a pouch in which their young develop. *Where do most marsupials live?* Most live in Australia. *What was Pangaea?* It is a possible supercontinent in which all of earth's current continents fit together. *Name some of the animals that are marsupials.* Kangaroos, koalas, wombats, possums, opossums, marsupial moles, bandicoots, bilbies, sugar gliders, Tasmanian devils, and Monito del Montes are all marsupials. *What are marsupial young called?* They are called joeys. *What is the difference between a wallaby and a kangaroo?* The only real difference is their size – wallabies are smaller than kangaroos. *Do animals that are herbivores always stay herbivores?* No. We have already observe some change their eating habits over time. *Why is it wrong to refer to the cute Australian animals as "koala bears"?* They are not bears. *What do koalas do most of the day?* They sleep most of the day. *How is the Tasmanian devil like a hyena?* They are scavengers that consume every part of an animal. *How many species of marsupials live in North America?* Only one marsupial lives in North America – the Virginia opossum. *Explain the defense mechanism of the Virginia opossum.* It "plays dead" hoping most animals will think it has been dead too long to be a healthy meal. *How can some marsupial joeys develop without a pouch?* They live in warm areas and just cling to the mother to develop.

Lesson 6

Picture on page 90: The one lying down is higher in the social structure, because it is being groomed by the other. *How are primates different from humans?* Their teeth are different, their facial expressions are different, their sense of smell is better than their sense of sight (opposite for humans), their brains are small compared to human brains, they are not designed to walk on two legs, they cannot change their surroundings the way people can, and they are not created in the image of God. *Explain how primates are similar to other wild animals.* They have teeth like a lion's, they can sit and stand like bears, their hands are similar to raccoon hands, they use tools like many other animals, and they commit infanticide. *Are most primates social or solitary?* Most primates are social. *What single feature is used to classify the major groups of primates?* The nose is used to classify primates. *Name a New World monkey.* Tamarins and marmosets are two New World Monkeys. *Name an Old World monkey.* Proboscis monkeys, colobus monkeys, langurs, leaf monkeys, baboons, mangabeys, mandrills, drills, guenons, patas monkeys, and macaques are Old World Monkeys. *What is the difference between monkeys and apes?* Monkeys have tails, while apes do not. Ape arms are designed for swining, monkey arms are not. Apes have larger brains than monkeys. Apes are more diverse than monkeys. *Which animal is considered a lesser ape?* Lesser apes are also called gibbons.

Lesson 7

"Try This" on page 122: A. hare, B. pika, C. rabbit *What is the main thing that makes an animal a rodent?* Rodents are characterized by teeth that need to gnaw. *How are rodents helpful to the world?* They are food for many animals, disperse seeds, can be used as test subjects by the military and medical fields. *How are they destructive?* They chew on almost anything, and they can carry diseases. *Into what three groups do scientists divide rodents?* Many scientists split them into mouse-like rodents, squirrel-like rodents, and cavy-like rodents. *Name three members of order Insectivora.* Hedgehogs, shrews, solenodons, and treeshrews are in that order. *Which mammals are poisonous?* Shrews and solenodons are poisonous. You could say hedgehogs, but they technically use other animals' poison. *What are the differences among rabbits, hares, and pikas?* Pikas are small, have short, round ears, no tail, and are very vocal. Hares are larger than rabbits, have longer legs, and have longer ears (often tipped in black) than rabbits. Hares are also born precocial, while rabbits are usually born altricial. *Why are animals like the platypus and echidna difficult to classify as mammals?* They lay eggs rather than giving birth to live young. *How is the echidna like a marsupial?* It has a pouch. *Which animal in order Edentata really has no teeth?* Anteaters have no teeth. *What disease do armadillos sometimes carry?* They sometimes carry leprosy. *How is an aardvark similar to an anteater?* It digs in termite heels with its claws and eats what an anteater eats. It also has the same general shape as an anteater. *Describe some differences between the two animals.* The aardvark is smaller than most anteaters, its hair is not as thick, and its snout is flattened. Aardvarks also have teeth.

Lesson 8

What are the different uses for an elephant's proboscis? Elephants use it to inhale water, spray water or dust, pick things up, break branches, scratch, move things out of its path, "shake hands" with other elephants, tear up food, smell, and defend themselves. *Why do elephants blow dust?* The dust covers the skin, acting as sunscreen and insect repellant. *How are mammoths like elephants?* They had about the same size and shape, including both tusks and a trunk. *How are they different?* They were covered with hair, and their tusks curved upward. *How do mammoths help us understand how the ice age might have happened?* Since their remains are found in Siberia, we know Siberia must have been warmer to supply them with the food they needed. This fits in with a warm ocean that would have warmed Siberia and provided the evaporation needed for an ice age. *What kind of habitat did the mastodon live in?* They lived in forests. *How are horses and ponies different?* Adult ponies are smaller than adult horses. Ponies also have thicker hair, thicker manes, thicker tails, a stockier build, and for their size, they are generally stronger than horses **What** *does it mean when a horse is labeled hot-, cold-, or warm-blooded?* Larger, gentler horses used for working and hauling are cold-blooded horses, smaller horses built for speed are hot-blooded horses, and warm-blooded horses have the athletic skill of the hot-bloods and the gentler personality of the cold-bloods. **Identify** *the following: filly, colt, foal, stallion, mare, and yearling.* A filly is a female horse that isn't fully grown, while a male horse that isn't fully grown is called a colt. A foal is any horse that isn't a year old yet. A stallion is a fully grown male, while a mare is a fully grown female. A yearling is any horse that is between one and two years old. *Explain the main differences between donkeys and horses.* Donkeys are smaller than horses, with larger ears, a loud voice, and a much less compliant personality. Their mane is stiff and upright, and the hair is coarse. A donkey's tail is more like a cow's tail, covered with short body hair for most of the length, and ending in a tasseled switch. *How are zebra stripes like your fingerprints?* Each zebra has its own stripe pattern, just as each person has his or her own fingerprints. *How are zebras like donkeys?* They have the same smaller, stockier frame; a thick, coarse mane that stands up straight; rather large ears; a powerful kick; a fierce bite; and they usually try to outrun predators. *Why are rhinoceroses endangered?* They are hunted for their horns. *What is a rhino's horn made of?* Rhino horns are made of the same material found in hair and fingernails – a chemical called keratin. *How are tapirs like elephants?* They have a long proboscis. *How are they like pigs?* They have the same general shape.

Lesson 9

What is rumination? The process by which an animal chews its food, swallows it, and then it come back up the throat to be chewed and swallowed again. *Are deer a part of the antelope group?* No. *Which animals migrate with wildebeests?* Gazelles and zebras migrate with them. *What do impalas do when they are frightened or startled?* When they are frightened or startled, the whole herd starts leaping about in all directions. *Where are zebu cattle found?* They are native to India. *Tell the basic history of bison.* They used to be abundant in the United States but were hunted almost to extinction. However, they were protected as an endangered species, and now they are so plentiful that the are no longer endangered. *What special features do camels have that enable them to survive in the desert?* They have humps that store fat. They can survive for a long time with no water, and when they finally find it, they can drink 20 or more gallons of water at one time! Their eyes have long lashes that keep out dust; and their nostrils are mere slits that can close up during a dust storm. Also, their two-toed feet are wide to provide more padding and stability when walking on shifting sand. *Why might you find a set of antlers with no deer attached?* Deer lose their antlers every year. *How do giraffes give evidence for our Creator?* They have amazingly-designed systems that alter their blood pressure when they raise and lower their head. *How did God protect the Israelites by telling them not to eat pig meat?* Pig meat can contain many disease-causing parasites if not cooked and handled properly. *How are peccaries different from pigs?* Peccaries have long, thin legs, and tend to be smaller and thinner than pigs. Their tusks grow straight down, while a pig's tusks curl away from the face. Peccaries live in herds that include the males and have a powerful musk gland on the top of the rump. Pigs are indigenous to the Old World, while peccaries are indigenous to the New World. *Which is the most dangerous animal in Africa?* The hippopotamus is the most dangerous animal in Africa.

Lesson 10

What do all reptiles have in common? They are ectothermic, are covered in scales, and must molt to grow. *What kinds of animals are in order Squamata?* Squamata contains lizards and snakes. *Why don't snakes blink?* They don't have eyelids. *How are their eyes protected?* Their eyes are protected by a transparent layer of skin. *How do snakes consume their prey?* They swallow them whole. *What tooth does a reptile lose after its first molt?* It loses its egg tooth. *Why don't you find molted lizard skins, even though you can find molted snake skins?* Their skin molts in patches, coming off a little at a time. Also, many lizards actually eat their molted skin. *What is unique about gecko feet?* A gecko's toes are covered by millions of setae which can lie across any surface and get so close that they can actually stick to the molecules that make up the surface! This design is so amazing that to this day, human science cannot come close to imitating it.

What is the difference between a tuatara and a lizard? Tuataras have no ear holes, and they also love cool weather. *If a legless lizard looks like a worm, why isn't it considered a worm?* They have eyelids, ears, and a tail that can break off. *How do tuataras give us evidence for the Flood as described in the Bible?* Despite the fact that their fossils are found only with dinosaurs, they are alive today. This indicates the layers of rock in which fossils are found do not represent millions of years of time. Instead, they represent stages of the Flood.

Lesson 11

What are the differences among turtles, terrapins, and tortoises? A turtle spends most of its life in water, a tortoise lives mostly on dry land, and a terrapin spends a lot of time both on dry land and in water. *Can snapping turtles pull their head into their shell?* No. *How do they protect themselves?* They stay in the water most of the time and are super-aggressive. *How does the alligator snapping turtle catch prey?* It keeps its mouth open underwater and wiggles its tongue, which is a bright pink. Like a lure, this attracts fish right into its mouth. *What is interesting about the snake-necked turtles of America and Australia?* Their method for catching prey is interesting. When a fish happens past, the turtle opens its mouth wide, thrusting its head in the direction of the prey. When it opens its mouth, its throat opens and fills with water, which both pulls the turtle's head forward and pulls the prey into the mouth. *Explain the differences among the different kinds of crocodilians.* When an alligator or a caiman closes its mouth, you cannot see many of its teeth. However, even with its mouth closed, you can see a crocodile's and a gavial's teeth. Alligators and caimans have U-shaped snouts, while crocodiles and gavials have V-shaped snouts. Alligators have a bone that separates the two nostrils in the nose, while caimans do not have such a bone. Caimans have a lot more bony plates protecting their underside than do alligators. A gavial has a very long snout with a bump on the end. Crocodiles and gavials have special glands that help them to get rid of excess salt in the body. Alligators and caimans do not have those glands. Crocodiles have DPRs over almost their entire body, while alligators and caimans have them only on the skin around their jaws. *How do crocodilians care for their young?* The mother carries her babies to the safety of a shallow pool and then watches over them carefully for while. *Explain the stages in an amphibian's life.* The spawning stage is when the amphibian lays its eggs, and the egg stage is the time in which the amphibian develops in the egg. When the amphibian hatches, it enters the tadpole stage, where it typically lives in water and breathes with gills. Over time, it transforms into the adult stage, where it can breathe air and looks like its parents. *What is the main difference between a salamander and a newt?* Newts are specific salamanders that have rougher skin that is not as slimy as that of a salamander.

Lesson 12

"Name Game" on p. 216: A. *Corythosaurus* B. *Monolophosaurus* C. *Monoclonius* D. *Dilophosaurus* *What evidence do we have that dinosaurs lived during the same time as people?* There are ancient drawings that are incredibly good representations of dinosaurs, and soft, unfossilized tissue found in dinosaur bones indicate that they cannot be more than a few thousand years old. *What's the difference between dinosaurs and other reptiles?* Lizards have a sprawling stance, where their legs are positioned out to the sides of the body. Dinosaurs have legs that are more directly under their bodies. **What are the two main groups of dinosaurs?** Dinosaurs are separated into two groups: Saurischia and Ornithischia. *What are some special features of sauropods?* Sauropods were large herbivores that walked on all fours. They usually had a long neck topped with a small head that had nostrils placed on top, close to their eyes. *Which animal does Behemoth best describe and why?* It best describes a sauropod, because it is described as large animal that has a tail that swings like a cedar. Also, it spent at least some of its time in water, as did many sauropods. *What are some special features of theropods?* Theropods walked on two legs and had sharp, serrated teeth. They typically had five fingers and five toes, and there were usually three large fingers or toes and two smaller ones. Their toes all had claws, but usually only the three long fingers had claws. *In which group of dinosaurs is Stegosaurus placed?* Stegosaurus was an Ornithischian placed in the thyreophora group. *In which group are the duck-billed dinosaurs placed?* They were ornithopods put in the hadrosaur group. *What are some possible reasons for the extinction of dinosaurs?* The Flood-induced ice age might have killed them off. Some must have survived, but they were probably hunted extinction.

Lesson 13

How can you identify an arthropod? They have a tough exoskeleton and a segmented body. *How can you tell the difference between an insect and an arachnid?* Arachnids have eight legs, while insects have 6. *What are the two most dangerous spiders in the United States?* The two dangerous spiders are the brown recluse and black widow. *How do spiders consume their prey?* They must liquefy their prey and drink it. *Name some of the things spiders do with their silk.* They use it to help protect their young, catch food, create a home, and help them move around. *From where does the silk come?* It comes from spinnerets that are most often found at the very back of the abdomen. *What are some of the different kinds of webs that spiders build?* They build orb webs, funnel webs, tangle webs, and sheet webs. *What are* *some ways spiders capture their prey?* Some capture prey in webs, others make traps, others hunt, and others ambush. *What are harvestmen?* Also called a "daddy longlegs," it is an eight-legged arachnid with only one body part. It has two eyes, does not produce silk, and can eat solid food. *How do they defend themselves?* Harvestmen can detach legs to escape predators and can spray foul-smelling fumes. *Why are harvestmen good for your garden?* They eat aphids, flies, mites, decaying plant and animal remains, animal waste, and some kinds of fungi. *What animals eat scorpions?* Elf Owls, grasshopper mice, pallid bats, desert shrews, some snakes, lizards, centipedes, tarantulas, and meerkats eat scorpions. *What are the acarina?* They are mites and ticks that are mostly parasites. *Name some specific kinds of acarina.* Specific acarina are scabies mite, harvest mites (chiggers), mange mites, dust mites, hard ticks, and soft ticks. *Why are ticks dangerous?* They transmit lots of diseases. *Name some differences between centipedes and millipedes.* Centipedes are aggressive carnivores that have one pair of legs per segment, while millipedes are docile herbivores that have two pairs of legs per segment. Centipedes fight to defend themselves, while millipedes roll up into tiny balls. *Where do woodlice live?* Woodlice live in moist environments. *How do they defend themselves?* They roll up into a ball.

Lesson 14

What are the meanings of the two Greek words that form the name "Gastropoda"? They mean "belly" and "foot." *Why do slugs and snails produce mucus?* The snail's mucus not only helps it crawl around; it is also a great defense. *How do slugs and snails eat?* They eat by scraping food into their mouth with their radula. *Name the three basic types of worms.* The three basic types are flatworms, roundworms, and segmented worms. *How does a tapeworm get inside a dog or a cat?* The dog or cat eats an infected flea. *Explain the tapeworm life cycle.* When an infected animal (or an egg) is eaten by another animal, that animal becomes infected. Once inside its final host, the tapeworm inserts itself into the intestine, attaching itself to the intestinal wall. Its skin absorbs the nutrients from the already digested food in the intestines. As the tapeworm continues to absorb nutrients and grow, it begins to add segments to its body. Each segment produces its own eggs. When the segments leave the body, the eggs can be eaten by animals to start the process all over again. *Which of the three basic worm types are pinworms?* Pinworms are roundworms. *What are some ways you can avoid getting parasites?* Wash your hands, especially after touching animals. Also, cook meat thoroughly. *What kind of worm is an earthworm?* An earthworm is a segmented worm. *Why are earthworms important to people?* They make soil more fertile. *How do earthworms move from place to place?* The earthworm has bristles called setae on its underside. When the worm decides it needs to go somewhere, it makes itself as long as it can, then it anchors its front setae into the soil. After this, it releases its back setae and pulls its tail end forward, making itself short and thick. Once the tail end is set in place, it anchors its rear setae into the soil. The front setae release, and the worm stretches out, propelling the front end forward, bumping against the solid dirt or tunneling into it as it stretches out farther and farther. Once the dirt is moved, it releases the back setae and starts over

Photograph and Illustration Credits

INDEX